DATE DUE			

Slavery in
Tennessee

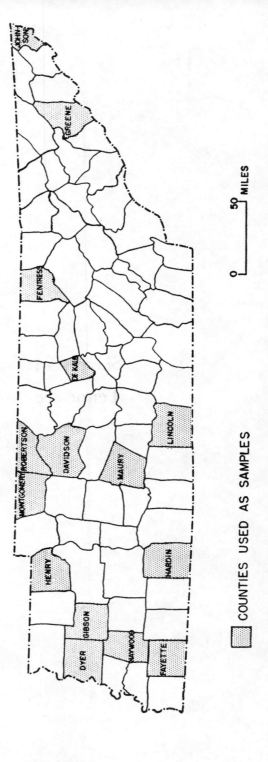

TENNESSEE IN 1850

☐ COUNTIES USED AS SAMPLES

0 — 50 MILES

Slavery in Tennessee

by CHASE C. MOONEY

Department of History
Indiana University

NEGRO UNIVERSITIES PRESS
WESTPORT, CONNECTICUT

301.4493
M77s
92499
Mar.1975

To all those who have helped to make this study possible and especially to my colaborers in the manuscript Federal census schedules

Foreword

MUCH OF the history of the United States has been written upon untested assumptions which, when later subjected to systematic research, prove to be partially or entirely unsound. Many such assumptions deal with the very grass roots of history—community, county, and state history; yet the writers of our national histories have seldom or never extended their researches to the community and county level. They have usually scorned the writing of "purely local history," and have been content to rely for their information upon the writings of the untrained county patriot, an occasional personal document, newspapers, and travel literature (almost totally unreliable). It should be needless to point out that generalizations based upon such sources are untrustworthy—they may be sound and again they may be wholly unsound. One can therefore be fairly certain that because of the neglect of the grass roots of American history, the works of our national historians have, of necessity, many unsound areas.

Of all the unsound parts, those dealing with the South are the most numerous. This is understandable: to begin with, many historians have approached the South with an unconscious, inherited prejudice; they have not had easy access to personal manuscript collections; there have been few good local histories for them to utilize; and of greater importance, they have had little understanding of the importance and the use of the official records of the county and community.

In recent years, especially in the field of Southern history, important progress has been made in the grass-roots study of the history of that region. Great collections of personal manuscripts have been made at several of the Southern universities, especially for the ante-bellum period; and trained scholars have undertaken the study of county and local areas. Land tenure, the migratory pattern of the Southern rural population, the disposal and settlement of the public domains, the productions of agriculture, the history of slavery on local and state levels have been and are being subjected to intensive scrutiny; and the county, church, and other local records have been systematically studied. It should be observed in this connection that the Federal manuscript census reports for 1850 and 1860 have been the greatest single source for the quantitative study of land tenure, slaveholding, and agricultural production on the county and community level.

Professor Mooney in his history of slavery in Tennessee has levied upon personal manuscript collections, farm and plantation account books, state codes and statutes, trial records, and newspapers, in the manner of Sydnor, Flanders, and Phillips. His systematic and thorough use of the county records and the manuscript census reports of 1850 and 1860 has, however, enabled him to penetrate not only to the county level but to the individual slaveholder and nonslaveholder on a quantitative basis heretofore not attained. It is only by such systematic and quantitative studies reaching to the individual level that a knowledge and understanding of a state and region can be attained. And, finally, when such is done, especially in the South, it is needless to say that much and drastic revision of our national history will be needed.

F. L. OWSLEY

UNIVERSITY OF ALABAMA
June 8, 1955

Contents

Contents

Tables

xi

Introduction

STUDIES of slavery have been made for nearly every southern state and for the South[1] in general, but the institution as it existed in Tennessee has been neglected, except for scattered articles on certain phases of slavery and slave life. Many of these articles need rewriting in the light of later research, as do some of the studies for the several states. Slavery and its relation to agriculture, however, has not been touched upon in the Volunteer State.

Parts of this study will appear new only in that they pertain to Tennessee. The chapters on the legal status of the slave, antislavery sentiment in Tennessee, slave life, hire and sale, and fugitive and stolen slaves contain the same general type of information as that found in other studies on the subject. But the earlier students of slavery omitted a most important body of source material, and it is only in the last decade and a half that a few scholars have made careful use of the vital statistical information found in the unpublished United States census schedules.[2] These more recent studies deal primarily with the nonslaveholder, but their findings lead one to question, and then to challenge, the conventional picture of slavery as it existed in the lower South, as well as in the upper South and the border states.

Census records have offered the most complete and valuable material for the study of slavery in Tennessee. The published census gives statistics for the state and county on population, on landholding and value, on livestock and value, and on agricultural productions and value, but the unpublished schedules reveal a more intimate picture of each individual head of a family. Three of the unpublished schedules have been used in this study. Schedule IV, "Productions of Agriculture," of the Seventh and Eighth Census of the United States for the years 1850 and 1860, was used in the original, the volumes having been borrowed from, or consulted at, the Duke University Library. Foundation, or master, charts were made including every person in the counties studied, the size and value of their landholdings, the number and value of their livestock, the value of their farm implements, and the amount of each of their agricultural products. Schedule I, "An Enumeration of Free Inhabitants," and Schedule II, "An Enumeration of Slave Population," for 1850 and 1860 were microphotographed at the Census Bureau in the Department of Commerce in Washington and studied on a projector. Schedules I and II were checked with Schedule IV, and to the master charts was added the following information: whether the individual was a landowner; the number of slaves held by each and every one listed on the agricultural schedule (if he or she was a slaveowner); the number of slave houses in 1860; and other information not used in this study.[3]

The cross-checking of the schedules revealed discrepancies between I and IV. Many persons listed as farmers on Schedule I did not appear on Schedule IV. This may have been, in some instances, due to the carelessness of the enumerators; in many more instances those were probably sharecroppers, tenants, squatters, or day laborers. The day laborers are often so marked, but the category in which many of these so-called farmers belonged could not be definitely ascertained. Frequently they were children or close relatives of a landowning operator and lived with him.

In this study only individuals who were listed on Schedule IV are considered. These were thought to be the *bona fide* agricultural producers, and even some of these were eliminated. A person living in, or on the edge of, a town and owning a cow and an acre or so of unproductive land was rejected as not belonging to the true agricultural class.[4] The criterion generally followed for such rejection was that the individual be listed on Schedule I as engaging in some other occupation or profession. Those who were definitely producers, however, even though they had another vocation or avocation, were included. Also, only the slaves belonging to the agriculturists were considered. By the above method many slaves and freemen are excluded, but in this manner a more accurate picture of the actual agricultural operations is obtained. Then, too, for those farmers listed on Schedule I and not on Schedule IV the only information obtainable is that they were farmers, who either did or did not hold slaves, and that they owned real or personal property valued at so many dollars. Nothing of the size of their landholdings or the amount of their agricultural productions can be ascertained.

Mechanical computing devices have been used in making all counts and for calculating percentages in this study; but even so, absolute accuracy is not claimed for the figures presented herein. Circumstances forbade such exactness. The physical condition of portions of the unpublished census made them almost illegible. Small parts of the schedules which were microphotographed were so watermarked that it was impossible to read the film. In some instances the enumerators were careless about the order of the names; in others the schedules were incorrectly bound; consequently, the order of names in the three schedules does not always correspond. This lack of regularity sometimes necessitated searching for a name through an entire county; obviously oversights were probable and even inevitable. Poor spelling and bad writing added to the difficulties. In spite of the above-named failings of the unpublished schedules, the shortcomings are not serious enough to affect materially the general picture. The unpublished schedules are not available for the years previous to 1850; part of this study is, therefore, confined to the decade preceding the Civil War.

Since it was neither possible nor necessary to study every Tennessee farmer to obtain a fairly accurate knowledge of slavery in Tennessee, fifteen sample counties were used. Counties predominated by nonslaveholders, counties in which slaveowners and nonslaveowners were about equally divided, and counties in which the slaveholders were the dominant agricultural group were selected. Another criterion of selection was the type of economy—stock and grain, cotton, tobacco, or diversified farming—on which the major portion of the farming class depended. The different economic modes of life were determined by the topographical and geographical conditions in the various sections of the state.

The three sections of Tennessee were so distinct that the early census returns were given separately for East, Middle, and West Tennessee. Then, too, there are definite geographical differences within these three major divisions, which make, altogether, eight different geographic and geologic areas in the state. At least one county from each of these areas was studied. Beginning at the eastern boundary of the state is the Unaka region, the mountainous area of which Johnson County is a part. The ruggedness and thinness of the soil prevented extensive cultivation, although there were interspersed fertile spots. In this country the nonslaveholder predominated; no money crop was produced; the farmers raised produce for home consumption and drove their livestock to the seaboard or the lower South. The valleys of East Tennessee form the second geologic division. There is more and better soil—containing limestone, shale, and sandstone—in this area, and the usual farm crops are more easily and profitably produced. The soil is well adapted to the culture of the cereals, especially wheat. Greene County in this area depended on a stock-grain economy, was one of the fairly prosperous counties of the state, and was materially aided by internal improvements which made markets more accessible.

Fentress County forms a part of the Cumberland Tableland. It is one of the poorer counties of the state, and in 1850 and 1860 many of the farmers produced only enough for home consumption. Unimproved land, though inferior, was plentiful, and cattle raising was fairly common. The unprosperous condition of Fentress and other counties in this area cannot be explained solely by the infertility of the soil; the inaccessibility of markets was a contributing factor.

The Highland Rim is very similar in shape to a question mark and partially surrounds the fifth division or the Central Basin. De-

Kalb County, lying in the central eastern part of the Rim, was not unlike Fentress in the crops produced, although the general farm crops were more easily grown in the rich soil at the foot of the knobs and ridges. The counties on the northwestern part of the Rim, such as Montgomery and Robertson, were prosperous tobacco-producing areas and resembled their sister counties of the Central Basin in development. In this part of the Rim the soil was drouth-resisting; the presence of marl in the ground was helpful for tobacco production; and the Cumberland River served as a means of reaching first-class markets. Lincoln County, in the southeastern part of the Rim, also resembled the counties of the Central Basin. In Lincoln, however, the soil was not as rich as it was in the Basin, and that county was not as prosperous as Davidson or Maury.

The Central Basin was in many ways the best agricultural division of the state. The fertile soils, admirably adapted to the growing of the cereals and grain, produced abundant crops. This section, a diminished replica of the Lexington Basin, is the only area in Tennessee where bluegrass grows luxuriantly. This grass made livestock-raising a profitable activity. Also, Nashville was a prominent commercial center, and the Cumberland and other rivers were more accessible to inhabitants of this region than to those of the northern and western Rim. Davidson and Maury, quite similar but exhibiting notable differences in type of economy, were studied in this area.

The sixth division, the western valley of the Tennessee River, represented in this study by Hardin County, was not as good a farming section as the Central Basin or the land still farther west in Tennessee. The production in this valley was moderate; the land was not suited to tobacco or cotton, but grasses were grown with comparative ease and in relative abundance.

In addition to the above area, West Tennessee has two distinct divisions. The northern Plateau Slope is similar to the northern and western part of the Highland Rim in Middle Tennessee. Some of the counties in this section, such as Henry, were large tobacco-producing units. Gibson and Dyer counties lie more or less between the Plateau Slope and the Mississippi Bottom. Gibson, today placarded as the "nationally known county of diversified crops," was predominantly a county of small slaveholders, and in the 1850's and 1860's practiced diversified farming. Cotton, however, was the chief money crop. Dyer, lying west of Gibson and bordering on the Mississippi River, produced cotton as the money crop in 1850. By 1860, however, the Dyer County farmers depended on a split cotton-tobacco economy.

The Mississippi Bottom region, primarily the two tiers of counties in the southwestern part of the state, was best suited to cotton production. The soil was the most recently formed in the state, and being of a sandy quality was admirably adapted to the culture of cotton. Corn and cereals did not, and will not, grow well in this soil. Land was to be had in greater quantities than in other parts of the state; there was a lack of population pressure; and the Mississippi River made New Orleans a not-too-distant market. Haywood and Fayette were used as representative counties in this section, and they were prosperous as long as cotton prices remained good.[5]

ONE

Legal Status of the Slave
in Tennessee

THE LEGAL status of the slave in Tennessee was determined by
North Carolina and Tennessee legislation, as well as by such
ordinances and regulations as were made from time to time by
the local governmental agencies. Some of this North Carolina
legislation dates as far back as 1715, and since it had prevailed in
the Tennessee region for many years, it was declared to remain
applicable to the Southwest Territory by the act of Congress creat-
ing that governmental unit.[1]

The system of slavery had for several decades been controlled
by custom in North Carolina, but in 1715 it was placed on a legal
basis,[2] and it is not surprising to see the Old North State protecting
the transmontane interests of her citizens by a proviso in the act
ceding the Tennessee country to the Federal government. The act
of cession as finally accepted by Congress on April 2, 1790, stated,
in part, that

. . . Congress . . . shall protect the inhabitants against enemies, and
shall never debar or deprive them of any privileges which the people
west of the Ohio enjoy, Provided always, that no regulation made or to
be made by Congress shall tend to emancipate slaves.[3]

Thus the newly created Federal government was not to interfere
with an institution which the toppling Confederation had prohibited in the Northwest Territory.

7

Tennessee emerged from her territorial chrysalis in 1796, but her constitution made no reference to slavery—except regarding taxation—and some North Carolina statutes regulating the institution were effective in Tennessee until 1865. Tennessee built upon this legislation and modified it until the slave in that state was granted more rights and privileges as a person than he received in some of the states of the lower South.

The policy inherited from North Carolina was a liberal one but this liberalism waned with the rise of the abolition crusade, the threat of insurrection, and the increasing heat of sectional controversy. The slave became subject to more severe restrictions, yet retained certain rights which distinguished him from a pure chattel in the eyes of the law. It is the purpose of this chapter to discuss only those features of the legislation which have significant bearing upon the characteristics of the government of a slave state, and to show the effects of the abolition attack and other events upon this legislation.

As in the other slave states, a master in Tennessee was held responsible for the economic security and well-being of his slaves, although he had complete power over them with the exception of the taking of life or limb. He could recover damages for a slave unlawfully killed and he was responsible for the thefts of his slave if it could be proved in court that insufficient food or clothing had prompted this pilfering.[4] An owner who permitted his slaves to go about "so naked and destitute of clothing, that their organs of generation and other parts . . . which should have been clothed and concealed, were publicly exposed" was fined $25 and costs in 1842.[5] As to the man who castrated one of his slaves, the court held: "We utterly repudiate the idea of any such power . . . of the master over the slave, as would authorise him thus to maim his slave for the purpose of his moral reform . . . the malice sufficiently appears . . . at least by legal implication. . . . "[6] The only instance where the slave could legally refuse to obey his master was when he had been commanded to perpetrate a crime.[7]

The Tennessee legislation relative to the killing of a slave contained a proviso that "smacked of irony." Any person who "willfully or maliciously with malice aforethought kill[s] any negro or mulatto slave whatsoever" shall be deemed guilty of murder and "suffer death without the benefit of clergy, any law, usage or custom to the contrary notwithstanding." If the slave so killed was the property of another and not of the offender, the latter's "goods, chattels, lands and tenements . . . shall be liable to the payment of the value of such slave . . . to be assessed by a grand jury. . . . " This law was not applicable to a person killing a slave outlawed by the General Assembly or "to any slave in the act of resistance to his lawful owner or master, or to any slave dying under *moderate* correction."[8] Evidently this was the "due process" clause of this portion of the Tennessee slave code.

In 1813 anyone who "wantonly and without sufficient cause beat or abuse[d] the slave or slaves of another person" was made liable to indictment. This indictment was to be conducted under the same rules and involved the same penalties as the commission of a similar offense upon the body of any white person.[9]

The responsibilities of the master were as great as could be expected under the prevailing system, and the slave, in return, had to yield almost completely or be subject to the legally sanctioned punishment of his "overlord."

Runaway slaves constituted one of the most serious problems, economic and otherwise, with which the government of a slave state had to contend. Despite stringent legislation, the desire for freedom always lured some of the enslaved from their masters. Part of the time, of course, they were persuaded to this flight by others.

In North Carolina[10] two justices of the peace were to issue a proclamation against any slave who ran away or "lurked out" and to announce the same at the place of worship in the locality. If the slave did not "immediately return home," he was declared an outlaw whom anyone could legally kill.[11] Any person apprehending and returning a fugitive was to receive 98¾ ¢ if the runaway was within ten miles of the master's dwelling, and 3⅛ ¢ were allowed for each additional mile. Perhaps overzealous fulfillment of the right to kill an outlawed slave prompted the legislature to repeal this statute in 1819.[12]

The runaway who refused to make known the name of his owner

was to be committed to jail and duly advertised by the sheriff. Any slave whose owner was not thus located could be hired out by the jailor after consultation with the County Court.[13] Either an individual or a corporation could hire these slaves, but the hirer must first promise to treat them properly and to return them on request of the owner or at the expiration of the jail term. These promises were secured by bond for twice the value of the slave.[14]

As the slave was a valuable piece of property, the officers of government were charged to take exceedingly good care of any who came into their custody. If the runaway's master was known, the slave was to be whipped before a justice of the peace and sent from constable to constable until he reached his home. Each constable on receipt of the slave was to give a statement in writing to that effect or else forfeit $2.50 to the church wardens. Any officer —justice, sheriff, patroller, constable, jailor—who willfully and negligently allowed a slave to escape was liable to the party aggrieved.[15]

The reward for the return of a runaway was raised to $5 in 1831,[16] and later to $25 for out-of-state fugitives.[17] It appears that the higher bounty proved too great a temptation and that the patrols, sheriffs, and constables abused their powers of arrest and subjected the masters to useless fees for the returning of slaves who were not real runaways.[18] To prevent this "usurpation" it was declared in 1852 that the slave was to have the freedom of the town in which his master resided, and any apprehended Negro who could not account for himself was to be detained at some place other than the jail.[19] A slave who ran away in 1847, and was advertised as a fugitive, was "picked up" by two men and sold in another state. The plea of the offenders was that the slave was, at the time, in the possession of no one, and thus they were not guilty of stealing the Negro. The court, however, did not hold this opinion, and said that a slave ". . . cannot be, lost in the sense in which . . . even a horse, may be lost."[20]

Inextricably interwoven with the problem of the runaway were the officers commonly known among the Negroes as the "patterollers." A basis for the patrol system was laid in the North Carolina

statute of 1733, although few details were set forth.[21] The great
fear of servile insurrection during the American Revolution produced legislation intended to make the organization more effective. The patrollers were exempted from muster, jury, and road
service, and were required to search slave quarters once a month
for weapons of all kinds, to seize and turn over to the court any
weapons found, and to take up any slave who was "out of place."
Service was made practically imperative, for anyone who refused
to serve or neglected his duty as a patrol forfeited $250.[22]

This legislation applied to Tennessee until 1806, when the
power of appointment of patrollers was vested in the captain of
each militia company. Under the law of 1806 the captain was
to appoint patrols "as often as it was deemed necessary," and these
officers were empowered to search all Negro dwellings within the
territorial limits of their military company. Any slave found at
one of these houses, or off his master's plantation, without the
required pass was to receive fifteen lashes on his bare back and
be committed to jail if his master was not promptly found.[23] The
several "beats" of the company were to be so laid out that a
patrolman might be on duty as often as circumstances required.
Penalty for refusal to serve or neglect of duty was reduced from
$250 to $5 for each offense[24] thus loosening the law in one respect
while tightening it in others.

Soon, in 1817, the plenary power of the militia captains was
lessened, and magistrates, when they deemed it advisable, were
empowered to command the captain to order out a patrol, and to
continue the same until he was notified that such patrol was no
longer necessary.[25] The magistrate was given the additional power
in 1831 of appointment of patrols in his district if the militia
captains refused to appoint them at the regular time.[26] The justice,
constable, patroller, or any other "authorized person" could get
assistance and inflict twenty-five lashes on the several members of
a group of "suspicious looking slaves at a suspicious place" at
unlawful hours, if the meeting did not promptly disperse when
told to do so.[27] Again the fear of an insurrection brought exemption from muster, road, and jury service for twelve months to the

patroller who faithfully performed his duty for three months. He was also to receive such pay as the county court thought proper.[28] This act of 1831 also provided that:

Hereafter it shall be the duty of the patrollers . . . to search and patrol in their respective bounds in the day as well as in the night time, and have and exercise the same power to arrest and punish all slaves found under suspicious circumstances off their master's plantation without a pass in writing in the daytime as heretofore in the night.[29]

Nashville was incorporated on September 11, 1806, and among other rights was given "full power . . . to establish night watches and patrols."[30] Apparently, it was many years before the city felt the necessity of exercising this power, for it was not until January, 1837, that provision was made for the appointment of patrollers by the mayor and board of aldermen at the regular April and October meetings. The terms of the patrols were six months and expired on April 1 and October 1. The duties of the watch were much the same as those set forth by state law, but they must walk, not stand or sit, and not enter any shop except in discharge of duty. They were to break up all meetings of persons of color or else treat the offenders as suspicious characters, that is, arrest, whip, or commit them to jail, depending on the seriousness of the offense and the discretion of the watchman.[31] The mayor was given authority to increase the patrol for a "few nights" if he thought it necessary.[32] Two weeks later, January 25, 1837, an act was passed which forbade any gathering of slaves at any time for any purpose whatever (except worship under the supervision of a "discreet" white) within the corporate limits. Nor were slaves, nonresident or not employed in the city, to remain within the corporation on Sundays or after sundown, unless on business, when they were to be allowed "a reasonable time to complete said business and return."[33]

The Tennessee act of 1856, the most comprehensive since 1831 and the last legislation of an affirmative character concerning patrollers, well summarized and knit together the whole system. The power of appointment was vested in the county courts which were to name not more than three patrols for each civil district of the county. The duties, privileges, and exemptions of the patrols were the same as under existing laws except that the exemption from road service was repealed. Their terms were lengthened to twelve months and their compensation, which was never to exceed $1 per day, was to be determined by the county judge. Also, the master, mistress, or overseer was constituted a patrol for his or her premises.[34]

The exercise of the patroller's power was always limited by the written pass from the slave's owner or employer. The slave had no strictly legal privileges without a pass, for he could not legally leave his master's plantation, or premises, day or night,[35] could not carry a sword, gun, club, or other weapon,[36] or enjoy other privileges of a free person of color. The provision relative to the carrying of a gun did not prevent the employment of one slave as a huntsman for each and every distinct plantation, conditional upon the owner's securing a certificate from the county court. This certificate had to be carried by the hunter at all times or else he became subject to the punishments of the patrols.[37]

The potential danger of a slave with a gun was realized in 1753 when it was enacted that no certificate for hunting should be granted until the owner gave bond for the slave's good behavior, and anyone injured by the hunter might sue on this bond. The punishment for a slave who did not have a certificate and hunted with dogs in the woods, even though he had no gun, was fixed at thirty-nine lashes.[38]

Any slave who forged a pass or certificate was to be whipped with not exceeding thirty-nine lashes;[39] any person giving, or causing to be given, to any slave a forged pass or certificate purporting to be a pass of freedom, or any other instrument of writing intended to aid the slave in escape from his master was to suffer imprisonment for not less than three nor more than ten years.[40]

In 1857 a Nashville ordinance provided that no slave was to pass about the city after 7 P.M. from October 1 to April 1 nor after 9 P.M. from April 1 to October 1. The penalty for violation of this regulation was ten to twenty lashes at the discretion of the captain of the police.[41] Later in the year the time was extended to 9 P.M. on Sunday nights for worship under the superintendence of some "discreet white person," and in the following year was further extended to 10 P.M. from April 1 to October 1.[42] In Memphis nine taps of the bell in the court square designated the hour "when the darkies must go home" and all "prudent white men should retire." Another Memphis ordinance of this same year, 1856, forbade the religious or other teaching of Negroes without the written consent of the mayor, and under the supervision of the police; nor could a Negro preach in the city. Penalties for the violation of the above ranged from $150 to $500.[43]

The right of a slave to engage in trade or traffic of any kind was dependent upon his having a written permit from his owner. The first act relative to this subject (a North Carolina statute applicable to Tennessee) provided that anyone buying, selling, or bartering with a slave without a proper permit was punishable by a fine treble the value of the transferred article and $15 in addition. If the offender was not able to pay, he should be sold as a servant for the debt.[44] This penalty was reduced, for a free person, to $25 in 1788 and an insolvent could be imprisoned "for as long as three months."[45] Also, in that year it was enacted that the slave who proffered articles for sale without a pass was, on complaint of anyone, to be whipped on his bare back not exceeding thirty-nine lashes. The penalty for trading with a slave without a pass enumerating the articles to be transferred was increased to a fine of from $10 to $50 in 1803.[46]

The above regulations related to trade in general, but the provisions carrying the harshest penalties concerning commercial intercourse with slaves were those relative to the prohibition of the sale of intoxicating liquors. In 1830 the slave selling liquor without his master's consent was to receive from five to ten lashes, and if he even possessed liquor in any place other than his own house, the punishment was from three to ten lashes. No merchant, tavern keeper, distiller, nor any other person could sell liquor to a slave who did not have a permit. Violation of this provision brought imposition of a fine of from $5 to $50[47] and, later, imprisonment for from one week to thirty days.[48] The master who knowingly permitted his slave to sell intoxicating liquors, without the written permit, forfeited to the "person who may sue for the same" not

less than $50 for each offense.[49] In 1859 Memphis supplemented
this legislation with an ordinance which made it a finable offense
to sell or give liquor to minors or Negroes, slave or free. Even
admission into "any liquor establishment, or confectionary or
even to a soda fountain on Sunday" was termed an offense under
this act.[50]

In 1842 the Court of Appeals affirmed the decision of a lower
court fining a man $50 for violating a trading-with-slaves regu-
lation, and the Court said "we . . . direct that, in addition . . . the
defendant be imprisoned one week."[51] The Nashville recorder was
considerably more lenient; in 1860 he fined one McGoldrick only
$3 on each of five charges of selling liquor to slaves.[52]

Any person who gave liquor to slaves was subject to a $5 fine
for the first offense and the discretion of the court was the limit of
the fine for all subsequent violations. Also, in 1852, the person
who sold liquor to slaves was made punishable at the discretion
of the court.[53]

The legislation dealing with rebellion and "insurrection in-
citers" is interesting, for in it is well exemplified the legal attempt
of a slave state to offset or counteract the vitriolic attacks of the
northern abolitionists. By the North Carolina statute in force in
Tennessee for a number of years, the conspiracy of three or more
slaves to rebel or to murder was declared a felony to be punished
by death.[54] Subsequently, in 1819, it was provided that punishment for this "offense" should not extend to life or limb.[55]

In 1803 the Tennessee legislature enacted a statute stating
that anyone publicly or privately uttering any words within hearing
of a slave or person of color "which in their nature will have a
tendency to inflame the minds of any slave or induce him or them
to insurrection or absent him or herself from the service of their
owner" shall for each such offense forfeit $10. In explanation it
was said that "such words must be directed to, and in favor of
general or special emancipation, or . . . to persuade any slave . . .
to rebel against the person or the lawful commands of his master
. . . or directly encourage any plot or combination against any of
the laws of the United States or this State. . . . "[56]

The effect of the abolition crusade is seen in the increase of punishments provided for conspiracy to rebel. In 1831 it was enacted that in cases of conviction for this offense, the court could inflict punishment according to its discretion—jailing, whipping, standing in the pillory, death—and no appeal was to be allowed.[57] Abolition "literature" soon fell under the legislative hammer and any person who aided in drawing up incendiary or "rebellion inciting" literature, paintings, or other matter, was to be imprisoned for from five to ten years for the first offense, and from ten to twenty for the second. The same penalties were provided for being connected with the circulation of such material, and attempting to incite by speech, or persuading someone else so to speak.[58] This statute went into effect immediately and the names of the plaintiffs were not necessary for prosecution of offenders.

It is possible that the law concerning the circulation of abolition materials was prompted by an incident which occurred in 1835, the year before the act was passed. Amos Dresser, a former student at Lane Seminary and member of the American Anti-Slavery Society, went to Nashville, so he said, to sell "Cottage Bibles" to help complete his education. When he sent his barouche to be repaired in the capital city, he left some antislavery tracts and other pamphlets in it. None of these had been given to "any person of color, bond or free, nor had I any intention of doing so," although he had sold a copy of John Rankin's *Letters on Slavery* near Gallatin. The repairers of his vehicle made known the fact that such materials had been found, but Dresser went about his "Bible" selling for a few more days. Meantime, the excitement was constantly increasing, and Dresser was arrested on August 21. Brought before a vigilance committee of sixty prominent citizens, Dresser said that he had not distributed any of the material, but "sought the good both of the master and the slave; contemplated emancipation through persuasion; and that in his few interviews with slaves he had recommended to them quietness, patience, and submission."

The committee established the fact that he was a member of the Ohio Anti-Slavery Society, and that he had in his possession periodicals published by the American Anti-Slavery Society; and they believed that he had "circulated those periodicals, and advocated the principles inculcated in them." Dresser was sentenced to twenty lashes on his bare back and given twenty-four hours to get out of town. Mr. Braughton, the principal police officer, administered the punishment on the public square before a "goodly" crowd, and Dresser left the city in disguise before the expiration of his allotted time. The Ohioan must have been doing something besides selling "Bibles," and he left so hurriedly that he failed to take all his personal belongings with him.[59]

In 1858, after the scare caused in some parts of the state in the previous year by a reported uprising, it was enacted that when "any slave or free negro shall be convicted of being engaged in, or aiding, abetting, or advising any insurrection of slaves . . . he, she, or they shall be punished by death." It was the duty of the judge to convene court at any time for the trial of such cases.[60]

Economic interest prompted severe penalties for stealing, enticing away, or harboring slaves. By a North Carolina statute of 1741 (applicable to Tennessee), to tempt or persuade a slave to leave his master with "intent to convey him out of the government," or to harbor or conceal him with such intent, was punishable by a fine of $62.50. An insolvent offender was to serve the owner of the slave for five years. Actual conveying from the state was a felony and punishable accordingly.[61]

Slaves were not allowed to congregate at night or on the Sabbath at the house of anyone without a pass from their owners. In 1803 any person permitting such congregation was fined from $2.50 to $10. If the offender was a free Negro or mulatto, and was insolvent, he was hired out to the master whose slave he had entertained.[62]

After 1833 no stage contractor, or driver, owner, or captain of any steamboat or other watercraft was to transport in intrastate or interstate passage any slave who did not possess a pass or whose master had not made previous arrangement. To do this was considered an attempt to steal, or to conceal stolen goods, and was punishable by a fine of from $200 to $500 and from three to six months' imprisonment.[63] The penalty for outright theft of a slave was rather more severe, to wit: "Whoever shall steal any slave, the property of another, with or without the consent of such slave, shall undergo confinement in said jail and Penitentiary house for a period not less than five nor more than fifteen years."[64] The same penalty was provided for stealing free persons of color or for harboring or protecting a known runaway. Later in the same year these penalties were lowered. The minimum punishment was three years' imprisonment and the maximum ten years'.[65]

Before one could be convicted of violation of the above, the case seemingly had to be clear. A Mr. Jones was acquitted of a charge of harboring simply because the "indictment must aver that the harboring was without the consent of the owner."[66] And a Mr. Duncan "did not receive the negro, and when he ascertained that he was on board of his boat, he made use of all reasonable exertions to secure him, and he fled and could not be overtaken."[67] Morehead and Bryant, however, were convicted of theft when they took up a runaway and sold him; for a slave "cannot be, lost in the sense in which . . . even a horse, may be lost."[68] In his report to the House of Representatives in 1838, John M'Intosh, keeper of the penitentiary, said that five of the 122 inmates were confined for Negro stealing.[69]

Nashville prohibited a slave from living in any house other than that of his master. The slave who violated this was to be lashed twenty times, and anyone who rented to a slave any house, lot, or room without permission was to be fined from $10 to $50.[70] The *Republican Banner* cautioned the slaveowners about this last prohibition by citing the case of a master being fined $10 and costs for allowing his washerwoman to occupy a house off his premises for the purpose of taking in washing.[71]

A North Carolina statute relative to the type of persons that could be brought into the state remained in effect in Tennessee throughout the slave period. This act provided that no "christian person be imported into this state to be a servant without an indenture," and any person bringing in and retaining or selling as a slave anyone that "shall have been free in any christian country" shall forfeit and pay to the party from whom said free person recovers his freedom double the sum for which the "slave" had been sold.[72]

An 1806 statute required that every free Negro or mulatto

. . . shall be registered and numbered in a book to be kept for that purpose . . . which register shall specify the age, name, color, and stature of such free negro or mulatto . . . by what authority he or she was emancipated or that such negro or mulatto was born free.[73]

A copy of this registration was to be given to the Negro or mulatto, and any one of them found living on any lot, not in the occupancy of some white person, without this "pass" was to be taken up and dealt with as a runaway.[74]

Fear of the free Negro expressed itself in the legislation of 1831 which forbade a free person of color coming to Tennessee to live, under penalty of a $10 to $50 fine and one to two years' imprisonment. If, thirty days after his release, he was not out of the state, the penitentiary sentence was to be doubled.[75] Eleven years later an amendatory act provided that the county court could at its discretion allow emancipated slaves and free persons of color, who had moved to the state prior to January 1, 1836, to remain on condition that bond be given "with two or more good sureties" in penalty of $500 to keep the peace and not to become a charge of the county.[76] A legislative provision of 1854, repealing one of February 27, 1852, declared that ". . . any free person having the right to reside in this state and of whom bond is required for good behavior and who fails to give such bond within two months, shall be termed a slave," and shall be subject to treatment as such.[77]

Tennessee, in 1826, forbade the bringing in of slaves for "personal use" who had been convicted of crime, and prohibited interstate slave traffic by declaring it unlawful to ". . . import into this state any slave or slaves, either for life or for a shorter period, for the purpose of selling or disposing of them or any of them as articles of merchandise within this state." In case the violator of this act did not give bond for his own and his slaves' appearance in court, the sheriff was to keep the slaves and sell them at the next court session.[78] Interstate trading again became legal in 1855,[79] and those who had been carrying on the trade under cover now came out into the open where they could reap much more substantial rewards.

Emancipated slaves constituted a problem that apparently worried the legislature to some extent. The first restrictive legislation on this subject, a North Carolina statute of 1777, provided that any slave set free by any method other than prescribed by law—will, deed, contract, state legislation—was to be taken by any freeholder, delivered to the sheriff, jailed, and, by order of the court, sold. The former owner who did not claim such a Negro within five days was forever barred.[80]

In November, 1801, the state legislature complained of too many petitions praying for emancipation, and passed an act vesting that power in the several county courts. Before the court was permitted to grant freedom to a slave, the master must set forth his intentions and motives for manumission and give bond "in such sum as the court may think proper to reimburse such damages as the county may sustain in consequence of such slave or slaves becoming chargeable." No petition was to be received unless nine justices were present, and the concurrence of six was necessary for emancipation. The freedman became heir to all the privileges and immunities of other free persons of color, and, if unable to support himself, was to be maintained by the county in which he was set free.[81] If the emancipation provisions of wills were not carried out, the slave could sue for his freedom in the Chancery Court.[82]

The fear engendered by the Nat Turner uprising and the defense attitude built up to offset the attacks of the abolitionists manifested themselves in this phase of slave legislation. In December, 1831, it was enacted that it was thereafter unlawful for any court or owner of any slave to emancipate such bondsman except on the "express condition, that such slave . . . shall be immediately removed from this state." The owner was to give bond equal to the value of the slave for the fulfillment of this requirement.[83] In 1833 there was quite a fight in the legislature to repeal the provision requiring that emancipated slaves be removed from the state. James W. Wyly, senator from Washington, Cocke, Greene, and Sevier counties, speaking on September 22, told the members to place themselves in the position of dying masters who wanted to free their slaves, but could not provide for their getting out of the state. "Would not their last dying accents denounce its provisions as revolting to humanity, justice, and the constitution of their country?"[84] Edward B. Littlefield, a slaveholder from Maury, said he was not an advocate of slavery as an abstract principle; he advanced the thesis that it was the only solution as long as the Negro remained in the area, and said he was unwilling to increase the facilities for emancipation except on the condition of colonization.[85] Leonard H. Sims (Rutherford and Williamson counties) took the same stand as Littlefield, and agreed with him, also, in contrasting the condition of the slave and the free black—much to the favor of the slave. He also noted the position of the free black as an agent or commission merchant in receiving and vending the articles that the slaves stole. Sims was in favor of emancipation, but "let them go to Africa, or to some place where they can enjoy their freedom."[86] No change was made in the 1831 act at this time.

Emancipated slaves were granted the right to remain in the state by an act of 1852, provided the courts appointed trustees for them.[87] This legislation was not to go into effect for two years; but three days before the expiration of this time the above provision was repealed, and no matter how a slave acquired his freedom, he was not only to be removed from the state, but must be sent to the western coast of Africa. If the liberator did not provide funds for passage and six months' support, the clerk of the court was to hire out the slave until the money was raised.[88] Emancipation restrictions in Tennessee remained in this status until slavery perished by the sword.

It is interesting and enlightening to glance at a decision of the Tennessee Supreme Court of Errors and Appeals—the final authority on all slave controversies in Tennessee. Joshua Hadley had freed his Negroes, but because of the restriction in Tennessee, had hired someone to take them to Illinois. In a short time some of them wanted to return to Tennessee to wait on their former master during his dying days. The clerk of the court in Illinois had told them they could safely do so. They came back, but after Hadley's death were taken into possession by a Mr. Blackmore, apparently the beneficiary of Hadley's will. Latimore, who had conveyed the slaves to Illinois, with the intention of their becoming citizens of that state, was a party to the suit of Phill for his freedom. The court held that once free in Illinois, the return to Tennessee does not replace them in the condition of slaves. . . . If it be true as contended, that the original design was to evade the laws of Tennessee, and that the return of the plaintiff . . . is inconsistent with our policy, still that will not place them in the condition of slaves. . . . If this State designed to make such acts . . . nullities, then express enactments should be shown.[89]

These justices of 1835 would not have agreed with the decision of the United States Supreme Court twenty-two years later.

The slave was substantially the equal of his free brother in the eyes of the law, but for many years enjoyed only a summary trial for his offenses. By a North Carolina statute of 1741, Negroes, mulattoes, and Indians, bond or free, were competent witnesses in the trial of slaves. If any of these witnesses were convicted of perjury, they were to have their ears nailed to the pillory and then cut off. Also they were to be given thirty-nine lashes on their bare backs. A special court of two or more magistrates and a jury of four slaveholders was the first tribunal for the trial of all slave cases.[90] In 1783 a single justice was declared competent to try cases that were punishable by whipping only, but if the offense was greater, the slave must be committed to jail and tried by the above means.[91]

The Assembly of the Southwest Territory stipulated that Negroes, mulattoes, Indians, and all persons of mixed blood descended from Negro or Indian ancestors to the third degree (although one parent of each generation be white), whether bond or free, were incapable of being competent witnesses in any case whatsoever, "except against each other." Also, no person of mixed blood in any degree, who had been liberated within the previous twelve months, was to be a competent witness against a white person.[92]

Tennessee was one of the five states that allowed the slave the right of jury trial.[93] In 1819 the legislature provided that in all trials of slaves where a jury was required by law it was the duty of the sheriff to summon three justices to preside and twelve "housekeepers being owners of slaves" to serve as a jury. All jailor's fees and trial costs were borne by the several counties.[94]

Later, if the juror was not a slaveowner, the master had just grounds for challenge, but not a basis for a new trial. In all such cases he could challenge four jurors, and if his slave was on trial for an offense involving the death penalty, he could challenge as many jurors "as a free white under similar circumstances." The slave could also be bailed as could a free white, except in cases of capital offenses "when the proof is evident or the presumption great."[95]

Eleven years later, 1836, the circuit courts were given exclusive original jurisdiction of all slave offenses that involved capital punishment, provided that no slave be tried until he had been indicted by a grand jury, and that the owner not be held liable for court costs. The state was to furnish counsel if the master did not, and any person could serve as a juror who was competent to occupy the same place in the trial of a white person.[96]

In an appeal case before the Supreme Court of Errors and Appeals in 1839, Elijah was on trial for assault and battery with intent to commit murder in the first degree by killing Puryear, a white man. A true bill was returned against him, but he pleaded not guilty, and his master concurred in this testimony. The lower court had rejected the master as an incompetent witness and sentenced the slave to be hanged. The decision was set aside and the prisoner remanded to be tried again, but the court ruled that:

in a case like this the law, upon high grounds of public policy . . . takes the slave out of the hands of his master . . . treats the slave as a rational and intelligent human being . . . and gives him the benefits of all the forms of trial which jealousy of power and love of liberty have induced the freeman to throw around himself for his own protection . . . the objection must be held to extend to the credit not to the competency of the master.[97]

This was an instance in which the court felt that personal economic interest interfered with the ability of a witness to present competent evidence.

The slave, of course, was never granted the right of suffrage, but, as other property, he was subject to executory sale for the payment of debts. The Panic of 1819, however, and the attendant hardships fostered legislation to "prevent the sacrifice of land and slaves" sold under the legal hammer. It was provided that slaves sold in this manner could be recovered within two years by payment of the money bid plus ten per cent interest.[98] This was not a too liberal stipulation, but it did allow the slaveowner a period of grace in which to regain his economic footing.

Shortly afterward no slave could be sold under execution unless the purchaser gave bond—twice the value of the slave assessed by "two good freeholders of the county unconnected with either party"—that the slave should be forthcoming at any time during the period stipulated for recovery. If the buyer did not give this "recognizance," the sheriff was to readvertise and resell, and the sheriff who delivered a slave without the required bond was to forfeit and pay a sum equivalent to the full value of the slave.[99]

The acts of 1820, 1821, and 1823 were repealed in 1825, but an owner (by paying the auction price) could still recover within two years a slave who had been in jail for twelve months and then sold after thirty days' notice had been given.[100] Any public official who sold land or slaves under any circumstances was required to advertise the same in the county paper at least three times, and the first advertisement was to appear not less than thirty days previous to the sale.[101]

One method by which the slave gained his manumission was the hiring of his own time; but this, like other privileges, was soon circumvented by legal restrictions. After 1823 any person who hired to any slave the time of that slave was to forfeit and pay not less than $1 nor more than $2 for each day that the offense was committed.[102] The illegality of self-hire was reiterated in 1839 and the penalty raised to $500 for each offense. A similar penalty was imposed on anyone who permitted a slave under his control to enjoy any of the privileges of a free person of color, that is, living to himself, owning hogs, cows, horses, mules, or other description of property, and spending his time as he pleased.[103]

Slaves, like other property, were subject to taxation, and it is worth while to note the gross inequality of the state tax on the different species of property. A few comparisons will suffice to show that the land speculator played a major role in taxation problems in Tennessee until 1834.[104] The first session of the first territorial assembly enacted that:

. . . all free males and male servants between the ages of 21 and 50 years; all slaves, male and female, between the ages of 10 and 50 years . . . shall be subject to the payment of public taxes . . . the public tax on . . . all white polls 25¢; on each and every negro poll 50¢.[105]

And the same statute said that land was to be taxed at 25¢ per hundred acres, regardless of value, and town lots at the flat rate of $1! The second session of the assembly cut all tax rates in half.[106]

The Constitution of 1796 provided that the tax on an area of one hundred acres was to be no higher than the tax on another area of the same size, and the tax on town lots was to be no higher than the tax on two hundred acres. The tax on freemen was not to exceed that on one hundred acres, and that on slaves should not be higher than on a town lot.[107] An act of the following year made a slight change in the tax rates, to wit: 12½ ¢ per hundred acres, 25¢ on town lots, and 25¢ on Negro polls. The counties were authorized to levy an equal tax.[108] These rates remained substantially the same for the next thirty-seven years.

When the democracy of the small farmer under the leadership of Governor William Carroll finally gained the upper hand, a more reasonable tax provision was put into effect by the Constitution of 1834. This document provided that all land and other taxable property should be prorated according to value, which value should be ascertained in such manner as the legislature should direct.[109] After this date the question of taxation was not such a controversial one, and the tax problem concerning slaves seemed to hinge on the issue of whether the hirer or the owner should bear this expense. It was finally provided that slaves were to be assessed to the owner in the county in which he resided, whether the slaves were hired out or not; but if the owner had farms in different counties, the slaves would be assessed where they resided.[110]

The penal code concerning slaves was specifically defined in 1819, when it was declared that murder, arson, burglary, rape, and robbery—and only these—were capital offenses, and a slave convicted of any of these was to suffer death by hanging.[111] It was from these offenses that many of the most interesting of the slave trials developed. There was the case of Tom, who ran away and hid in the woods; Haley, a hunter, came unexpectedly upon Tom, who promptly shot him in the arm. The lower court found the slave guilty of assault with intent to kill and sentenced him to be hanged. The appeal court held that although the prisoner must have felt Haley to be in pursuit of him, it is

no offense for any individual to arrest a runaway slave . . . if he resist and slay . . . he is guilty of murder in the first degree. . . . It may be painful to the feelings to hold such doctrine, but it is a necessary incident to the institution of slavery . . . no pretence whatever for the assault, however the prisoner no doubt thought otherwise . . . however much we regret the consequences, we must affirm the judgment.[112]

One other quotation will suffice to show the general attitudes of the court in determining a slave's guilt on a murder charge, as well as to throw light on what was not considered provocation. In the case of Jacob v. State, the master, Robert Bradford, had been killed by the slave; intending to punish him, Bradford had postponed the penalty for some time and had not allowed Jacob on the place until he was willing to be whipped. In affirming the sentence of hanging, the court laid down the following principle as to the master's control of his slave:

the right to obedience . . . in all lawful things . . . is perfect in the master; and the power to inflict any punishment, not affecting life or limb . . . for the purpose of . . . enforcing such obedience . . . is secured to him by law, and if in the exercise of it, with or without cause, the slave resist and slay him, it is murder . . . because the law cannot recognize the violence of the master as a legitimate cause of provocation.[113]

Trials for rape, or attempt to rape, were rather frequent compared to others involving the death penalty, but it is difficult to agree with the court's reasoning in some instances. Sydney, a slave boy, was dismissed for attempting rape of a six-year-old white girl, because "the Legislature did not mean, by the word woman . . . a child under the age of ten years."[114] In a later case Dan was found not guilty on a rape charge, but this time the court noted that an attack on a white girl under ten was not a capital offense: "a singular omission by the Legislature."[115]

An 1822 statute prohibited cohabitation of persons of color and whites; but the court held that the law was so worded that the penalty could be imposed only on the white, and that the colored person had not been guilty of violation of a statutory prohibition.[116]

What then was the status of the slave in Tennessee? By civil law he was a chattel and by common law a person, but these two systems of jurisprudence were so combined in this state that he had characteristics of both. As a chattel he was personal property with no legal right to hold property himself; he had neither civil marriage nor political rights; his movements in the community, his time and labor, were subject to the control of his master; his punishments were usually whippings; he had no control over his offspring; and he was subject to sale, as any other piece of property, to the highest bidder.

As a person the slave could be a party to a suit for his freedom, for which he could contract during the early period of the institution in Tennessee; he could represent his master in various transactions; his children were not illegitimate but took the status of their mother; he was held responsible for murder, arson, rape, and other offenses; and he possessed the cherished privilege of trial by jury. He was also protected by law in other ways, but these were his most important privileges and immunities.

It is also fitting to note that the slave was eligible for life insurance at a lower premium than the white person. It seems that not many of the slaves were insured, though, and this protection was provided chiefly against the "dangers of the river." The northern companies, however, were willing to take the risk of insuring them, and stated that losses would be "promptly adjusted."[117]

Though Tennessee prohibited the interstate slave trade for many years, the slave naturally had no right to choose his master and was subject to sale in the same manner as was other property. Consequently, numerous regulations concerning the hire and sale of slaves were invariably upheld by the judicial tribunals of the state.

Attention should again be called to the great change that occurred in the legislation of Tennessee after 1831. In nearly every instance, punishments were increased and privileges and immunities were lessened and circumvented. Many of these laws seem to have been enacted as precautionary measures, being more honored in the breach than in the observance. They were part of the code so that they might quickly and easily be enforced should the necessity arise. Slaveowners often violated the slave code when it was to their convenience to do so.

TWO

Hire, Sale, Flight, and Theft
of Slaves

IT IS only natural that nonslaveowners and owners who did not
have a sufficient number of workers to meet their labor demands
would desire to, and did, hire or buy Negroes from those who had
more than enough for their immediate needs. Likewise, there were
a few persons who did not hesitate to steal slaves either for their
own economic benefit or for the purpose of freeing the slaves,
while some Negroes, prompted by a desire for freedom or en-
couraged by individuals of allegedly benevolent attitudes, fled
from the services of their masters.

No attempt will be made to determine the exact amount paid for
the hire of slaves during any particular period, nor the price of
slaves, nor the number of fugitive or stolen slaves. A number of
cases will be given in each category so that the reader may arrive
at reasonably accurate approximations in each instance. County
records show many cases of sale and hire, but these are so
numerous and so nearly identical one to the other that they would
do little toward clarifying the picture. Personal papers and newspapers have been the chief source of information for this chapter.

HIRE OF SLAVES

Hiring was a practice which was beneficial to both parties to
the contract. The person hiring the slave could thus get reasonably
cheap labor, while the owner would profit by having his slave

employed in a certain remunerative capacity when he was not needed at home. General economic conditions—supply and demand, price of staples—seemed to have affected the monetary value of a slave's work as well as the value of the slave.

The term of hire usually expired on January 1 following the date of agreement. The person hiring the slave generally gave him his "keep"—that is, food, shelter, and clothing—but there was no fixed practice as to responsibility for medical attention. If the slave hired on a yearly contract basis should become disabled, or even die, before the expiration of the year, the hirer was still bound by the terms of the agreement, for "the temporary owner . . . is subject . . . to all the casualties . . . so far as his interest reaches, unless there be stipulation in his favor to the contrary."[1] The privilege of sub-hiring was denied unless the owner gave his consent;[2] and the hirer must not excessively chastise the rented slave. The Supreme Court of Errors and Appeals said that if the hirer punished the slave he "must always, at his peril, be able to show . . . reasonable grounds for the chastisement, and that it did not . . . exceed the bounds of moderate correction. . . ."[3]

Joseph Hooper and his wife hired Negroes from John Claybrooke, Davidson County, in the 1790's and early 1800's. Their accounts from 1794 to 1804 show that they paid $180 for hire of Lettice for nine years, $146 for Tilda for ten years, and $466.67 for two-thirds of the hire of Nan and Bess for fourteen years. Claybrooke had only a two-thirds interest in Nan and Bess; they were valued at $400 each, and each had brought their owners $350 in fourteen years—a profitable investment from the standpoint of modern business. The price paid for the services of Lettice and Tilda was very low, and Claybrooke did not receive all of that. A $20 reduction was made for "administering and attending" to Lettice while she was sick during most of the year 1796; $10.50 also was allowed the hirer for bed clothes during the same period.[4]

At times slaves were hired for the purpose of learning a trade. Early in 1821, John Overton hired Matilda to Joseph Wright. She was to follow weaving on these terms: Overton was to receive $22 in weaving; Wright was to clothe the girl "by furnishing

her with two full suits of clothes suitable to the season"; and at
the end of a year Overton should be furnished a loom, at a reasonable price, of the kind to which Matilda had been accustomed.[5]

Often a desire was expressed by the owner for husband and wife
to stay together, and the rural section was preferred to the city.
Such was the case with Mrs. Sarah McLean, living three miles
east of Nashville, when she offered a Negro man and his wife,
and a "very valuable negro fellow" for hire in 1818.[6] The following
year she proposed to hire two Negro men and one Negro cook,
possibly the same three Negroes.[7]

It frequently happened that the administrator of an estate let
out the slaves of the deceased. In 1820 forty men, women, boys,
and girls were to be hired at the store of Sanders and Chandler
near Clover Bottom, Andrew Jackson's racing grounds. Field
hands seem to have constituted the major portion of these, but
there were "tobacconists, coarse shoe makers, etc." among them.[8]
Thirty Negroes of the late Benjamin Phillips were offered for hire
in February of the same year.[9]

Field hands practically always hired at a rate comparable to the
wages of the unskilled white; the more skilled laborers com-
manded a higher rental wage and were more in demand. Ellis
Maddox advertised in 1804 for an apprentice to the blacksmith's
business, and a "Journeyman who understands his business, and
has good recommendations for honesty, industry, and sobriety. A
black man will not be rejected" in either instance.[10]

Of the skilled laborers, blacksmiths were probably hired more
than any other type, as they were essential to the functioning of a
well-rounded plantation. Since they were not required all the
time, their period of hire was frequently less than a year. Edward
Ward wished to hire Henry, John Overton's smith, for "about half
the season." Ward said he would take Henry by the week, two
weeks, or the month. Ward placed faith in Overton's sense of
justice; he said to send Henry, "set your price, I'll give it believing
you will ask nothing that is unreasonable."[11]

James Winchester had some difficulty over a blacksmith that
McBride, proprietor of the Gallatin Cotton Mill, had hired from
him. The trouble lay in McBride's failure to perform the services

that he promised in return for use of the smith. Winchester did not consider McBride a "very worthy person."[12]

The slave bringing the largest known return to his master was Harry, the blacksmith of Samuel P. Polk. Harry was sent from Tennessee to Mississippi, where he earned more than would have been possible in the former state. He was the father of eleven children and a "friend" of the Polk family, and he earned $350 for his master in 1841. In 1852 Polk received $487.76 for Harry's services, and, in addition, Harry did all the smithing for the Mississippi plantation.[13]

House servants were generally very much in demand, as evidenced by the number of people advertising for them. What one might consider a typical advertisement was the notice of R. and B. B. Winn in 1806. They wished to hire a Negro woman until January 1, 1807, who must be "well recommended" and "acquainted with house business." They offered a "generous price" for such a servant.[14]

John Overton also hired other Negroes besides the blacksmith, Henry, and the weaver, Matilda, and his slaves seem to have had a good reputation. In 1824 Samuel Stackens wrote Overton expressing a desire to hire Bob as a fireman for the steamboat *Rambler,* which was to leave Nashville the next day. Bob was to be given the "customary wages."[15] It is not known what "customary wages" were, but pay for this type of work was much higher than that for a field hand. Also, a man from Columbia wanted to hire Overton's "good mulespinner" for six or twelve months.[16]

The hirers of slaves were required to give bond and good security, and, as stated above, to furnish them with clothes suitable to the season of the year. Some persons, however, did not scruple to hire Negroes without the consent of the owners. On August 9, 1819, Morgan Brown inserted a notice in the Clarksville *Town Gazette and Farmers' Register* to the effect that his Negroes had been working at night "for such persons as will employ them, to the great injury of their health and morals." Brown forbade such practice without his written permission, and also cautioned against trading with, buying from, or selling to them; he threatened strict enforcement of the law "without regard to persons."[17]

The only official statistics relative to the price of labor in Tennessee for the first half of the nineteenth century are found in the reports of the keeper of the state penitentiary. Estimates are based on the earnings of convicts working at mechanical trades. These figures show that the average mechanic earned about $500 per year, or slightly more than the average plantation overseer. Unskilled labor was valued at $10 per month and "keep," and slaves rented for $80 to $100 per year, plus "keep."[18] This was for semiskilled slaves, but it does not quite agree with the offer of Macy and Stewart to give $20 per month for four or six "Negroes or White men to work at the steam mill."[19] The work at the mill, however, was dangerous; skill was required; and nothing is said about providing food and clothing. R. H. Barry wrote John Claybrooke on October 13, 1835, that Negroes were hiring for $120 per year: "I expect . . . much higher than you would like to give. . . ."[20] One hundred dollars, food, and clothing was probably a fair price at this time for the services of an unskilled slave for a year.

The price of slave labor naturally fluctuated with the market value of the slave, the type of work, and the profits which the hirer expected to make. By 1858 the Memphis and New Orleans Packet Line was paying $40 per month for the Negroes who worked on the boats.[21]

Unfortunately, not all the census takers in 1860 indicated whether slaves were hired or owned by the individual to whom they were credited. Of the fifteen counties used as samples in this study, the hired slaves are designated in only four—Davidson, Fayette, Haywood, and Lincoln. In these counties the number of hirers and hired slaves, respectively, were: Davidson, 44 and 160; Fayette, 49 and 136; Haywood, 5 and 10; Lincoln, 14 and 29.[22] This makes a total of 112 hirers and 335 hired slaves. There were probably more slaves hired than the census indicates, but again the lack of adequate training of the census takers must be considered.

Although the exact number of hired slaves cannot be ascertained, it is apparent that the practice of hiring was followed— as in the other slave states—without an unusual amount of friction between owner and hirer, and sometimes to the satisfaction of the slave himself. Self-hire or the right of a slave to hire his own time, however, was declared illegal in 1823, and severe penalties were later provided for infringement of this statutory prohibition.[23]

SALE OF SLAVES

Sale or exchange of slaves was a natural accompaniment of slavery, and the price paid for Negroes in Tennessee approximated that in the other states. As in the case of the hiring of slaves, no attempt will be made to present a complete picture, but a few transfers will be cited in order to indicate the almost uninterrupted increase of slave prices.

On July 9, 1792, Frederick Stump, one of the signers of the Cumberland Articles of Agreement, sold to John Overton a Negro man "March, about twenty three or four years of age," for £ 100.[24] Possibly March was a skilled laborer, for the price is rather high for the period, and, of course, slaves were still not numerous in the region. Three years later, Thomas Overton wrote John Overton that he would buy Captain Ben Williams' land and "pay him down provided he will take negroes in payment. . . ."[25] Negroes served as payment for practically everything, and, in turn, nearly anything was taken as payment for Negroes. While many farmers or planters, however, were selling their "excess" land and buying Negroes, Thomas wished to do the reverse.

John Overton might be classed as a slave trader—but not of the coffle-driving type—for he both purchased and sold quite a number of Negroes. Some of his purchases follow: Robin and Pol, $530; Sam, Phyllis, and Ezekiel, $1050; Mathew and wife (slaves of John Coffee, purchased through the United States marshal), $710; Charles, $180 in "horse flesh, and one hundred and ten dollars in notes"; Lewis, $400; Betty, $800; Elijah, $450; Wood, $600; Bob, $500; Huldy, $375; Tom, $300; Ben, $385; Arthur, $315; Washington, $340; Adam, $500; Martin and Oliver, $365; and "two negroes," $700.[26]

The sale of a slave was accompanied by the guarantee from the seller that "he is sound and healthy, and not in the habit of running away or stealing or in other words that he is not a rogue or a runaway."[27] Overton had a little difficulty with one of his slaves on the first count. Seth L. Hardeman of New Orleans wrote Overton on March 6, 1830, that the boy, Elbert, whom he had purchased had "come down" with the rheumatism three or four days after leaving Nashville. Hardeman's first reaction was that nothing was wrong with the Negro "except his opposition to coming to this place." The purchaser said that if he could not cure Elbert, he did not intend to pay for him unless compelled to do so. He did not think that Overton had intentionally practiced a fraud on him, but he did want to know what Overton wished done with the Negro.[28]

Overton must not have replied, or else replied to the effect that the Negro had been sold, and he would like to have the money for him. A few months later Seth's father, Eliazar, wrote Overton that he did not intend to keep the Negro, even if he recovered from his sickness. Hardeman told Overton that "You could not give him to me unless yould [sic] make me a compiments [sic] of his wife to take care of him neither would I be instrumental in parting them." He added a postscript, part of which was incoherent: "you may make his securities pay all that I now [owe?] and if you are determined to do so the sooner his business will be settled for I am determined never to do it [that is, pay for Elbert] nor . . . to encourage any man in the slave trade."[29]

Finally, though, the money for Elbert was received, and R. H. Barry communicated this information to Overton, who was in Knoxville, on August 13, 1831. Also, Barry said he had not been able to find a Negro to "suit" Overton, and suggested that the latter buy one or two in Knoxville—if he had not gotten any in Virginia. Barry himself wanted one or two slaves, and quoted Overton some prices to the effect that Negroes were rather too expensive around Nashville.[30]

Another purchaser, John W. Walker, felt that he had been cheated in a deal with Chapley R. Wellborne of Fayetteville, Tennessee. Walker had bought the Negro at night, only to be informed later by his overseer that *the fellow had no toes on his feet.* He wrote Wellborne that "you have practised on me a base and monstrous imposition." Walker said that he had personally inspected the Negro, and learned "the anecdote of the cotton so cunningly stuffed in the front for show. . . . An honest man can never be guilty of such an act. . . . Much as I abhor lawsuits, I shall hold myself bound to expose you before a jury of your country unless you come down speedily, take back your negroes, and repay me my money. . . ."[31] The outcome of the case is not known.

One of Overton's Negroes, Nelson, became diseased, and R. H. Barry—who seems to have looked after Overton's affairs when the latter was away from home—was quite provoked at "old Stephen for not having told long since of his having applied to him for something to cure him." Nelson, so Barry wrote, said that he "must of caught it from a pare of panterloons that was given to him by some person but I know that he must ly about it as he must of caught it from some of these dirty devels about town. . . ."[32] A little while later, Philip Shute made an offer of the original purchase price, and Barry advised Overton to sell Nelson "as he has behaved so badly about the disease."[33]

Overton was not the only one buying and selling Negroes outside the state in violation of the statute of 1826.[34] In 1834 Barry wrote John Claybrooke that he had not been able to sell the latter's boy and he did not wish to put him up at auction. Barry said, "I have not been able to see James Perkins or to sell him to any of the traders in this place [Nashville] as I think the price is somewhat on the decline."[35] In the fall of the same year, 1834, Barry informed Claybrooke that Perkins had been home two weeks with eleven Negroes for Jackson. Jackson was late returning, however, because one of his Negroes ran off at Abingdon, Virginia, and "kept him 2 weeks longer than he would of been negroes are very high in Va   Jack pd as high as $615 for a man who was only 20 to be a tanner   other men $550."[36]

Barry was disturbed over the high price of slaves and noted that "our country must under go a great change before Long as we cant stand things as they now are." Only "a few days since" there had been a sale of Negroes, and a "young fellow" sold for the "small sum of $1,504 and others . . . equally high."[37] At the same time *The Anti-Slavery Record* stated that in Tennessee the price of slaves was "never known to be higher" nor people "ever more madly bent on continuing the practise of slavery."[38]

Many people wishing to purchase slaves inserted advertisements in the papers to that effect. In 1823 Baxter and Hicks, of the Tennessee Iron Works, advertised for "20 likely young Negro Fellows between the age of 18 and 24 years; also 2 or 3 good Blacksmiths, and 2 or 3 women."[39] "Pike's Intelligence Register" of November 7, 1831, listed 20 people who wished to buy, sell, or hire Negroes, and to some of the advertisers the price was "no consideration."[40] People felt that the institution was here to stay and they wished to profit as much as possible by it.

Naturally some slaves brought higher prices than others. In Memphis, in 1846 and 1847, carpenters sold for $2,500; a hammerer, or a helper, for a blacksmith for $1,114; painters for $1,005; field hands from $750 to $1,000; boys about 12 years of age for $700; and girls between 12 and 18, from $600 to $800.[41]

The prices paid for slaves at a chancery sale in Lebanon in 1859 were considerably above the average. A description of the slaves sold and the prices paid follow: Jerry, 16, one arm defective, $1,125; Harriet, 19, and a little child, $1,675; Judy, 30, $905; Lewis, 15, $1,406; Jacob, 34, $1,305; Jane, 26, and two small children, $2,050; Sally, 8, $1,051; Emeline, 7, $1,051; John, 14, $1,575; Paralee, 22, and two small children, $2,280; Tom, 21, $1,656; Hannah, 19, and suckling child, $1,687; Tabby, 15, $1,051; Emeline, 25, unsound, $700; Prince, 10, $860; Bob, 7, $800; and Hasty, 60, $100.[42]

Slave buying and selling were naturally dependent, to an extent, upon the general economic conditions prevalent in the various sections of the country and the attendant demand, or lack of demand, for this "commodity." The price of slaves fluctuated with material prosperity. In 1790 the average value of slaves was from $150 to $200,[43] and in 1795 they were worth from $300 to $400 upward in the upper and lower South, respectively. Eight years later the price range rose to $400 and $600 "in consequence of the initial impulse of cotton and sugar production and of the contemporary prohibition of the African slave trade by the several states."[44]

The period of prosperity immediately following the War of 1812 caused slave prices to increase about $100 per slave, and by 1818 the average price ranged from $500 to $1,000. By 1823, however, prices had declined to substantially the level of 1814. The prosperous years following the disappearance of the effects of the Panic of 1819 were accompanied by an increase of prices, so that by 1837 slaves sold for $1,300 in the purchasing markets and $1,100 in Virginia. "The general panic of 1837," however, "began promptly to send them down; and though they advanced in 1839 as a consequence of a speculative bolstering of the cotton market that year, they fell all the faster upon collapse of that project, finding new levels of rest only at a range of $500-$700."[45] A final advance set in during the middle 1840's and continued until the highest levels on record were reached on the eve of secession and war.[46]

How closely did the prices in Tennessee correspond to this general pattern? The amounts that Overton paid for his Negroes seem to follow the same trend, but not enough data are available for the period before 1836 to say definitely whether there is a close correlation. The Tennessee Comptrollers' reports, however, give more definite information for the period from 1836 to 1859. After 1836 the trend of prices in Tennessee was the same as that outlined by Phillips for the South as a whole. By that year, 1836, the average value of slaves in the Volunteer State was $584. This decreased to $540 in 1838, rose to $543 in 1840, and then declined to a low of $413.72 in 1846. After 1846 there was a rapid increase to the all-time high of $854.65 in 1859.[47]

Phillips says that the "heyday" of the slave trade was just prior to the Panic of 1837, for "thereafter the flow was held somewhat in check, first by the hard times in the cotton belt and then by an agricultural renaissance in Virginia." The role of Tennessee in the interstate slave trade was a negligible one until the late 1850's, for participation in that traffic had been legally forbidden Tennesseans from 1827 to 1855.

Previous to the re-legalizing of the interstate trade, private citizens of Tennessee often expressed the wish that the slaves they were offering for sale be kept within the county, or, by all means, within the state. One owner, advertising in 1831, wished to sell a woman and her children together, if they would be kept in Tennessee. If a purchaser could not be found who would do that, the slaves would be sold separately in the county.[48] Another advertiser offered to sell, "on good terms," a family of six to some person who would keep them "in the county; or if carried out of the state would not separate them."[49] The feeling seems to have been that if the families must be separated, the individual members should not be taken far from their habitual environs.

The first evidence of an interstate slave trader operating in Tennessee is contained in an anonymous and undirected letter from Knoxville on January 24, 1795. The writer stated that on arrival

I took the earliest opportunity to prepare to Bring you the Negroes. . . . I shall depend upon you to take them. I intend to bring some others, with me for sale, if you make any, Engagements for me, I shall ever be bound in acknoledgements, Governor Blount is my friend and will aide me—I intend Carrying on the Business, Extensively. Your Pattronage in Kentucky will be—Gratefully Solicited. . . .[50]

It would be incorrect to say that no slave trading between Tennessee and the surrounding territory was carried on at this early date, but to state that the "North Carolina and Virginia pioneers in Davidson County brought with them their slaves, and the sale of slaves was continuously carried on between this settlement and those of Illinois and the lower Mississippi Region"[51] gives a false impression, and is a generalization on insufficient data if the recording of slave sales is to be taken as an indication of the extent of such transactions.[52]

A Mr. Haley may have engaged in the interstate traffic, for in 1835 John Claybrooke was apprised of the fact that Haley had "some $40,000 to lay out in negroes . . . but was willing to take your money if he could lay it out so as to get home by the 1st of Sept."[53]

Joseph Meek of Nashville, however, was definitely in the business, and his partners remained in Virginia while he moved about in Tennessee, Mississippi, and Virginia. Meek formed a partnership by correspondence early in 1835. Samuel Logan of Abingdon, Virginia, was the initiator of the plan that was finally adopted. On February 9, 1835, Logan wrote Meek that he and others had already purchased six or eight slaves at a very good price, "say 500$ for likely fellow," and he thought that from twenty to fifty more Negroes could be bought on the same favorable basis. Logan told Meek that he would not be able to raise more than $1,000 or $2,000, and consequently had but "little interest in the business" for the time being. C. Haynes, Logan's law partner who wished to become a partner in the slave-trading firm, was also in need of funds.[54]

Logan thought that he and Haynes could raise a "considerable" amount of money in a few weeks, but by that time the other slave traders would have returned to the purchasing field and prices would be up again. Meek was asked to state his terms of entering into the business and furnishing from $5,000 to $10,000. Meek had formerly asked Logan to enter into partnership with him, and Logan reminded him of this fact. Logan said that he was not acquainted with the business and Meek was; previously lack of capital had hampered them. At the time of the earlier attempt to form a partnership Meek had only a little money, Logan had none, and the latter had "damned little yet." The Virginians would be forced to sell what slaves they had in six weeks or two months if they could not secure capital, but they wanted Meek's advice before they made any partnership.

In the same communication Logan proposed that his and Haynes' participation in the sought-for partnership be kept secret; knowledge of their slave-trading activities would interfere with their law practice. A third Virginian, Magee, was suggested to Meek as the "front" for the traders in the buying market. Magee was Haynes' merchandizing partner, and these two had done some Negro speculating the previous summer. Logan told Meek that they had made from $50 to $100 profit per Negro, and he thought they had shown "skill and judgment."[55]

Meek replied rather promptly; Logan received the letter on March 1 and answered it four days later. In this letter Logan repeated Meek's terms as he understood them. They were: (1) Meek was to furnish as much money as Logan, Magee, and Haynes together; (2) the latter three were to purchase and Meek was to market and sell the Negroes; (3) losses, expenses for clothing, suits for freedom (if any), or any other litigations were to be borne by the partnership; and (4) profits, if any, were to be halved between Meek and the other three.[56] The "purchasers thought the terms fair," and requested that the money be sent "some how as soon as possible." Already they had bought ten or twelve slaves upon better terms than Meek had indicated in his letter, but the influx of traders had raised prices to what Meek considered a "safe" buying level. By this letter the final arrangements of the partnership were concluded.

Shortly thereafter Logan forwarded to Haynes a letter from Meek requesting information on the progress of purchases. In reply Haynes told Meek that things were moving along nicely; fortyseven Negroes had been bought for $19,800, an average of $421. Among these were a family of nineteen for $6,200; a blacksmith with a fifteen-year-old boy and a seventeen-year-old girl for $1,-650; "Susan—24—not fleshy but weighs 170 lbs. Yellow"—for $500; and "Jac—30 large and Likely—180—$600."[57]

Haynes realized that some had "cost high," especially "Julian motatto [sic] handsome face Smart 17 competition $550."[58] Inflation of prices was attributed to a Kentucky trader, but Haynes' practice of allowing the seller to keep the Negroes until August 1 gave the Virginia owners an incentive to sell to Meek's partners rather than to the other traders, who took immediate possession. Haynes said they still had money on hand, and that they planned to purchase about thirty more Negroes. The slaves would be ready for the road by August 10.[59]

Slave speculation at this early date was not without its troubles, as Haynes revealed to Meek about three months later. Magee, who had gone to Kentucky, returned "without one negro," and Haynes had some trouble getting slaves for whom he had already contracted. A certain Gearhart had "run all his (except some

children) off and had them hid."[60] Half the purchase price had
been paid Gearhart, but, instead of delivering the Negroes on
August 1, he wished to return the money. Haynes said he was
unwilling to let Gearhart go without suing him for delivery of the
slaves; he would have done so by the last mail if he had known
where the nearest Federal Court was located.

Also, Logan had not been at Abingdon to receive Graham's
and Batty's Negroes and nobody knew anything about them. These
unfortunate occurrences had reduced the number on hand to about
fifty and no wagon would be needed for them. The youngest was
eight years old.[61] Haynes, Logan, and Magee still had "mony a
plenty," but did not seem to be able to get the Negroes they wanted.
No further information is available concerning the activities of
1835; the troubles must have been overcome for the business was
continued the next year.

Prices had increased by 1836, and sixty-one Negroes cost
Messrs. Meek, Haynes, Magee, and Logan $42,420, an average
of $695. Included in this group were Elisha, 22, $1000; three
men, 23, 21, and 19, $2,850; Billy, a blacksmith, $1,200; and
two men, 25 and 19 (one a shoemaker), $1,900. The situation
of the previous year was reversed; this time the money was "nearly
out," and the "Negroes are plenty."[62] One of the Negroes did not
want to leave Virginia and had cut off his hand. He had cost
$450, but could now "be counted as nothing," and an attempt was
to be made to exchange him.

More Negroes were bought before the drive was started about
August 15. Haynes, Magee, and Logan were the drivers as far as
Bean's Station.[63] Up to this point thirteen of the men had been
chained, and when the Virginians left the coffle, the Negroes were
going on "very cheerfully, peaceably and safely." Price, Jesse
Haynes, and Simms were to conduct the ninety-eight slaves on
to Nashville. Meek, in a letter previous to the beginning of the
drive, had expressed a desire that C. Haynes accompany the
Negroes all the way, and Haynes said that had he gotten the letter
in time, he "would have certainly" done so. He, however, would
continue to buy.[64]

The slaves apparently reached Nashville safely, but some of those that Haynes bought after he returned to Virginia ran away, and Haynes was busying himself trying to capture them. In a letter to Meek on October 6, 1836, Haynes explained the situation relative to the fugitives. A friend of Haynes had seen the Negroes on the previous Saturday night and would see them again the next Saturday night. This "intermediary" was to make an arrangement to meet the Negroes some week night, and would notify Haynes, who would send assistance to take them. Haynes thought the Negroes could "be got." Additional purchases, ranging from $675 to $1,000, had been made and some of these slaves were to be started in two weeks. Haynes must have put other buyers in the field, for he stated that Hickman and Clevinger were still buying and would not start until a week or so after the first group. Hickman was also having trouble with runaways.[65]

Toward the latter part of 1836 and early 1837 misfortune dogged the heels of the traders. In November of the former year Logan's wife died and left him with a small child. Logan then planned to sell his own slaves, but said he "must keep some woman that gives suck."[66] Financial difficulties followed. Logan was glad to see Meek selling for cash and short-term credit, but he had borrowed heavily and still owed money. John M. Preston, their biggest creditor, was going back into business and wanted his $11,505. Tankerly was due $1,016.67 and Hugh White $350. White had been the slave traders' security for $5,000 or $6,000. He had been released at his own request, much to the dissatisfaction of Logan, who said, "I never want to have anything more to do with him."[67]

The last evidence obtainable on the transactions of these four traders is contained in a letter from Logan to Meek on May 28, 1837. The panic had come; Logan did not know what kind of notes to take "one day before hand"; all the banks had stopped payment. He advised caution in the trading for that year, requested from $5,000 to $10,000 in specie if possible, and closed by saying that "we are among the damndest population upon the earth for the slander of mens circumstances."[68] By this statement he evidently meant that his fellow Virginians were prone to talk about his financial well-being as well as the activities in which an individual engaged.

Meek is the only individual who is known to have been carrying on interstate slave trading from Nashville at this time, but there must have been others. A letter from John M. Bass, president of the Union Bank of Tennessee at Nashville, to M. D. Cooper of Columbia on February 1, 1837, substantiates this assertion. Bass wrote Cooper, in part,

> . . . it has been a common subject of complaint against the Union Bank that too large amount of its accomodations have been extended to Negro traders & other speculators to the exclusion of the Planter and Merchant—It is the intention of the Board at least not to *merit* this imputation in future.[69]

Tennessee was well situated to be a slave-trading state and to serve as an entrepôt between the border states—primarily Kentucky—and the lower South. Memphis was a first-class market, but Nashville's mart never rose above second-rate and the capital city was chiefly a point of dispersion.

The legal prohibition of the interstate trade in Tennessee and the social stigma attached to slave trading prompted many of the Nashville dealers not to use the term "slave trader" in their notices during the "prohibition" years. An advertisement in the *Daily Nashville True Whig* of November 12, 1852, referred those who wished to purchase "valuable family servants" to Andrew Ewing on Cherry Street or to Henry Williams "living at the place formerly owned by Jos. F. Williams, dec'd."

In 1853—prior to the re-legalizing of the interstate traffic— Glover and Boyd advertised as "Agents and collectors for the sale and purchase of real estate, negroes, etc., and collectors in the City-Office, 50 N. Cherry St."[70] Dabbs and Porter also advertised as agents for the "purchase and sale of real estate and negroes," while Ballowe and Scruggs were agents for the "purchase and sale of property."[71] Apparently, Glover and Dabbs quit the business by 1854, for, in that year, W. L. Boyd, Jr., and R. W. Porter, former members of the firms of Glover and Boyd and Dabbs and Porter, advertised as rival Nashville slave dealers in the *Southern Business Directory* of Charleston, South Carolina.[72]

The interstate slave traffic was re-legalized in Tennessee in 1855. By 1857 Boyd's establishment had become a "general agency" and H. H. Haynes was a "clerk" at 33 Cedar Street.[73] Two years later this "clerk" would buy or sell slaves on commission and had "a good and pleasant yard and safe rooms for keeping them."[74] On the eve of secession Nashville's slave traders had increased to six. They were: Lyles and Hitchings, "dealers in slaves," 33 Cedar Street; Webb, Merrill and Co., "negro dealers," 8 South Market Street; H. H. Haynes and Co., "dealers in slaves," 16 Cedar Street; E. S. Hawkins, "slave dealer," 18 Cedar Street; G. H. Hitchings, "negro dealer," 72 Broad Street; and W. L. Boyd, Jr., "general agent and dealer in slaves," 50 North Cherry Street.[75]

E. S. Hawkins was probably the most extensive advertiser among the Nashville dealers. In 1859 he attracted attention thus:

NEGROES! NEGROES!

For Sale

I have on hand three families of negroes which I wish to sell to good homes in this or adjoining counties. They are all good servants— Cooks washers and ironers, etc. Also four or five good field hands. I have a good man who is a fine house servant; all of which I will sell low for cash. Call and see for yourselves at 18 Cedar St.[76]

Will Boyd, Jr., was the next most extensive advertiser in Nashville papers, but his notices were not as "catchy" to the eye as were those of Hawkins. Boyd said

I have several likely negroes for sale. Among them is a superior cook, washer, etc. about 20 years of age.

I.wish to buy all the good young negroes that is offered in this market, and have got the money to pay for them. Call and see me before you sell.[77]

He apparently would have liked to have a monopoly of what must have been a profitable but degraded business.

Webb, Merrill and Company would at "all times purchase NEGROES suited to the N. O. market."[78] Although Bancroft says that this company and Lyles and Hitchings were the leaders in the Nashville trade,[79] the fact remains that their advertisements in the local papers were infrequent when compared to those of Hawkins and Boyd.

Buyers from other states must have felt that Nashville was a good "mid-point" in the interstate slave trade, for the *Republican Banner* of January 6, 1860, carried advertisements of dealers from both Kentucky and Louisiana. Lucas, a trader of Lexington, was endeavoring to get Tennesseans to purchase in the Blue Grass State, and Hatcher of New Orleans was trying to attract Tennesseans who had intentions of selling in Louisiana.

Nashville's market never rose to prominence, but Memphis, more strategically situated from the standpoint of accessibility to the lower South, and being rather centrally located in the cotton region of Tennessee, Arkansas, and northern and western Mississippi, enjoyed a more flourishing trade. Bancroft says that Memphis had by far the largest slave trade of any city in the central South.[80]

Trading in Memphis also was carried on illegally, and in 1836, I. L. and W. H. Bolton, Negro dealers, dissolved partnership by mutual consent.[81] These Boltons, with their two other brothers and Dickins, were later to become the largest traders in Memphis. M. C. Cayce and Company were dealing in Negroes, among other things, before the re-legalizing of the interstate traffic. In 1845 Cayce said:

NEGROES

We have on hand a choice lot of Negroes, which we offer at such reduced prices, that those wishing to purchase Men, Women, or Boys, would find it to their interest to give us a call, and be in a hurry

Hats

Just received a lot of wool Japan hats. Where are the Planters. Will you call?[82]

Seven years later Cayce had a "sale and livery stable and was an auctioneer."[83]

S. and A. Fowlkes were others who practiced slave trading in addition to their dealing in fancy and staple dry goods, hardware, saddlery, Queensware, hats, boots, shoes, etc.[84] W. H. Bolton also followed the trade in this year, 1846—one can scarcely imagine that he kept it confined to Tennessee—and advertised that he had an eighteen-year-old woman, "a first rate Cook, Washer, and Ironer," her six-month-old child, and a "first rate plough boy 12 years old . . . I intend keeping on hand a constant supply of negroes through the season; and will have another supply in 40 or 50 days."[85]

W. E. Eliot had a "likely lot" of young Negroes on hand in 1846 at his place on Howard's Row and referred people to Messrs. W. W. Hart and Company or Major W. B. Morris.[86] One wonders if David Saffarans and Son, prominent businessmen, actually wanted the two hundred slaves "in families" for their personal use as advertised. Saffarans said that letters addressed to Gallatin or Memphis would receive prompt attention, and requested that the Louisville *Journal*, Baltimore *Sun*, Richmond *Enquirer*, Raleigh *Register*, Charleston *Courier*, and Holly Springs *Gazette* publish his advertisement to the amount of $10.[87]

The only Negro trader listed in the *Directory* of 1849 was Z. H. Curlin of Adams Street, "about Main and 3rd."[88] W. H. Bolton, however, had become more active and formed a partnership, Bolton, Dickins, and Company. This concern expressed a desire to purchase one hundred Negroes, for which the "highest price" would be paid. One of the partners, so the advertisement explained, could always be found at the Negro mart on Adams Street or at Bostick's Hotel.[89] Four months later the public was notified that the firm had forty or fifty Negroes for sale and that two buyers in the market would keep the stock "monthly replenished" until the close of the season.[90]

Bolton, Dickins, and Company were the largest of the Negro traders in Memphis, and have been called "the most extensive negro traders in the world."[91] At one time or another Isaac, Jefferson, Wade, and Washington Bolton, and Thomas Dickins, son-in-law of Isaac, were connected with the organization. They had markets in New Orleans, Vicksburg, Mobile, Lexington, and Memphis—the last being the home office. Dickins did much of the scouting around; Washington was at Lexington; Isaac spent most of his time at Vicksburg; and Wade looked after the Memphis office.[92]

In 1852 this group purchased the Herron House—lately occupied by Marsh and Hill—as a Negro mart. They promised always to keep a supply of Virginia Negroes on hand, and said "we will sell as low as good negroes can be afforded anywhere. . . . In a short time we will have a jail completed as safe as the County Jail."[93] Two years later, 1854, they were offering to give "from $50 to $100 more a head for all good negroes" than any other buyer in the state, and would soon have Negroes from Virginia, Kentucky, and Missouri.[94] In 1854 their specialty seems to have been Virginia and North Carolina Negroes, for the traders believed "with the Southern Planters that the Virginia and North Carolina Negroes give more satisfaction, less trouble and make the best servants South."[95]

Trouble was to come to this prosperous firm in 1857. Washington Bolton, who was at Lexington, bought the unexpired term of a free Negro apprentice from James McMillan, a Kentucky trader. The Negro was sent to Memphis and sold as a slave—a crime against the apprentice, a violation of the state law, and a fraud on the purchaser. It is not known whether Bolton knew the Negro was free or whether McMillan misrepresented the facts. Somehow the Negro obtained a lawyer and was freed, and the Boltons had to refund the purchase money.

Not long after, when McMillan was in Memphis, Wade Bolton enticed him to the slave mart by letting him think that he, Bolton, wanted to buy a "yellow" house boy. McMillan, "after some misgivings," went to the Boltons' place and was confronted by Isaac, whom he did not know. Words followed; McMillan was shot four times and died that afternoon in the slave mart next door. Memphians were enraged and came near taking Bolton from the jail and hanging him. Bolton, however, secured a change of venue to Covington, evidently bribed the jury, presented perjured testimony, and was acquitted.

This murder and trial caused trouble within the company. The members fell to quarreling as to who should pay the expenses of the trial. Isaac was asked to reimburse the partners, but he refused on the grounds that it was all a partnership affair. The $300,000 which had been spent for bribery and legal aid had greatly reduced the assets of the traders. Their business fell away "almost like water when a dam breaks," and a feud developed "which ultimately involved the lives of 13 men" according to Hallum, who was counsel in one or more of the cases that resulted.[96]

The slave mart in which McMillan died was that of Nathan Bedford Forrest, who, like others, had risen from a horse trader to a Negro dealer. Bancroft says that by 1853 Forrest was a "typical interstate trader, traveling extensively and scouring Kentucky for slaves."[97] Forrest was employing the above McMillan as a purchasing agent, and giving him one-fourth of the profit on the slaves he obtained.[98] In 1854 Forrest formed a partnership with Josiah Maples, but this relationship lasted for only about eighteen months, and Forrest returned to his "lone wolf" dealings.[99] He advertised, in 1856, for two hundred Negroes saying that he had the "most comfortable quarters" but was not responsible for "accidents or escapes."[100] The following year he said that he would be in monthly receipt of Negroes from North and South Carolina.[101]

Forrest was a successful trader, and after the decline of the Bolton firm, he had, by 1860, become "one of the best known and richest slave-traders in all the South." His five brothers, except possibly the youngest, were, according to Bancroft, engaged in the business with him. John, William H., Aaron, Jesse, and possibly Jeffrey associated themselves with Bedford in the order named.[102] It was not, however, until 1860 that Bedford formed his partnership with William H. Forrest of Memphis and S. S. Jones of De Soto, Mississippi, and there were no more notices of new partners in the papers for 1860. Combined with the advertisement of his new partners was the following:

FORREST, JONES & CO.

Dealers in Slaves

They board and sell on commission and keep constantly on hand a good assortment of Virginia, Georgia [! !] and Carolina Negroes.

500 Negroes Wanted

We will pay more than any other person for No. 1 Negroes suited to the New Orleans market.[103]

Soon after this Forrest must have closed his slave mart; the 1860 *Directory* does not list him or his brother as slave dealers. He had accumulated a large fortune for the time, and he put much of it in cotton lands. Bancroft says of his money-making:

> . . . Forrest was one of the largest traders of the decade, and after the downfall of the Boltons he was unmatched in Memphis. It seems conservative to believe that in some of his best years he sold over 1,000 negroes. A 20 per cent profit on only 600 at $800 would be a net gain of $96,000. At that time this was a fabulous income, yet it was within the reach of the largest traders.[104]

Another rather extensive advertiser among the Memphis dealers was the firm of B. and M. Little, who wished to purchase Negroes, would pay "as high price as any other buyer," would buy and sell on commission, and let rooms to traders.[105] A seemingly larger trader was Byrd Hill. In 1856 he notified the public that he had established a slave mart "upon a basis more liberal and accommodating in its character than heretofore introduced into the South . . . very best negroes that several markets can afford." Hill said he would have both private sales and auctions with no "sham sales, by-bidding," and that he would sell on commission.[106] In 1859 he advertised that thereafter he would hold an auction sale every Thursday during the year.[107]

These four, the Boltons, Forrest, the Littles, and Hill, were probably the largest dealers in the Bluff City, although the Littles never appeared in the *Directory* as slave dealers. There were many others at Memphis in addition to the "big four." In 1855 one finds Anderson Delap and William Witherspoon of Delap and Witherspoon, Isaac Nevill and A. J. Cunningham of Nevill and Cunningham, and George N. Noel listed as traders in slaves.[108] There were no additions in 1856, but three years later John A. Denie and A. Wallace advertised as being in the business.[109] Quite a few changes took place by the next year; Nelson and Norman Delap had displaced Witherspoon; Damascus G. and William M. James became associated with Nevill in place of Cunningham; and J. C. Butler, John Staples, and Edward H. Word had established separate marts.[110]

This is not a complete list of the Memphis traders in Negroes, for many "auctioneers" also bought and sold for profit. Such a one was Ketchum, who in 1856 had nine Negroes for sale: "likeliest, stoutest, and healthiest Negroes ever offered for sale in this market." He said they were raised on a West Tennessee farm and that the family would not be separated.[111] Also, there were a number of brokers, like A. Wallace, who had "Negroes! Negroes! 35 North Carolina and Virginia Negroes just rec'd."[112]

One of the accusations leveled at the border states, and at the slave states in general, was that slaves were bred for the market. Was Tennessee a slave-breeding state? The Reverend Philo Tower has so classed her by saying that "Not only in Virginia, but also in Maryland, North Carolina, Tennessee, and Missouri, as much attention is paid to the breeding and growth of negroes as to that of horses and mules. Further South they raise them both for market and for use."[113]

Slaves were seldom sold under ten years of age, and if a state were breeding to sell, one would expect to find a greater proportion of slaves under ten in that state than in a buying state. Collins, by use of the census, shows that there was not a vast difference in this respect in any of the states, and the "buying States which had a greater number of slave children in proportion to their slave population in 1860 than Virginia, Maryland, and Delaware were Georgia, Arkansas, Tennessee, Alabama, Texas, and Florida."[114] Perhaps, it would be better to class Tennessee as a buying and selling state—a "transferring" state—rather than a breeding state.

How many slaves were sold from Tennessee to the lower South? Bancroft estimates that the Volunteer State exported 2,568 annually from 1850 to 1860.[115] This would be less than 26,000 for the decade preceding the war, and is small when compared to an estimate of the Negroes sold South by some of the other states. The *Republican Banner* of January 20, 1861, said that 12,000 slaves had been sold South from Virginia alone during the year 1860! Tennessee was far, far behind the Old Dominion State; interstate trading was nearly always present but was on a secondary scale, and it is impossible to determine the number of slaves involved.

FUGITIVE SLAVES IN TENNESSEE

The problem of the runaway was one of the most serious with which the owner had to contend. It would be impossible to determine the number of fugitives from bondage, but some instances will be cited to show the different methods of advertising escape, rewards for capture, and attitude of the owner toward the runaway.

Robert Cartwright did not offer much for the apprehension of his Sam, "commonly called Porters sam," when he escaped in 1799. Sam was about six feet tall, thirty years of age, had on tow linen trousers and shirt, and had a "waddling walk." The apprehender was to receive $3 and all "reasonable" expenses.[116]

Andrew Jackson was more specific in the description of his absconder. The fugitive was a mulatto man, about thirty, five feet one, stout, active, talked sensibly, stooped in his walk, and had "a remarkably large foot, broad across the root of the toes." He was suspected of having obtained certificates of freedom, and would "make" for Detroit through Kentucky and Ohio or the upper part of the Louisiana Territory. Jackson also described the extra clothing which the Negro carried. Fifty dollars would be given if the Negro was taken in Tennessee, $50 and "reasonable" expenses if taken outside the state—"and ten dollars extra for every one hundred lashes any person will give him to the amount of three hundred."[117] Jackson had his own ideas of how to keep them from running away again.

Two of William B. Robertson's slaves ran off in December, 1819, and in the following August he was still offering rewards for them. He described Clem as over six feet, a good wrestler who had never been "thrown down by black or white and seldom beat at running or jumping." A reward of $300 was offered if Clem was caught "west" of the Ohio, $150 if "east" of the Ohio, and $100 if he was still in Tennessee. The corresponding rewards offered for Dave were $200, $100, and $50.[118]

Some ingenious ways of escape, or attempted escape, were devised by the slaves or their assistants in flight. On June 8, 1825, a box marked "John Bennett, Louisville, Kentucky" was deposited by a free black on the wharf boat of A. B. Shaw and Company at Memphis. Directions were to ship on the first boat and to handle with care. An hour or so after the box was deposited a voice was heard calling out to "open the door." Much consternation followed, and spectators "thought his Satanic Majesty had taken temporary lodgings in the inside of the box." After some deliberation, the package was opened with a butcher's cleaver, and out rolled a "strapping negro fellow nearly dead with suffocation and steaming like the escape pipe of a steamboat." Upon reviving, he gave an account of his attempted flight.

The Negro said he belonged to John Lewis of Germantown, but had been hired in Memphis. The scheme which had nearly cost him his life was concocted some time before by John Bennett, "a free black rascal, well known to many of our citizens." The plan was to ship the slave to Cincinnati from whence he would be conveyed to Canada by the abolitionists. A number of plates, a quantity of moss, and a few dozen water crackers had been provided. Air holes had been bored in the box, but the water supply had been overlooked. The "boxed-up" said he would have soon died had he not been extricated; the offending free black was soon arrested.[119]

Slaveowners did not have much sympathy for men who would entice away their slaves. Andrew Cavit of Bolivar offered $50 for the return of Ned, who had forged papers, and a "similar sum for bringing the scoundrel to punishment who has seduced him off."[120] The Robertson brothers of Dickson County offered $75 for the jailing of Bill, $100 for his delivery, and $50 for the apprehension of William King and John W. Marshall "in whose co. we think he is." Bill was a recent purchase, formerly had hired his own time, and would probably be found on the White, St. Francis, or Arkansas River.[121]

"Old Yaller," slave of General Stokes of DeKalb County, was

a frequent absconder and hider in the hills. On one of his sojourns he discovered Colonel James Tubb's residence on fire and put it out before much damage was done. In appreciation Tubb purchased him; this was pleasing to "Yaller" since his wife was one of Tubb's slaves.[122]

Early in September, 1845, the Shelby County jail was quite well supplied with runaways. James A. Harrell, jailor, advertised that he held in confinement the following: Wesley Ballard's Flick of Tipton County, William Armor's Becky of Shelby County, Buck Winn's George of De Soto County, David Little's Tom of Marshall County, and William Terlis' Ned of Yalobusha County.[123] The last three were from Mississippi; Memphis was well suited for runaways from Arkansas, Tennessee, and Mississippi, for there they could mingle with a rather large free colored population and not be so easily recovered.

Forrest and Maples offered the largest known reward for one of their escapees. They would pay $500 to the deliverer of Richard—if taken in a free state—a Charleston-reared carpenter about thirty years old who could read and write well.[124]

Interesting stories of runaways and their future lives are told by Levi Coffin, Benjamin Drew, and some of the refugees themselves. Coffin became acquainted with Robert Burrell of "sober and intelligent appearance" some months before Robert told him that he was a runaway from East Tennessee. Robert's story was to the effect that he had married a free woman and was happy until he learned that he was to be sold down the river. He ran away, hoping he could make enough money to purchase his wife and children.[125] Burrell obtained a job in a linseed oil mill where he was paid "extra wages for his care and good judgment."

Contact was made with John Rankin—whom Robert knew in East Tennessee—and Rankin said it would cost $40 to get Robert's wife and children to Ohio. The plan was not successful the first time; Robert's wife thought it was an attempt to betray her husband, and could not be taken into confidence. Two years later the transfer was accomplished; Coffin, who furnished the $40, purchased the Negroes a home at Newport, which Robert paid for by his work. There they lived until the Fugitive Slave Law of 1850

was passed; then they left and went to Canada for greater security.[126]

John W. Lindsey was born free, but was kidnapped at the age of
seven by S. G. and taken to West Tennessee, so Benjamin Drew
says. His escape was accomplished relatively easily, after twenty-
one years of slavery, as people did not know "whether he was
black or white."[127]

John Warren of Wilson County escaped by writing passes for
himself,[128] but Williamson Pease's freedom was gained by just
walking away. Pease was born in Hardeman County, but moved
to Haywood when he was seven. He said he had heard his father
was a white man and his mother a mulatto. As a house servant,
his owner tried to teach him to read and write, but "I would get out
of the way . . . being small and not knowing the good of learning." This "white man with blue eyes" suffered "nothing except
for want of education," and was the only slave not promptly sold
by his first master's grandson. In 1850 he went with his young
master to California, where he got about $80 worth of gold; then
he tended a dry goods store in New Orleans before he was hired
to keep a "billiard saloon." The owner was finally forced to sell his
last Negro, but no one in New Orleans would buy him because he
was "too white." Pease was sold to an Arkansan who made him a
"trusty" in March, 1852. In January, 1854, when Pease was about
twenty-one, he thought his master intended to whip him, so he
walked to the Mississippi River and escaped.[129]

J. W. (Jarm) Loguen, future agent of the Underground Railroad, was the mulatto slave son of David Logue of Mansker's
Creek, Davidson County.[130] Not many years before the war Jarm
ran away, and on February 20, 1860, his owner, Mrs. Sarah Logue
of Bigbyville, Maury County, wrote him to this effect: Cherry, your
mother, is "as well as common," but we are in financial straits as a
result of your running away. The mare you escaped on was recovered, but was ruined; I have had an offer to sell you but did not
see fit to take it. If you will send $1,000 and pay for the mare, I
will forward your bill of sale to you.

Mrs. Logue then told Jarm that his brother and sister, Abe and
Ann, had been sold, as had twelve acres of land. Jarm was threat-

ened with sale unless he complied with her request. Mrs. Logue asked him, since he was a preacher,[131] what would become of the thief if he did not repent, and said that Jarm had been raised as one of her children, and was never abused; also, when he was asked if he would like to be sold to someone else, his reply was a definite negative.[132]

Loguen's reply from Syracuse on March 28 was a scathing rebuke: he was glad to hear about his mother; he would send no money to redeem land; if he sent any, it would be to buy his brother and sister. He did not agree that he had been reared as one of Mrs. Logue's children, at any rate, not for the same purposes. He continued:

. . . I had a better right to the old mare, as you call her, than Mannasseth Logue had to me . . . human rights are mutual and reciprocal, and if you take my liberty and my life, you forfeit your own . . . I meet the proposition with unutterable scorn and contempt. The proposition is an outrage and an insult. I will not budge one hair's breadth. I will not breathe a shorter breath, even to save me from your persecutions. . . . If your emissaries and venders come here to re-enslave me, and escape the unshrinking vigor of my own right arm, I trust my strong and brave friends . . . will be my rescuers and avengers.[133]

Entirely different in tone is Jourdan Anderson's reply of August 7, 1865, to a request from his "old master," Colonel P. H. Anderson of Big Springs, Tennessee, to return "home" and become his tenant. Jourdan was glad he was not forgotten and that the Colonel wanted him to return. The freedman said that he had

. . . often felt uneasy about you. I thought the Yankees would have hung you long before this, for harboring Rebs. . . . Although you shot at me twice before I left you, I did not want to hear of your being hurt, and am glad you are still living. It would do me good to go back to the dear old home again. . . . Give my love to them all. . . . I get twenty-five dollars a month with victuals and clothing; have a comfortable home for Mandy,—the folks call her Mrs. Anderson,—and the children—Milly, Jane, and Grundy—go to school and are learning well. . . .

Sometimes, Jourdan's children would be hurt by the remark that "them colored people were slaves," but Jourdan would tell them it was no "disgrace in Tennessee to belong to Colonel Anderson. Many darkeys would have been proud, as I used to be, to call you master."

Mandy, though, was afraid to come back without some proof that they would be treated kindly. As assurance of such, they requested their "wages" for their period of slavedom: $25 per month for thirty-two years for Jourdan, and $2 a week for Mandy for twenty years, or $11,680. Jourdan said that interest on this sum should also be paid, but that deductions for clothing and doctor's bills would be allowed. Jourdan also wanted to know if there would be any "safety for Milly and Jane, who are now grown up, and both good-looking girls," and whether any colored schools had been opened. He closed with the request to "Say howdy to George Carter, and thank him for taking the pistol from you when you were shooting at me."[134]

Part of the above letter sounds as if it were written by some unscrupulous individual who thought he might make a little money in the transaction. Colonel Anderson could hardly have been expected to meet Jourdan's conditions of return, but he must have retained some feeling of kindness for this "old time negro."

Louis Hughes made several unsuccessful attempts to escape his owner. In 1844 he was sold, at Richmond, to Edward McGee [McGehee] of Pontotoc, Mississippi, who had already bought sixty others.[135] Six years later, twenty-five slaves were sent to Memphis —Hughes was cook—to make bricks for McGee's new home there. The slaves rejoiced in their master's good fortune; they could no longer be pointed to as belonging to "po'r white trash."[136]

Louis had heard his master read of slaves going to Canada, so one morning when the "Madam," in the absence of "Boss," threatened to whip him, he stowed away on a sugar boat in Memphis. The third night on board he was discovered by the second mate, taken to Louisville, and recovered there.[137] Three months later he was given a "terrific beating" for attempting to escape.[138]

The farm at Bolivar, Tennessee, was Hughes' next residing place, and two attempts to escape from there were unsuccessful. He was a slave until the end of the war, learned to read at the Sherman House and School for Freedmen in Chicago, became a nurse and traveled rather extensively. He spoke kindly of his master, though he tried four times to escape from him.[139]

How many slaves were successful in escaping from their masters in Tennessee? The Census for 1860 shows that from all the slave states, 1,011, or one in every 3,165, escaped during the year ending June 1, 1850, and only 803, or one in every 5,000, made successful their flight for freedom during the twelve-month period preceding June 1, 1860. Of these fugitives, 600 came from the border states in 1850 and 300 in 1860. Tennessee furnished seventy of the fugitive slaves in 1850 and only twenty-nine in 1860. The greatest increase of escapes occurred in Mississippi, Missouri, and Virginia, while the decrease was most marked in Delaware, Georgia, Louisiana, Maryland, and Tennessee. The census states that the complaint of the slaveowners was a "result of misapprehension," that the loss to southern states was less in proportion to the capital involved than the "daily variations which in ordinary times occur in the fluctuations of State or government securities in the city of New York alone," and that escape occurred "independent of proximity to a free population, being, in the nature of things incident to the relation of master and slave."[140]

The slave population of the border states declined between 1850 to 1860, and it is scarcely correct to suggest that this rapid decline was due to the large shipments of slaves to the lower South, without at the same time suggesting that proximity to a free population and numerous lines of the Underground Railroad might have been responsible for such shipment. It was not the loss that the slaveowner particularly resented; he would not have complained excessively if slave prices had decreased as the New York securities fluctuated; but he did resent the fact that men in the North were, in reality, accomplices to the crime of theft of his Negroes. Siebert does not think that the census tells the whole story relative to fugitive slaves:

The concurrence of evidence from sources other than the census reports, and the agreement therewith of part of the evidence gathered from these reports themselves, constrains one to say that those who compiled the statistics on fugitive slaves did not secure the facts in full; and the complaints of large losses sustained by slave-owners through the befriending of fugitive slaves by northern people, frequently made by Southern representatives in Congress and by the South generally, were not without sufficient foundation.[141]

THEFT OF SLAVES

As stated above, the southern slaveholder resented the theft of his slaves, whether it be by another for his own personal use or profit, or to gain the freedom of the Negro. In May, 1819, Michael Campbell advertised for Lewis who left Nashville with a John Black, said to be of New Orleans, but did not, as most advertisers, offer a reward for the apprehension of the decoyer.[142]

John Wright of Rutherford County offered $100 for the seizure of John Coleman, "about 21 and very large," who had walked away with his Lawrence.[143] Not many notices contained expressions of suspicion that Negroes were enticed away until the 1830's when there seemed to be an epidemic of thieving. In 1833 Andrew Cavit of Bolivar offered $50 for bringing the "scoundrel to punishment who has seduced him [Ned] off," and C. and B. Robertson of Dickson County offered a similar reward for the apprehension of William King and John W. Marshall in whose company they thought their Bill was.[144]

In the early 1830's John A. Murrell and his gang of desperadoes were operating in the western part of Tennessee and "throughout the Southwest." Murrell and his cohorts were probably the greatest of the Negro stealers.[145] Their scheme was shrewd; both the whites and blacks were victims. Phillips describes their activities thus:

They would conspire with a slave, promising him his freedom or some other reward if he would run off with them and suffer himself to be sold to some unwary purchaser and then escape to join them again. Sometimes they repeated this process over and over again with the same slave until a threat of exposure from him led to his being silenced by murder.[146]

Murrell was finally caught by Virgil A. Stewart in a rather ingenious manner. He was taken to Jackson, Tennessee, in February, 1834, found guilty of slave stealing, and in July was sentenced to the penitentiary for ten years at hard labor.[147] He was, however, pardoned after six years because of ill health.[148]

It was probably part of Murrell's clan against which the Randolph *Recorder* warned in 1834:

. . . Horses, negroes, cattle, and every species of property is their prey; and such is their adroitness and so impregnable their marshy skulking places, as to make their detection almost impossible, burying themselves when pursued, in the almost impervious canebrakes.[149]

These thieves hid out in Arkansas—which had been Murrell's hide-out—but twenty-five or thirty of them had been captured, some of whom were beaten, and some spared because of the secrets which they promised to divulge.

George W. Penn of Randolph had seven slaves who absconded (or who were stolen) in 1835. One, Hannah, was still missing in September; four had been recovered, and two, trying to swim away from their captors, were drowned. Lowel, one of the recovered Negroes, said that they had been under the guidance of Anson Moody, who had lately received one hundred lashes and a brand on the right cheek with the letter "R" for Negro stealing around Brownsville. Moody also had a recent knife wound in the right arm near the shoulder. Penn offered $250 for the Negro and Moody, or $200 for Moody alone.[150] In the same paper, O. Shelby of the same town offered $300 for the conviction of "any white man" harboring his runaway Moses.

In his report to the House of Representatives in 1838, John M'Intosh, keeper of the penitentiary, said that five of the inmates were confined for Negro stealing.[151] One of these was Murrell.

Richard Dillingham is more deserving of pity for his "rashness." Some colored people of Cincinnati persuaded him to go to Nashville to get some of their relations from a "hard master." He succeeded in getting three of them in a closed carriage, which he accompanied on horseback, as far as the Cumberland River bridge which was still within the city limits. There he was arrested on December 5, 1848. He was tried on April 12, 1849, confessed his guilt, and said that he alone was "responsible for the error into which his education and his feelings of philanthropy led him," and had expected to derive no monetary gain from freeing the Negroes. Dillingham was sentenced to three years in the penitentiary. His strength gave out and he was relieved of hard work after nine months, but died of cholera about August 1, 1850.[152]

More dreaded than the slave thief was the person who endeavored to incite the slave to insurrection. Tennessee was not much troubled by servile uprisings, but there were times when such disturbances threatened. The first of these took place in 1831 —possibly a repercussion of the Nat Turner episode—but was quelled speedily by information obtained from a female slave.[153] Even this minor threat contributed to a considerable tightening of the patrol system.

Four years later insurrection again threatened, and this time, according to some reports, it was to be widespread. Murrell, unaware at the time of the real identity of Stewart, outlined to him the plan of his clan for an uprising on December 25, 1835. Murrell's men were to help start the insurrection and then fire the towns and rob the banks "while all is confusion and dismay." The clan had not "taken in every negro they saw," but only those who seemed the most "vicious and wickedly disposed." These Negroes' minds were poisoned; they were reminded of the pomp and splendor of their masters; and told that when the uprising was over they could all marry white women.[154]

The trusted Negroes had been sworn in with pomp and ceremony and were shown a painted picture of the monster who would deal with them should they fail to keep faith. These slaves were the "missionaries of rebellion" who talked with other Negroes and kept the clan leaders informed of their progress. When the time came, the various groups of Negroes would be "forced" to rebel by being told that their brothers everywhere else had risen against their masters. If the insurrection were not successful, the "emissaries" were to be taken to Texas where they would be free, but, Murrell said, "we never talk of being defeated." Should a leak in the plan perchance occur, the leaders would crush the rebellion rumor at once by ridiculing the idea and the fears of the people.

"All things," according to Murrell, "would be accounted for to the satisfaction of the community in short order."[155]

It is difficult to believe fully this plan of a concerted uprising, although there was uneasiness among some of the citizens of Tennessee about Christmas, 1835. At Clarksville, the danger from Negroes employed in the iron works was considered so great that arms were procured from the state capitol in preparation for a special guard during the holiday season.[156]

The following letter from F. S. [?] to John Claybrooke on July 14, 1843, contains some information relative to slave troubles, but, unfortunately, the manuscript was mutilated:

Branches negroes have since you left made another confession implicating about thirty negroes and some white men, which story has thrown the whole c . . . in utter confusion, among . . . company implicated are Mr . . . boys, I shall set off . . . and am anxious . . . you before I start.[157]

There is some evidence that an insurrection was talked of in 1856 and again in 1857. Goladay, Cheatham & Company of Clifton, Tennessee, wrote M. D. Cooper of Columbia on December 16, 1856, that the "many reports" which had reached them relative to a servile uprising were in reality unfounded. The letter continued:

. . . we are satisfied that there has been no Insurrectionary movement or feeling among our hands, but on the other hand, increased confidence on their part as well as ours, so much so that we could calmly sleep in their midst after arming all of them—We apprehend no difficulty—among them, and think you may rest calmly and gently upon this subject. . . .[158]

Some evidence lends credence to the report that an effort to secure freedom by forcible means was to be made in Kentucky, Tennessee, Missouri, Arkansas, Louisiana, and Texas. The general servile uprising, however, did not materialize. In Tennessee the scheme was discovered in November among the employees of the Cumberland Iron Works. "More than sixty slaves in the Iron

Works were implicated, and nine were hung, four by the decision of the court and five by a mob."[159] No actual outbreak occurred.

It appears that concern over an insurrection in 1856 was directly associated with the election of that year. That most of the trouble was in the panic realm and not in actual insurrection prompted one individual to rather sarcastic and satirical comments:

We are trying our best in Davidson County to produce a negro insurrection without the slightest aid from the negroes themselves. Whether we shall succeed remains to be seen, but it is certain no more effectual means could be pursued than our wiseacres have adopted. The rack, the thumbscrew, and the wheel are looked upon, it is true, as instruments of justice belonging to the dark ages of barbarism—but then the lash properly administered is quite as efficacious. It breaks no bones, while it satisfactorily elicits whatever confessions or disclosures, the ministers of extra-legal justice are anxious to procure.

There is in sober seriousness, no shadow of foundation for any belief of domestic plot or insurrection. But the popular mind is in that excited state requiring the most trivial cause to set everything in a blaze. Our better citizens are at work and I hope will succeed in preventing an outbreak—among the *Whites*.[160]

There were the above mentioned minor difficulties with the slaves in Tennessee, but no serious servile insurrection ever occurred. When the war came, the Negroes in Tennessee followed very much the same course that they did in the other slave states.

THREE

Antislavery Sentiment

THE INDIVIDUALS in Tennessee who worked for a slave insurrection were few; but the people who opposed the institution were far more numerous. Tennessee as a whole was never an antislavery stronghold, but the eastern part of the state carried on an organized activity against slavery during the first quarter of the nineteenth century. This activity waned, however, in the 1830's, and after that date organized antislavery sentiment in Tennessee was practically nonexistent. Among the many factors which contributed to this decline, the most important were the northern abolition crusade, the Nat Turner insurrection, the turning of the southerners to a defense of the institution, and the shifting of the center of population in Tennessee to an area better suited to slavery.

It has been stated that petitions bearing two thousand signatures "coming from all settlements in the state (territory) were presented to the Constitutional Convention in 1796, asking that a provision be embodied in the constitution prohibiting slavery in the state after the year 1864. This was the voice of prophecy coming out of the *Western Wilderness.*"[1] Be this as it may, no such petitions have been found; there is no record of this in the journal of the convention; and the constitution, as drafted and ratified, contains no statement concerning the status of slavery in the new state. Seemingly, the institution was accepted as a matter of course. Slaves were, however, made the subject of taxation. Sentiment against the perpetuation of slavery was soon to become articulate. A letter from Thomas Embree, on January 23, 1797, to the Knoxville *Gazette* said that citizens of Washington and Greene counties were planning a meeting to form abolition societies modeled after those of Philadelphia, Baltimore, and Richmond. The purpose of these societies was to labor for the

relief of such persons as are illegally held in bondage, to effect their relief by legal means alone, without any intention to injure the rights of individuals . . . not to take negroes from their legal masters and set them free, as some have vainly imagined; but by lawful means to vindicate the cause of such of the human race as are lawfully entitled to freedom, either by mixed blood or any other cause.[2]

The communication proposed more liberal emancipation laws, and expressed the desire and goal of general emancipation when the Negro had been adequately prepared by education. Since no further information concerning these proposed societies has been found, it may be assumed that they were not formed.

The eastern part of the state, however, was soon to become one of the antislavery strongholds of the country. These East Tennesseans did not advocate immediate abolition, but recognized gradual emancipation "as the only safe and practical method of abolishing slavery."[3] The first evidence of a definitely organized antislavery effort appeared in December, 1814, when eight citizens of Jefferson County met at the home of Elihu Swain and effected the temporary organization of the Tennessee Manumission Society.[4]

East Tennesseans gathered at the Lost Creek Meeting House of Friends on February 25, 1815, and adopted the constitution of the "Tennessee Society for Promoting the Manumission of Slaves." This document provided, in part, that each member display in the "most conspicuous part" of his dwelling a sign reading: "Freedom is the natural right of all men; I therefore acknowledge myself a member. . . ."; that no member vote for any one for governor or legislator unless "we believe him to be in favor of emancipation"; that meetings be held every month; and that the "requisite qualification of our members are true Republican principles, patriotic and in favor of emancipation, and that no immoral character be admitted into the society. . . ."[5]

Soon after this, societies were formed in Greene, Sullivan, Washington, Blount, Grainger, Knox, and other East Tennessee counties. At first these organizations had constitutions of their own; but correspondence between them developed, delegates were chosen, and a state convention was held at the Lick Creek Meeting House of Friends, in Greene County, on November 21, 1815. Here the groups were welded together under a common constitution and given the name of the "Manumission Society of Tennessee."[6]

The leader of this Lick Creek meeting was the Quaker minister, Charles Osborn, originator of the first branch of the society and a material aid in the formation of the others. He was ably assisted by John Rankin of the Presbyterian Church. These two were rather inclined toward immediate emancipation, and, along with Jesse Willis and John Lockhart, moved to the Old Northwest between 1816 and 1825.[7]

Never did the Manumission Society of Tennessee declare for immediate abolition, but from the memorials and petitions it presented—or caused to be presented—it certainly embraced the cause of gradual abolition. Until 1819 practically all the petitions to the state legislature involved cases of individual emancipation, but in that year there was a "deluge" of memorials to the assembly convened at Murfreesboro. Thirty-five in number and bearing 1,975 signatures (but no counties or dates), these papers requested that some program of gradual abolition be adopted.[8] These documents were referred to the Committee on Abolition Petitions which reported on November 15, 1819, as follows:

. . . that in common with their fellow citizens, they regret the occasion which gave rise to the introduction of slavery in the United States, at this time however those regrets are unavailing. Slavery is established by law, and the owners of them will feel their rights are ascribed, whenever, it shall be attempted by law, to extinguish the right to, or lessen the value of, this species of property.

It appears . . . that to commence the gradual abolition of slavery would be to lessen the value of that species of property. . . . The power to lessen the value of a man's property is necessarily the power to render that property of no value whatever, and such a power as your committee would feel themselves unwilling to recommend the exercise of at the present . . . such a course would in many instances prove injurious to the slaves themselves, particularly to the female part of them. To declare that all the children of slaves born after a certain period shall be free, is to lessen the value of a female slave . . . the consequence . . . would be that in very many instances, the owner . . . would separate her from her husband and children and dispose of her in parts where such law did not exist. . . .

Your committee nevertheless are disposed to permit such as are willing to do so, to free their slaves . . . therefore . . . Resolved, that so much of the law as requires security from those disposed to set their slaves free be repealed.[9]

The same day, November 15, 1819, the House rejected the proffered resolution, and the following day the Speaker of the Senate marked the report as "Read and the resolution therein contained non-concurred in." The representatives of slaveowners and nonslaveowners were not yet ready for emancipation without safeguards, and future developments drove them to defend the institution as the only feasible solution of the race problem.

Earlier in that year, March, 1819, Elihu Embree, a slaveholding Quaker, began the publication of the weekly *Manumission Intelligencer* at Jonesboro, Tennessee. This paper was published under the auspices of the Tennessee Manumission Society, and was the only periodical in the country devoted exclusively to antislavery agitation.[10] In April, 1820, it became an octavo monthly, *The Emancipator,* but the death of Embree[11] on December 4 of the same year cut short the life of the paper. The increase in circulation of this periodical was phenomenal, for in the short period of eight months the subscription list had mounted to approximately 2,000.[12]

Embree was extremely resentful of the fact that the planters would send money to foreign lands for missionary purposes and allow their slaves to remain in a condition which he depicted as follows:

Not suffered to rise higher in the scale of being, than mules and asses, with which they have to labour; beating, driving, starving, and buying and selling them as if they were brutes in reality—whilst the bowels of these savage hearted christians yearn over the heathen world that is at a distance from them, and contribute large sums of money (the earnings of their poor emaciated slaves) to their conversion to christianity, when, in all probability, if they had these same heathen in their power, as they have their slaves, they would show them the same degree of mercy—Should one of these missionaries whom they have employed, turn about, and labour for the conversion of their negroes, he would be laid by the heels in prison, or banished from the benevolent country . . . I had almost said that such converts would be fit for neither Heaven or Hell.[13]

Again, attacking the statement of a Tennessee judge that "Christianity was a part of the laws of the state," Embree asserts that slavery is not only declared lawful, but "conscientious persons have their hands tied" so that before they can "perform the duty" which

. . . God and nature, and their own consciences require of them they have to leave the state . . . and go to a land where oppression is not one of the indispensable principles of law. . . . Justice is fled, and equity is kicked out of doors and knocked down in the streets, while oppression stalks, and struts through town and country, rules states and lifts its daring front in the national council! May Heaven overturn it![14]

These quotations show that Embree was not as violent as William Lloyd Garrison, but that he was sincere in his opposition to the perpetuation of the institution. Had he lived and continued his crusade—but probably not in Tennessee after 1830 or 1831, for such would have been merely inviting physical violence—his language would possibly have become more scathing as his ardor for the cause increased. Vitriolic and vituperative phrases, sarcasm, and irony were not foreign to the nature of Embree.

After the death of Embree, Benjamin Lundy, at the request of the inhabitants of the region, brought his *Genius of Universal Emancipation* to Greeneville, Tennessee, in April, 1822. He had been publishing the paper in Mt. Pleasant, Ohio, since January, 1821. Soon after he reached Tennessee, partly by water and partly by foot, he had a weekly newspaper and a monthly agricultural journal.[15] Lundy remained in Tennessee until August, 1824, when he went to Baltimore.[16] During one winter of his sojourn in the Volunteer State he rode to Philadelphia for a meeting of the American Convention for the Abolition of Slavery. He says that he was the "first delegate that ever attended . . . from any portion of the country as far south as Tennessee." Although Lundy stated that he went to Baltimore to increase the circulation of his paper, he said that he was threatened in "many ways" in Tennessee. Later, he was to move to Washington, for the "spirit of tyranny in Maryland became too strong and malignant" for him.[17]

During the years that Embree and Lundy were publishing their periodicals in East Tennessee, antislavery sentiment in that section was strong. In 1823 Tennessee had twenty antislavery societies with a membership of six hundred. Four years later, 1827, the number of societies had increased to twenty-five and the membership to one thousand. In all the free states in that year there were only twenty-four such organizations with a total membership of fifteen hundred. All the slave states at that time had 106 antislavery societies with 5,125 members, 4,000 of whom were in North Carolina and Tennessee.[18]

In 1823 the Tennessee Manumission Society embraced the colonization idea as a plan of gradual emancipation, and recommended it to the American Convention in its address to that body. The Tennesseans' proposal was to set aside a parcel of land in the United States for a Negro colony, and to educate the would-be freedmen in order to insure the success of the undertaking.[19]

John Rhea, on January 14, 1822, and January 20, 1823, presented memorials from the seventh and eighth conventions of the Tennessee Society to the House of Representatives praying that Congress take the "situation of the people of color of the United States . . . into their consideration, and provide by law for their relief." Also, it was hoped that Congress would "give every facility in their power to effect the final abolition of the system of African slavery within the United States."[20] The following year, 1824, John Blair of Tennessee presented a memorial asking the "prevention of slavery in the future in any State where it is not now allowed by law, as, also for its proscription in States hereafter to be formed and admitted into the Union."[21] These three petitions were "lost" in the Committee on the Judiciary.

The Tennessee Manumission Society at times adopted humanitarian measures and went on record as opposing the use of extra-legal means to end slavery. At the 1825 meeting it was resolved that "all slaveholding members who shall hereafter refuse or neglect to educate their slaves, so far as it is practicable [a saving clause!] be excommunicated, and no longer be considered members of this society."[22] Then, in 1827, the annual convention adopted, among other things, a resolution forbidding members "to assist in any way the escape of slaves from their legal owners." If they did such, the offenders should be tried by the local branch of the organization and expelled.[23] Evidently, the society was being criticised for activities of this kind, and the above position was considered the best answer to that criticism.

Thomas Dean, who delivered the address to the convention in 1827, made the following statements:

Slavery is unfriendly to a genuine course of agriculture, turning in most cases the fair and fertile face of nature into barren sterility. It is the bane of manufacturing enterprise and internal improvements; injurious to mechanical prosperity; oppressive and degrading to the poor and laboring classes of the white population that live in its vicinity; the death of religion; and finally it is a volcano in disguise, and dangerous to the safety and happiness of any government on earth where it is tolerated.[24]

The twenty-five antislavery societies of Tennessee had almost entirely disappeared by late 1831, and "no anti-slavery society . . . existed after 1837." Allen Leeper was the secretary and most influential member of the last antislavery society formed in the Volunteer State. This group was organized at Rock Creek in June, 1835, had eleven members, and was one of three such societies in the South at that time.[25] It, too, had gone out of existence by 1837.

The state society must have passed out of existence in the "early thirties" for "records of proceedings and memorials and addresses are no longer regularly found."[26] Why was this so? First of all, the organization was never radical, and it grew less so. The result was that a rather conservative program had no effect upon the minds of those who built up strong defensive attitudes against the violent abolition crusade. After the early 1830's, any plan of freeing the slaves was, rightly or wrongly, linked with the uncompromising opposition of the North. Other factors—those stated at the beginning of this chapter will bear repeating here— were: the most outspoken and aggressive members of the Tennessee Society moved to the Old Northwest; the Nat Turner insurrection and Garrison's *Liberator* struck fear and resentment into the hearts of the southern slaveholders; the center of population in Tennessee had shifted toward the West where slavery was more profitable and there was more plantation life; sectional lines began to be drawn tighter; and the southerner began to cling doggedly to the constitutional guarantee of property rights. "There seems to have been," says Martin, "a uniform impression among the great majority of the citizens of the state that the abolition movement was wrong as it stood related to the political fabric and that it had in it the germs of incalculable injury."[27]

Prominent among the Tennessee opponents of slavery were Peter Cartwright, Samuel Doak, Isaac Anderson, John Eaton, W. B. A. Ramsey, Seth Lucky, and William Reese,[28] but James Jones probably deserves more credit for long and continued service to the Tennessee antislavery movement than any other individual. He was president of the society for a large part of its existence, wrote many of the addresses delivered by the society, and, though his education was limited, he possessed a strong mind with a soul "wrapped in the cause." His death in 1830 probably contributed to the dissolution of the society.[29] Lundy in the *Genius* for April, 1830, said of him:

A great man has fallen, one of the brightest stars in the galaxy of American Philanthropists has set . . . James Jones . . . the steady, ardent and persevering friend of universal emancipation, is numbered with the dead . . . few men living can fill the station that he held with equal honor and usefulness.[30]

One other individual, Ezekiel Birdseye of Newport, Tennessee, is deserving of mention here because of his connection with Gerrit Smith. This East Tennessee abolitionist provided Smith with considerable information during the two decades preceding the Civil War.[31]

In a letter of January 25, 1841, Birdseye touched upon various and sundry happenings in the field of slavedom. He noted that he was trying to buy a Mr. Woodfin's slave to set him free. This Negro had tried repeatedly, for ten years, to escape, but he was "comfortably provided for and receives kind treatment." Also, he said that the Reverend Robert H. Lea of Jefferson County had discontinued his Sabbath School of "upwards of 40 most of them slaves" because he had been threatened with prosecution.[32]

The East Tennessean felt that the abolition crusade had had good effects upon the South, for he said that "an opinion is gaining ground . . . that slavery cannot continue long . . . barbarous punishments are less frequent." He then tells of the burning of a Negro in South Carolina near the plantations of John C. Calhoun and George McDuffie. "No language could describe his agony. The plain dealing of the Abolitionists has put a stop to this mode of execution I trust forever."[33]

The contents of the same letter of January 25, 1841, would lead one to believe that a manumission society still existed in Jefferson County. A Mr. Patterson, president of the organization, had told Birdseye that the society had over six hundred members, but had not "opened their meetings owing to the oppressive laws of the state." The section around Knoxville was described as the "most thoroughly anti-slavery part of the South." Birdseye and a Judge Peck owned the French Broad "for about 16 miles" and were anxious to establish improvements "wholly excluding slave labor."[34]

Proneness to violence, so the East Tennessean said, was the unhappy feature of slavery, and Nashville and vicinity had been the "most afflicted with these occurances [sic] . . . mostly among the aristocracy." As a matter of fact, that region had been "distinguished" for violence and assassination since the whipping of Amos Dresser.[35] Likewise, free Negroes had been sold into slavery, and, if the free colored had no rights in the slave states, Birdseye felt that slavery should have none in the free states. Thus the North should deal "firmly and decidedly" with persons attempting to re-capture escaped slaves. The people of the free states would then be respected, but if they "tamely yield their rights they will meet with insolence and insult."[36] Birdseye was in favor of bringing manufacturing and industry into the region, and also talked about making East Tennessee a separate state.[37]

In summarizing this aspect of antislavery sentiment in Ten-nessee, it is to be noted that organized agitation was confined almost entirely to the mountainous areas of the state, where the institution was not profitably adapted to the economic mode of life. The Quakers and the Presbyterians were the leaders of the movement. There were individuals in other parts of the state who openly advocated the inalienable equality of man with as much force as their co-workers in the eastern part of the state, but they were not so numerous, and their influence was less.[38]

Colonization played a minor role in the Volunteer State. On December 21, 1829, the Tennessee Colonization Society was formed at Nashville with Philip Lindsley as the first president. At the beginning there were only sixteen members, but before Josiah F. Polk, the American Colonization Society agent for Tennessee, Indiana, Illinois, and Alabama, left town, this number had in-creased to seventy-three.[39]

Polk's duty was to organize new colonization societies, but he met with a little difficulty in Columbia, Maury County. There he encountered "open, violent, and indecorous opposition, incited by a Lawyer lately from South Carolina." A society, however, of thirty members was formed. The agent on this occasion acknowl-edged the friendly support of Terry Cahal, a young lawyer, and the Reverend Mr. Maddin, a Methodist minister. "They both made very pertinent and animated speeches."[40]

Another agent of the American Colonization Society, Reverend O. S. Hinckley, addressed the Tennessee branch at the First Pres-byterian Church in Nashville on August 8, 1831. After the speech, "some resolutions toward furtherance of their work were adopted."[41] The next representative of the national society in this section was James G. Birney, who was appointed in early July, 1832.[42] Birney felt that there was considerable sentiment in Tennessee in favor of colonization and the ultimate extinction of slavery.[43] He said that the people's "consciences are too much awakened to sleep without some action."[44] Early in October he visited several towns in Tennessee and lectured on colonization.

The future candidate for president was even enthusiastic about conditions in Maryland, Kentucky, Virginia, and Tennessee. He ventured to say that "all that is wanting . . . to disburden them of slavery in a reasonable time is to defray the cost of a comfortable conveyance to a safe and pleasant home. . . ." He did not see any "sudden extinguishment of slavery," but felt that it would be "continually approaching its termination."[45] Birney proceeded to combat the idea of abolition until "every other feasible plan" had been tried; and he laid down the proposition that there is in society "an inherent power for self-preservation, which it is authorized to use *for the removal of any evil* . . . although it may be unavoidable that another evil be introduced. . . ."[46] This seems to assert the right of a state legislature to abolish slavery.

On October 14, 1833, he spoke to a meeting of the Tennessee Colonization Society in the Representatives' Hall in Nashville. Birney said that he spoke for about an hour and a half, and went beyond what he could do with propriety south of Tennessee by assuming the position "that slavery must not be regarded as a permanent condition among us. . . . My propositions were so much bolder than . . . elsewhere, that I was prepared to expect some complaint from the timid and the indolent lovers of Slavery. But there was none at all of which I have heard. . . ."[47] Large audiences also attended his speeches at Gallatin,[48] Franklin, and Elkton, but Birney was no longer enthusiastic, and felt that his efforts had been almost in vain. With this tour and the promotion of petitions asking aid from the state legislature, Birney's official relations with the Tennessee Colonization Society came to an end.[49] Even so, it is interesting to note that in May, 1835, he said at Boston that "there is less *negro hatred* in the slave than in the free States. They [the Negroes] are subject to more insult in the latter than in the former."[50]

The Tennessee legislature did not give the society as much aid as it expected, but, in 1833, $10 was allowed for each Negro sent to Liberia. An all-important proviso stated that not more than $500 could be spent in this way in any one year.[51] The same year the legislature was petitioned "to consider and adopt" the best means of colonizing free colored people. The Committee of Propositions and Grievances, to which this document was referred, made no comment as to its disposition.[52]

Individual and group contributions to the American Colonization Society by Tennesseans amounted to approximately $700 by June, 1858.[53] The largest single contributions were made by E. B. Littlefield and Andrew J. Polk, who gave $25 and $50, respectively.[54] Both of these were slaveowners.

The only instance discovered of a Tennessean actually carrying out the wish of a neighbor in respect to colonization was that of Samuel Henderson of Williamson County. On December 5, 1852, he went to Nashville to "fit off" the Negroes of the late General Logan Douglas. The Negroes were to leave Nashville on December 8, and would sail from Savannah, Georgia, one week later. On the latter date Henderson made an entry in his "Journal" to the effect that Elvin had gotten his wife to go with him by paying $300 cash and giving his note for $100. The note was to be paid in two years and W. B. Walton countersigned it for Elvin.[55]

Tennesseans did not colonize many of their freedmen, for from 1829 to 1866, inclusive, only 870 were sent to Liberia. Only fifty-five of these emigrated before 1841, and the banner years of colonization for Tennessee were 1853 and 1856. In those years 181 and 144, respectively, were sent across.[56]

The way to Liberia, however, was beset with troubles. A colored minister from Tennessee wrote that he and his family had been "highly favoured by Providence," and were ready to set out for West Africa. He said, "I believe my family are all quite willing to go. We are waiting with great anxiety to hear the words, Go on! to the place of embarkation."[57] Not all the free colored, though, were so desirous to leave this country. Lundy noted that on July 5, 1836, forty-seven colored persons from Tennessee and Kentucky left New York for Liberia. The original number was sixty-five, of which fifty had been emancipated only on condition that they go to Africa. Of this group ten escaped at Pittsburgh and eight at New York, "preferring to remain in this country."[58]

Mary Moore, "a citizen of Liberia," and her sister from Tennessee were experiencing difficulties in getting off to Liberia. Mary wrote to the American Colonization Society on February 28, 1849, saying that she did not think it right for her sister to have to pay her own passage to Africa. Furthermore her sister did not have the money for such a trip; nor could Mary finance them both. Mary said she knew it was "better" for her sister to go "to that country," but a few purchases had to be made in preparation for the voyage. The "Liberian" requested the Society to "fix it" so she could pay the passage fare after she got "home." She promised faithfully to repay the Society, and requested an "answer . . . in hast."[59] The outcome of Mary's dilemma is not known.

Why was not colonization more successful? First of all, that method of abolishing slavery was rather expensive; the cost of sending each Negro over was approximately $180. Secondly, and more important, the slaveowners disliked the idea because they naturally saw a connection between the colonization and the radical abolition movement. Anything that aimed at the immediate or ultimate extinction of slavery was opposed by the great majority of the southerners after the middle 1830's. Finally, the northerners did not support the movement as strongly as was anticipated. Some of them felt that by removing part of the free labor supply, slavery would become still more strongly entrenched. Had colonization been the only method of terminating slavery, it would probably still be here. Throughout the entire period the number colonized by all the states was less than the slave population of Davidson County in 1860.

The opponents of slavery did not confine their activities to various societies, but carried the fight into legislative halls when the Constitutional Convention assembled at Nashville on May 19, 1834. By this time their other attempts had proven futile, or practically so, and the advocates of extinction of the institution girded themselves for a supreme effort to abolish the system by constitutional means.

Thirty memorials from sixteen counties were presented to the assemblage with the chief abolition sentiment coming from East Tennessee. Only five of these counties were in Middle Tennessee and none in West Tennessee. These petitions had been signed by 1,805 people. The one hundred and five signatories who were slaveowners had only five hundred slaves, or less than an average of five each.[60]

The 1834 convention did not wish to consider these memorials in the Committee of the Whole, and on May 21, a motion of Jonathan Webster (Bedford County) to refer documents of this kind to a Committee of Propositions and Grievances of five members was adopted.[61] On June 6 William B. Carter, president of the convention, appointed J. A. M'Kinney (Hawkins County), Adam Huntsman (Madison County), and Robert Allen (Smith and Sumner counties) to draft the reasons that governed the convention in declining to act on these memorials in the Committee of the Whole.[62]

Thirteen days later, June 19, 1834, M'Kinney delivered the report of the committee. He stated that a majority of the members of the convention had been induced to "refuse to enter upon a lengthy discussion of this perplexing question" because of the "utter impracticability" of the plan proposed in the memorials. They did not see how such a plan "could have been accomplished," and felt certain that its discussion would produce "no result except the waste of time, the expenditure of money, and the destruction of harmony among the members, the preservation of which was so necessary for the accomplishment of the great work . . . of . . . the convention."[63] The assertion that slavery was an evil was admitted, but to tell how that evil could be removed was a question that the "wisest heads and the most benevolent hearts have not been able to answer in a satisfactory manner."[64]

M'Kinney noted that "the gates of society are just as effectually barred against him . . . after he becomes a nominal free man as while he is a real slave," and that his condition would be the "most forlorn and wretched that can be imagined." It was pointed out that the freedman would be beset with temptations, "strong, nay, almost irresistable, to the force of which in most cases he may be expected to yield." The result would be that he will be "degraded, despised, and trampled upon by the rest of the community."[65]

The chairman concluded his contrast of the condition of the slave and the freedman by saying:

. . . unenviable as is the condition of the slave, unlovely as slavery is in all its aspects, bitter as the draught is that the slave is doomed to drink . . . his condition is better than the condition of the free man of color in the midst of a community of white men, with whom he has no common interest, no fellow feeling, no equality. . . . The slave is almost wholly exempt from care, when his day's work is done he lies down and sleeps soundly. . . . He knows not at any time what it is to hear his children ask for bread when he has none to give them, they too are provided for. . . .[66]

M'Kinney continued to state clearly and logically that to banish slavery from Tennessee would not necessarily mean freeing the slaves. What was to prevent the owners from moving beyond the limits of the state and selling or settling their slaves elsewhere? Neither the convention, nor the legislature, nor the courts of justice could issue any mandate to prohibit such action. Besides, "it cannot be denied, that in Tennessee, slaves are treated with as much humanity as in any part of the world, where slavery exists"; they are "frequently taught to read" and "have access to religious instruction and the means of grace in common with the rest of the community. To this there may be some exceptions, but it is believed that they are *few and far between.*"[67]

Fear was expressed that the newly freed slaves would be "strongly tempted to concert plans" with their "brothers in chains" for the "extermination of the white race" and would take "possession of the country."[68]

The committee again stated that the chief ground of opposition of the majority of the delegates lay in the inexpediency of the plan, and asked the "friends of humanity" not to despair, and the memorialists not to "dread that slavery will be perpetual" for "Providence has already opened a door of hope [colonization societies], which is every day opening wider and wider."[69] M'Kinney

concluded the report by denouncing the northerners for their abolition agitation. He said:

And if misguided fanatics, in those parts of the United States where
slavery does not now exist, will only refrain from intermeddling in a
matter, in which they have no concern and in which their interference
can do no possible good and may do much positive evil, slavery, with
all its ills, will be extinguished as certainly and as speedily as the friends
of humanity have any reason to expect.[70]

This report reflects the tactics employed at this date, 1834, by
the Tennesseans in their defense of slavery. They had not yet, despite the abolition crusade, come to uphold the institution as a
positive good, but admitted that it was an evil, and confessed that
the trouble lay in their inability to adjust relations between the
whites and the freedmen and a fear that this attempted adjustment
could not be accomplished peaceably.

Abolition and emancipation advocates, chiefly Mathew Steph-
enson, John M'Gaughey, Richard Bradshaw, James Gillespy, and
Joseph Kincaid,[71] attacked the report by saying, among other
things, that the convention was "flaunting the public opinion" of
the state. Kincaid's motion of June 24 to strike from the records
that part of the report contrasting the condition of the slave and
free colored people was voted down, forty-two to twelve.[72] Terry
Cahal, a nonslaveowner of Maury County who had assisted
Josiah Polk in the formation of the Columbia Colonization Society
in 1830, spoke thus in behalf of the report of the committee:

Liberty, lovely as she is in my eyes, is not the only Deity at whose shrine
I desire to worship. There is another to be more adored. It is order. The
liberty I prize is a liberty regulated by law, which secures peace and
order. Liberate your slaves and attempt to elevate them to equality
with their masters, and she will soon take flight from this favored
land.[73]

In refutation of the charges of June 24, M'Kinney delivered another report on July 9, 1834.[74] Here he reiterated much of his
former report and said that "as far as they [the committee] have

been able to ascertain" the memorials came from sixteen of the sixty-two counties of the state, and the counties with the greatest number of signers were: Greene 378, Washington 273, Bedford 139, Lincoln 105, Overton 67, Maury 33, and Robertson 24. Some individuals "appeared to sign from more than one county." Also, only 1,805 of the "supposed" 550,000 whites of the state were signers and the committee "believe that there is something very uncandid in condemning others for not adopting a measure which the fault finders would have been the last to have adopted."[75]

The same delegates again protested against the report, but to no avail.[76] There was very little more controversy over the question, and the constitutional provision as finally adopted stipulated that "the General Assembly shall have no power to pass laws for the emancipation of slaves without the consent of their owner or owners."[77]

An issue closely allied with that of the eventual extinction of slavery was the question of Negro suffrage, and it took its place as the number two thorn of the convention. On May 27, William Ledbetter of Rutherford County introduced a motion that the right to vote be taken from the free colored[78] and that they be exempted from military service.[79] The question lay undisturbed until after the first M'Kinney report. Terry Cahal spoke to this motion on June 26, saying that personally he favored retention of the voting privilege by those who then possessed it, but he opposed sending free Negroes out of the country. The privilege of voting, however, should not be extended to any other freedmen, for if

. . . Tennessee become[s] the asylum for free negroes and the harbour for runaway slaves from other states, with the same right of suffrage, extended to the white and black man, with the influx of population which must ensue, because it is a sort of invitation to them to come, and the degradation and injury which we should inflict on posterity would call down on this convention its execration.[80]

W. H. Loving, delegate from Haywood and Tipton counties, was probably the most bitter opponent of Negro suffrage. He was "truly astonished and regretted" to see "old grey headed gentlemen" contending for the proposition to let free Negroes and mulattoes exercise the "highest right and privilege in a free government."[81] As in the case of emancipation, the question of granting the franchise to the free colored was not a question of right and wrong, but one of policy and expediency. Chiding the members of the convention for refusing to lower the voting age for whites and then contending for Negro suffrage, he asked, "Can they possibly have a deeper interest in the welfare of the government than white male citizens over the age of 18 and under 21 years?"

In answer to the assertion that the exercise of the franchise was a *"natural right—an inalienable and inherent right,"* Loving asked, "Who ever before . . . heard that the *right of suffrage* was a *natural* right? Is there any such right known in a state of nature beyond the pale of society?" Also, do not their "degraded condition, their general worthlessness of character, and idle and dissolute habits exclude all claims to any such right?" The West Tennessee delegate said that it was not his intention to run a tirade of abuse against these degraded people, but it was true, as Robert Weakley of Davidson County had said, that the free colored were "in the habit of trading with our slaves and corrupting them." He added that "many of the free blacks might be considered in the light of 'brokers' in the stealth of slaves" and "were the corrupt link between the debased of our own color and the slave."

Loving concluded by appealing to the superiority of the white race and expressing fear of a servile insurrection:

The same Almighty hand which separates Lazarus from Dives by an impassable gulph has fixed upon the negro race, a color of indelible hue, and pronounced upon Ham, the son of Noah, the curse "A servant of servants shall he be"—It was an evil example to our slaves of an incalculable extent to allow free negroes to exercise the right of suffrage. The slave can see no difference between himself and the free negro, no difference in color, none in moral and intellectual cultivation, and must think himself in every way as well qualified to exercise that right as the free men of color; and the only reason he can't do so, he has a master and the other none. These reflections must awaken and excite feelings in the breast of the slaves of a most delicate nature, embracing within their range, the overthrow or total extinction of the white race, one instance of which is yet fresh in our memory—that of the ill-fated Island of St. Domingo.[82]

The suffrage article as presented to the convention of 1834 granted the franchise to "every freeman of the age of twenty-one years and upwards" with the usual qualifications of citizenship and a certain period of residence within the state.[83] Reading and discussion of each clause of the proposed new constitution was commenced on July 28, and on July 31 Robert Weakley of Davidson County moved that the word "white" be inserted after "free" in the above article. The motion was carried by a vote of thirty-three to twenty-three, and the amended provision was adopted on that day.[84] The franchise was thus limited to free whites of twenty-one or more years with the proviso, introduced by J. A. M'Kinney, that "no person shall be disqualified from voting in any election in this state, on account of color, who is now by the existing laws . . . a competent witness in a court of justice against a white man."[85] Thus, persons of color who had only one-sixteenth non-Caucasian blood were allowed to vote.[86]

It will be noticed that all through this 1834 Convention practically the only argument set forth in favor of slavery was: it is the only practicable solution of the race problem as long as the Negro remains a part of the social order. The Nashville *Whig* in 1841 likewise stated that it was not slavery but the race relations attendant to liberation that constituted the major difficulty. It said, in part:

We have nothing to say in favor of negro slavery. It is a condition . . . we much lament. We would gladly be freed of them if we knew how. To free them and let them remain among us would aggravate the evil greatly. We would most willingly turn them over to our Yankee bretheren, if they would take them away and guarantee their good behavior. But whilst among us *ownership* is indispensable, and in the meantime we make their condition as comfortable as their situation will permit.[87]

Olmsted's East Tennessean expressed much the same view. He and his wife lived in the same house with the hired man, and said they had always wished there "hadn't been any niggers here . . . but he wouldn't like to have them free." He thought slavery was the best way of "getting along with them." They had owned three slaves but sold them to a speculator, because the Negroes "had a great fear of the mountains." Sale to a trader had been preferred to life in the "unknown" regions.[88]

Editorials from some of the West Tennessee newspapers reveal that the agitation created by the abolition crusade was bitterly resented, that the abolitionists were not respected, and that the West Tennesseans wished to have nothing to do with them. The Randolph *Recorder* of August 5, 1836, carried an article[89] which said that the paper was giving insertion to "one of the most scurrilous, insolent, and unwarrantable effusions that have ever fallen under our eyes." Some "unknown dastard of an Abolitionist" had written a letter to E. D. Tarver, Tennessee legislator, who had advertised for a runaway slave. In this communication Tarver was told to ". . . Blush, Tyrant, blush; Let confusion and shame mantle your face. Seek concealment in darkness, or retreat from civilized life. Be a beast." In commenting on this letter, the *Recorder* said:

We have never seen so much meanness, insolence, and disgusting Billingsgate contained in the same compass. And the writer pretends too to be a moral reformer! . . . Why does he intrench himself behind a feigned signature . . . ? Why does he remain in Cincinnati, if he feels such an interest in the freedom of the black? . . . But . . . they never go where there is any danger. Noble reformers these—bold Apostles of liberty![90]

Two years later, 1838, the Randolph *Whig* was requested to exchange with the *Emancipator*. The reply was not favorable; for "how we could be expected to exchange with such a concern, all filled as it is with the most insulting cuts, and base defamations, we cannot conceive."[91] The *Whig* termed parts of the antislavery paper as a "cut-throat piece of impudence," and the conclusion reached was:

. . . We cannot exchange with the Emancipator, or hold commerce with it in any shape or form. Under a disguise of patriotism and a love for mankind, the editor is a full-fledged monster who would disgrace the fingers of a public hangman, and be hooted from the society of a lawless banditti.

The *Whig* thought about as highly of the abolitionists as many of the abolitionists thought of the slaveholders.

Tennesseans took the side of the Federal Government in the Nashville Convention of 1850. This group assembled on June 3, and, with the fiery Robert Barnwell Rhett taking a leading role, adopted resolutions setting forth, among other things, the familiar doctrine of the equal rights of states in the territories and the newer doctrine of the duty of Congress to protect these rights.[92] Congress passed the famous "Compromise" of 1850 without regard to the demands of the Nashville assemblage, and the Convention reassembled—as had been agreed upon if the compromise passed—on November 11. The actions of the second meeting were historically unimportant.

The defense of slavery in Tennessee did not rapidly lead to opposition to the Union, and on February 9, 1861, the proposal to sever connections with the Federal Government was defeated by a vote of 69,675 to 57,798. The Sumter episode and Lincoln's call for troops helped to lead Tennesseans to the conviction that their chief interests lay with the states of the South. On June 8, 1861, the Volunteer State, by the overwhelming vote of 104,913 to 47,238, cast her lot with her sister slave states.[93]

What effect did the antislavery movement have in Tennessee? Though the number participating in this activity was small when compared to the total population of the state, some services were performed. The Tennessee opponents of slavery defended the free Negro in court cases and endeavored to better his standard of life; they attempted to ameliorate the condition of the slave and to prevent the separation of families. It is true that they did not wholly succeed in any one of these things, but they did succeed, in part, in all of them.[94]

Antislavery sentiment was strong in the eastern part of the Volunteer State during the first quarter of the nineteenth century, and it was "thought up to 1830 that Tennessee . . . would become a free State."[95] Then, however, came Garrison and the radical abolitionists, the Nat Turner insurrection, a shifting to the westward of the center of Tennessee's population, the southern defense of slavery, and a tightening of sectional lines. The result was that antislavery sentiment in Tennessee declined rapidly and was practically nonexistent before the decade of the 1830's was over. It should be noticed, however, that the great majority of Tennesseans did not defend the institution *per se,* but contended that it was the only practicable, sensible, and feasible solution of the race problem. If the Negroes were to remain, ownership was thought to be indispensable.

FOUR

Slave Life

ALTHOUGH the slave of Tennessee was subject to sale and hire —with the accompanying possibility of separation of husband and wife—his life was not, perhaps, as hard as was the life of the slave in the true plantation states. Yet, all the slaves of the South were far more secure—if security is the *summum bonum*—than were many of the free laborers of the North of the same period. There are, of course, exceptions to every generalization and the issue of liberty has been arbitrarily excluded from the comparison, but with the clamorous outbursts of those "clad in the armor of righteousness" having long since died away, this generalization may not grate too harshly on the ears of those who still maintain that the slave was driven, beaten, cowed, and mutilated by the blacksnake whip of heartless masters.

Tennessee, with the three major divisions of East, Middle, and West, presents a good cross section of the various types of slavery found in the southern states. In the eastern portion of the state there were relatively few slaves, and many of those were personal servants; the others who worked in the fields were almost invariably accompanied by their owners and masters. In Middle Tennessee, where the agricultural mode approached, in some counties, the plantation system, the holdings were larger and the slave occupations quite varied. In some of the West Tennessee counties, particularly Haywood and Fayette, plantation life bore

striking similarities to that of the lower South, though many of
the slaveowning class held fewer than five slaves.

The largest single group of slaveowners—even in the cotton
counties of the state—held only four or fewer slaves. The slaves
of these owners were the type of which James Stirling, the English
traveler, spoke when he visited the southern states. He pictured
them as midway between the house servants and the plantation
hands; they were neither spoiled nor abused, and were probably
the "best off" of all the slaves. These slaves often lived with their
master's family, worked in the fields with him, took an interest in
his affairs, and, in return, became "objects of his regard."[1] Also,
only very rarely did a person with fewer than ten slaves hire an
overseer, so the owners of from five to nine slaves might be included in the small proprietor class in Tennessee. In the fifteen
sample counties used in this study, 69.26 per cent of the slaveowners in 1850 had fewer than ten slaves; by 1860 the percentage
had decreased slightly to 67.69. Even if the ownership of thirty or
more slaves is accepted as the criterion for classification as a
planter, Tennessee cannot be made into a plantation state. In this
category there were 402 in 1850 and 485 in 1860 in the fifteen
counties studied. The total number of heads of families were
18,718 and 20,558, respectively! Harrod C. Anderson, of Haywood County, owned thirty-three slaves in 1860, but he generally
had only from six to nine field hands. He worked side by side
with the Negroes in the fields, rolling logs, building fences, and
doing other farm chores, although he had hired an overseer to
manage his slaves.[2]

J. H. Ingraham has portrayed very well, through the letters of
his fictitious governess, Miss Catherine Conyngham, at the home
of Colonel Peyton near Nashville, the life of the slave in Tennessee. Here the day began at 4:30 in the morning when the overseer rang a bell as a signal for the slaves to get ready for the day's
work. The domestic servants, however, were permitted to sleep
thirty minutes longer.[3] Then followed the regular daily routine:
breakfast in the field after a few hours' work; later on dinner in
the field or at the quarters—the latter if the slave were using a draft
animal; the day closed with the homeward trek about sundown or

in the twilight. If the Negroes were working on the task system, they often finished sometime in the afternoon. The above may seem like long hours, but the day of the overseer was even longer. He had to rise before bell time and see that the Negroes got to their chores promptly; then, after the slaves were through their work at night, it was his duty to see that all was well in the quarters.

Miss Conyngham tells of meeting about fifty Negroes on the avenue one evening at twilight. They were returning home from work, and the men seemed more cheerful than the women. One and all were clad in their Negro cloth, the men wearing straw hats and the women handkerchiefs. On Sundays the men put on their best Negro cloth, and the women replaced their weekday kerchiefs with some of gayer colors.

The governess fast became reconciled to slavery, for it did not "exhibit the revolting horrors I was taught in the North to discover in it." She said further:

I am almost ready to acknowledge that the African is happier in bondage than free! At least one thing is certain: nearly all of the free negroes I have seen in the north were miserable creatures, poor, ragged, and often criminal. Here they are well clad, moral, nearly all religious, and the temptations that demoralize the free blacks in our northern cities are unknown to, and cannot approach them.[4]

The transplanted Yankee was pleased at the division of labor on the plantation; each slave was trained from childhood in his own work, "hence the admirable, the *perfect* servants, one always finds on a well regulated plantation." Another portion of the letters tells much when one considers that she (in reality, Ingraham) had been taught to look for evils. It follows:

You will be interested to know that I have not heard a blow struck on this estate, and the Colonel says he has not punished one of his slaves in seven years. It is true all men are not like the good colonel, yet for most part the planters are kind and considerate toward their slaves. They often give them Saturday afternoons, and all day Sunday, when they appear in holiday attire, gayest of the gay.[5]

Not only did the slaves get Saturday afternoons and Sunday, but D. R. Hundley says that "nearly all masters give them certain established holidays, such as Easter Monday, the Fourth of July, the Eighth of January, and others."[6] Phillips notes that slaves were hired for the fifty-one weeks from New Year's to Christmas, "for every hireling went home for his traditional holiday. In fact, an employer was lucky if he recovered control before a week of January had elapsed."[7] Particularly was the latter true among the town slaves.[8] Elsewhere, Phillips states that Easter Monday and "a day or two in summer and fall," in addition to the Christmas season brought leisure to the slaves.[9]

Harrod C. Anderson's slaves had to "be *made* to work when the season comes for it, they seem not to see the present but are always putting off for some future days."[10] Anderson, however, rewarded his slaves when they worked well. In 1855 he gave them "a big dinner" on February 17, a holiday on May 5, "every Saturday afternoon (or part of it)," and four "working days" during the Christmas season. The following April 19 he "gave the servants a big dinner." The hands were given three "working days" at Christmas, 1856, and on the Saturday preceding July 19, 1858, they were given a dinner "in commemoration of their faithful working and expectation of a good crop of cotton." On November 22, 1859, Anderson states that the previous Saturday the hands had been rewarded with a full holiday and dinner for "their good picking of cotton." Anderson's diary is by no means a day-by-day account, and he possibly gave several more holidays than he mentions. Also, never once does the word "slave" find its way into his record, and "Negro" is used less than a half-dozen times. His usual designation was "hands," or they were spoken of by name. Anderson had a year or two of medical training in Philadelphia and administered to his own "hands."

Holidays were beneficial to the master as well as to the slaves, for on those days the Negroes could tend their "patches," or garden plots, which were generally allotted to each family. In this way they raised vegetables to supplement the rations from the "big house," or for sale to the master or on the market. In one more instance the master's loss from pilfering was lessened. The slaves often made money from their little pieces of ground, but almost as often they squandered it.[11] Some of the slaves were permitted to earn small sums of money by working on the holidays; they often used such earnings to buy whiskey for the Christmas season.[12] Many of the masters, however, furnished liquid refreshments for the yuletide period.

The Negro was quite sociable by nature, and had great capacity for enjoying himself. Ingraham noted that the happiest persons in the ballroom were the Negroes, and "you who live in a free state have no idea of the privileges this class are permitted in a slave state by the white people." The slaves moved about the room at pleasure; a favorite "aunty" would even ask, "Please, missis, stand dis way a little bit, so I can see!" The "missis" would comply as "readily as if a lady had asked her."[13] At this time a colored person could travel in the public conveyances in the slave states, but as late as 1864 colored servants attending white women and carrying white children were "driven from the street-cars in Philadelphia— a brutality without example in the South."[14]

A few cases will illustrate that all was not harsh feeling between master and slave in Tennessee. Colonel James Tubb of DeKalb County requested that Caleb, his body servant, be buried next to him. After the war and Tubb's death, Caleb cared for Mrs. Tubb and the youngest child until they died. Then he disappeared for several years, until one day he asked the stage driver from McMinnville to Smithville to let him ride. He was obliged, but died en route. James, Jr., carried out his father's wish and buried Caleb at the head of the family section.[15]

On one of his birthdays, Samuel Henderson's Negroes raised him to their shoulders and paraded around the house, singing as they marched. Later, Henderson made the following entry in his Journal:

Died on my farm near Franklin Tennessee May 7-1857 my Old Man Tom so well and favorable known in this community as Henderson Tom—seventy three or four years of age. He has been a regular member of the Methodist Church between forty-five and fifty years—and a more faithful and constant Christian either white or black I have seldom known. He lived like a christian and he died like he lived in full prospect of Immortality and Eternal life.[16]

Andrew Jackson was pictured as an "excellent master to his slaves, and never permitted his overseers to ill-treat them."[17] Many will recall that Alf, his body servant, is buried close to Jackson in the garden at the Hermitage. The proprietors of "Belle Meade," John Harding and his son, General William G., were paternal masters and opposed the entrusting of slaves to overseers. They never separated a family of slaves, and when the slaves became too numerous for the size of the farm, more land was purchased. Many of the slaves remained faithful during the war,[18] and lived their last years with "general." "Uncle Bob," tender of the horses, was probably the last of Harding's prewar Negroes.

Judge John Overton so trusted his slave Abram that he allowed him to visit his wife and children, who had recently been freed, in Evansville, Indiana. In the pass given on December 28, 1823, it was stated that Abram was to take from three to four weeks to make the trip, and "it is asked of all good people to assist his passage there and back." Abram stayed overtime, and on the reverse side of the pass Garrard Jones and Elijah King, on January 24, 1824, vouched for the fact that the Negro was detained because the Ohio River was so high that it was "impossible to pass the ravines on either side."[19]

The old Nashville Cemetery, located on Fourth Avenue South, began to be used as a place of interment in 1822. There was no discrimination as to color, and during the next thirty-eight years 7,170 whites and 3,913 Negroes were buried there.[20] It is assumed that a large majority of these Negroes were household or personal servants, though some were free Negroes.

In Tennessee, as in the other slave states, a number of slaves accompanied their masters to the Civil War. Byrd Douglas, prominent Nashville wholesale dry goods dealer, wrote Governor F. W. Pickens of South Carolina on January 18, 1861, offering the services of "three or four" of his sons, "if it be before their native State . . . shall require their services." Also, he had two "intelligent negro men" who would "willingly and efficiently fill any vacancy when one or more of their young masters may be disposed of by the enemy." Douglas was, perhaps, rather over-optimistic when he said there were "one hundred thousand more of the same sort of material in Tennessee."[21]

Ebenezer Jones, writing to his children on August 22, 1819, gave the following advice:

> Dear son and doughter may you ever mind
> and to your slaves be always very kind
> you soon with them on a level must meet
> when Christ doth call you to his judgment seat
> Christ will not ask if folks are black or white
> but judge the deeds and pass a sentence right
> The earth is not a place for our abode
> prepare prepare to meet a righteous God.[22]

There was a gay time among the Negroes at cornhusking parties where they were often fed delicacies. But, there was also trouble, as at the party given by a Mr. Jones. He had asked his neighbor, Allen, to send over his Negroes, so that altogether about seventy-five slaves and twenty-five whites were present. At ten or eleven o'clock all were fed and the Negroes instructed to go home. Isaac, one of Allen's Negroes, remained a few minutes longer to participate in the wrestling activities. An uninvited drunk white man mortally stabbed him while many were testing their strength and skill. The trial court said there was no direct evidence that Isaac went to the party with the permission or knowledge of Allen, and awarded Allen $1,050 damages. The case was appealed, and Justice M'Kinney, delivering the opinion of the appeal court, said, in part:

By . . . universal usage, they are constituted the agents of their masters, and are sent on their business without written authority. And in like manner . . . sent to perform those neighborly offices, common in every community . . . are allowed by universal sufferance, at night, on Sundays, holidays, and other occasions, to go abroad, to attend church, to visit . . . and to exercise other innocent enjoyments, without it ever entering the mind of any good citizen to demand *written authority* of them . . . verbal consent may . . . be implied from circumstances.[23]

The opinion of the lower court was reversed—written permission of the master was not necessary for a slave to attend such a gathering—and if Justice M'Kinney's opinion is a statement of fact, the Tennessee slave was not too closely hedged in by socially restrictive measures.

Some of the owners made it a rule for their slaves to find husbands or wives on the plantation, but this was sometimes violated. Mrs. Theresa Perkins tells how she forged the name of her father, Henry R. Ewing, to a pass permitting Jane to marry Willis, Mr. Mymms' Negro, instead of Peter of the "homefolks." Later, Mr. Mymms moved to Mississippi, but would not sell Willis, so Ewing, against his principles, sold Jane.[24]

Samuel Henderson's granddaughter recalls the gala occasion of the marriage of Loge, Henderson's body servant, to Sal, the housemaid at a neighbor's home. They were married in the dining room; little Negroes held candles to enable the preacher to read; then all were fed sumptuously. The next summer the "regular" Negroes were married in the backyard under the trees.[25] Louis Hughes, who made four unsuccessful attempts to escape, was given a "big wedding" by "Boss" on November 30, 1858.[26]

The white children and the slave children played together,[27] and still today many white children prefer—whether from an innate desire to "boss" or actually because the association is more pleasant is not known—colored playmates at a certain age. This practice during slave times nurtured many close relationships between young masters and their slaves.

Slaves hated to be called lazy and worthless, and they rejoiced in their masters' good fortune because they felt that they, too, had thus been lifted in the social and economic scale. Mrs. Perkins states that she used to hear the Negroes repeat, in "great scorn," the expression of a neighboring overseer: "Hurry up, you black rascal, you are as lazy as old squire Ewings trifling niggers, one half of them dances to their shadows while tother half leans on ther [sic] hoes and looks on."[28] Louis Hughes, the four-time fugi-

tive, said that a servant owned by a man in moderate circumstances was "hooted at" by the slaves of a rich man. "It was
common for them to say: 'Oh! don't mind that darkey, he belongs
to po'r white trash.' So . . . our slaves rejoiced in master's good
luck."[29] The "good luck" of which Louis spoke was the new brick
home that his master, Edward McGee [McGehee] built in Memphis in the 1820's. Louis had previously been an errand boy on
the Pontotoc, Mississippi, place, but now he was installed as butler
and body servant. In his new capacity he had to look after the
parlors, halls, and dining rooms, arrange flowers, wait on the
table, polish the silver, care for his master's clothes, go for the
mail, and "stone the steps."[30] He "felt big" in his "snowy white
linen"; no longer would he be "cowed and lashed," and although
the change was "merely for the gratification of my master's pride
. . . I thought I would do all I could to please Boss." Louis was
very fond of his "extra" chore of caring for the sick under the
supervision of McGee.[31]

Thomas, McGee's coachman, and Louis were fast friends. The
former took lessons at night from some plasterers in the neighborhood, but Louis was required to sleep in the house. Although
Louis was not freed until after the war—when he became a nurse
—he states that

it is, perhaps, but justice to say of my old master that he was in some
respects kinder and more humane than many other slaveholders. He
fed well, and all had enough to wear, such as it was. It is true that the
material was course, but it was suited to the season, and, therefore,
comfortable, which could not truthfully be said of the clothing of the
slaves of the other planters.[32]

Perhaps, the pride engendered by having belonged to a wealthy
man prompted Louis to berate the condition of the other slaves
as he had once been "hooted at."

Although the *Presbyterian Witness* could not see a "solitary
argument in favor of teaching a white man that might not as properly be urged in favor of enlightening men of color,"[33] common
sense tells one that the teaching of slaves was sometimes forbidden
to prevent their being able to write their own passes or to read

abolition literature. By no means, however, was it a general rule
that the Tennessee slave was denied the rudiments of education.

Education of the slaves was feared by some of the whites. This
is attested by the boyhood experience of "Reverend Rufus L.
Perry, Ph.D." At an early age, Rufus was sent to Nashville where
he was taught in the free Negro school by Miss Sally Porter. His
slave parents escaped to Canada when he was about seven years
old and left Rufus behind. His master then denied continuance of
his temporary freedom and took him back to the plantation. As
the boy grew toward manhood, his schooling made him contemp-
tible among his fellow bondsmen, and gained him a reputation
among the whites as a "dangerous nigger." So "dangerous" did he
become that he was sold to a trader in August, 1852, to be taken
to Mississippi. Rufus, however, escaped and fled to Canada in
three weeks.[34]

Edmund Kelly, later a preacher, wanted an education, so he
traded bonbons from his master's table for a speller and a few
lessons from some young people. For some weeks Edmund's owners did not know he was studying; when they found him with his
books, they did nothing about it.[35] Also there was Randall B.
Vandervall, of Davidson County, who attended school, was aided
in his studies by his master's son, John Vandervall, and paid for
his lessons by splitting rails. Randall began preaching when he was
only sixteen years old.[36] Newell Houston Ensley of Nashville was
the son of slaves, but was owned by his white maternal grandfather. His owner bought books for, and employed a man to teach,
the slaves. Newell was body servant and buggy boy for his master,
was treated "remarkably well for a slave lad, and often was he
commended for his capabilities." He played with the other grand-
children.[37]

Other slaves who were taught by their masters, or by their masters' children, were John Warren of Wilson County, Williamson
Pease of Hardeman County, and Uncle Cephas, a slave of Parson
Winslow. Cephas said that he was never "without books during
his stay with his master."[38]

These are only a few examples; the practice seems to have been
rather prevalent. Memphis prohibited the teaching of Negroes,

slave or free, in 1856, but there were Negro schools in Nashville.
Most of the teaching came through the masters and masters' children, however, and was, from conditions themselves, more common among the small proprietors. James Stirling noted that in
Tennessee and Kentucky he "heard little or none" of the "nigger
gibberish" and the "coloured men in America seem to speak better, or at least more agreeably to an English ear, than the whites."[39]
Nor was the slave denied religious instruction—except in rare
instances—as the abolitionists contended. Henry Ewing had "all
the negroes who wished to come in to prayer every Sunday night,"[40]
and

> In the Synods of Kentucky, Virginia, North Carolina, and West Ten-
> nessee, it is the practice of a number of ministers to preach to the
> negroes separately on the Sabbath or during the week. There are also
> Sabbath schools in some of the Churches for children and adults, and
> in all the houses of worship, with a few exceptions, a greater or less
> number of colored members and negroes form a portion of every Sab-
> bath congregation. In portions of the Synods the abolition excitement
> checked and in others retarded the work of instruction.[41]

One of the largest Negro missions in Tennessee in 1833 was
that of the African charge in Nashville under the guidance of the
Methodist minister, James Givin. In August he had just closed a
camp meeting which had been attended by about one thousand
colored people. During the revival thirty "professed to find peace
with God" and fifty-nine joined the church "on trial." The church
had a membership of seven hundred, "nearly all of whom profess
to be happy in their Saviour; and what greatly encourages me,
there is no opposition from owners of slaves." By the end of the
year the membership had increased to 819, and six years later,
1839, it was the third largest colored charge in the country.[42]
The Methodists were, perhaps, the most active denomination
in religious work among the slaves, and between 1829 and 1864
members of the Tennessee, Holston, and Memphis conferences
contributed nearly $237,000 for the advancement of the work of

the plantation missions. The annual amounts advanced were considerably larger after 1844, and the Memphis Conference was particularly adept at raising funds for this purpose.[43]

The slaves were not lacking in forceful preachers within their own ranks. Emanuel Mask of Fayette County was given a written permit by his master so that he might go around and preach. Reverend N. A. D. Bryant said that Emanuel did this to the "great pleasure of people everywhere, white as well as black. . . . I frequently invited Emanuel to my house to preach to my slaves."[44] Nelson Merry succeeded S. A. Davidson, white, as pastor of the colored Baptist Church in Nashville. Under his leadership, and with the aid of the whites, the church obtained a lot on North Spruce Street and erected a large brick building. The membership increased rapidly to 2,800. Merry was a "remarkable man in many respects," and when he died in 1884, a "preacher of every denomination (except Roman Catholic) came to his funeral and testified to his exalted character, wisdom, and prudence."[45]

Dr. T. L. Boswell, "a man of commanding influence in the Memphis Conference," tells of the fine relationship between Ned Davis and his body servant, Dennis. Ned had spent some rather "wild" days in North Carolina and other places, but Dennis was always compelled to accompany him on his escapades. When Boswell first knew master and slave at La Grange, Tennessee, in 1840, Ned had become religious; Boswell

often saw the two happy together, shaking hands and rejoicing on their way to the better land. Ned often spoke of the sinful ways into which he had compelled his servant to go, while tears of regret filled his eyes. It was indeed a goodly sight to see them together praising God.[46]

While there were a number of separate churches for the Negroes, the more usual practice was to give religious instruction to the slaves on the premises of the owner, or in the churches of the whites, where they occupied the back rows or the balcony. Perhaps not too many of the services were like the one which Levi Coffin describes in the crack-filled log cabin Methodist Church at Hamburg in West Tennessee. He pictures eight or ten whites, a half-dozen Negroes, and several dogs as the congregation. The men were spitting tobacco juice on the floor; the women were dipping snuff; while the dogs "quarreled and fought with each other. The sermon was good, but no one seemed impressed by it except an old negro woman, who sobbed aloud and rocked herself to and fro."[47]

The impression made on another northern visitor was much more favorable, and he saw more of the true side of slave life in the South. After a three months' sojourn, he wrote:

> The impression here made upon me, or rather confirmed and illustrated afresh, was, that the slaves, so far as I had seen, were unconscious of any feeling of restraint; the natural order of things proceeded with them; they did not act like a driven, overborne people, stealing about with sulky looks, imbruted by abuse, crazed, stupidly melancholic. People habitually miserable could not have conducted the musical service of public worship as they did; their looks and manner gave agreeable testimony that, in spite of their condition, they had sources of enjoyment and ways of manifesting it which suggested to a spectator no thought of involuntary servitude.[48]

If no higher motive was present, self-interest was a sufficient incentive to most masters to treat their slaves kindly. Anyone with a sense of values, much less a feeling for humanity, does not beat a horse, mule, or other work animal, to say nothing of a much more valuable slave, until it is rendered worthless by the lacerations inflicted by the whip. However, slavery was neither all good nor all bad; Ulrich B. Phillips has admirably expressed existing conditions: "All in all, the slave regime was a curious blend of force and concession, of arbitrary disposal by the master and self-direction by the slave, of tyranny and benevolence, of antipathy and affection."[49]

Mrs. Theresa Perkins, "an octogenarian of the Old South," recalled, with feelings of pity and sympathy for the freedmen, the slave days in her poem, "A Leaf from the Long Ago." It follows, in part:

I mused o'er my early childhood,
  My childhood friends, and lo;
There arose the forms of a people,
  From the dear dim long ago.

In my heart came a flow of pleasure,
  Quickly checked by a flood of tears,
As I remembered they are gone forever,
  Buried in the vanished years.

                *   *   *   *   *

Men called them slaves, and so they were,
  'Neath their country's law,
They who write of "slavery" now,
  Write fiction—nothing more—

Of suffering, toil and sorrow,
  Ever the saddest refrain,
See only the furrowed sweating brow,
  Hear only the cry of pain.

Had they but heard the laughter,
  Or hearkened to the shouts of joy,
Of the girl, who was never a woman,
  And the man who was ever a boy.

They would know that trouble, nor sorrow,
  Ne'er lingered in the heart of a slave,
Forgotten e'er the dawn of the morrow
  New joy or sorrow gave.

Food, clothes, a home was theirs,
  From the cradle to the grave;
No child of labor, so free from cares,
  Has penury ever made.

They recked not of the toil and trouble,
  Waiting for them on freedoms road,
Nor how their hearts would quake and tremble
  'Neath the unaccustomed load.

No 'Ole Marse' to control, or guide them,
  No kind 'Ole Miss' to call their own;
Poor, thoughtless, old, young children,
  "Treading the wine-press alone."[50]

The life of the slave in Tennessee was no harder than might have been expected under the circumstances. The great majority of the owners had fewer than ten slaves, and this type of owner was, by his economic status, brought into closer contact with the slaves than the more wealthy planters. The latter, however, were not very numerous in Tennessee. Slaves were often given religious instruction by his owner or the local minister. They were also frequently taught to read and write, but the interest of the owner sometimes demanded the abrogation of this type of training. Instances of cruel masters in the Volunteer State are very few; such men are found in any place at any time. The slave worked— if he had to be made to do so—but he also had some time of his own which he utilized for rest, pleasure, or the earning of a few dollars for himself.

FIVE

Land Tenure and Slaveholding, 1850 and 1860

TENNESSEE was admitted to the Union in 1796. In the preceding year the census taken for the purpose of determining whether the Southwest Territory was ready for statehood credited the region with 77,263 persons of which 10,613 were slaves.[1] The majority of settlers who came to the "new" country in the early decades were from Virginia, North Carolina, and South Carolina, with scattered numbers from other states and foreign countries. Men had sought homes on the frontier for various reasons. The exhaustion of farm land in the eastern states had prompted many to move westward.[2] The lure of financial gain by speculating in land provided the incentive for others, who, in turn, convinced still others of the desirability of moving to a new area. Still more were led to change their place of residence through hope of bettering their economic, social, and political status. A few sought only adventure and excitement.[3] By 1840 most of the sections of Tennessee had lost the characteristics indicative of the frontier, and the patterns—economic, social, and political—that the state was to follow, with slight modification, until 1860 had been fairly well set.

Following the introduction of slavery into the Tennessee country by the earliest settlers, the growth of the institution was not rapid until the opening of the Western District in the second decade of the nineteenth century, and at no time during the ante-bellum period did the slave population of the state exceed one fourth of the total population. In 1790 there were only 3,417 slaves in the Southwest Territory, constituting 9.7 per cent of the total population; by 1820 there were 80,107 in Tennessee, or 18.9 per cent of the total. Between 1820 and 1840 the slave population of the state more than doubled, and then continued to increase until it had reached 275,719 in 1860, while the proportion of slave to total population had risen to 24.8 per cent. That the pattern of distribution varied widely in the different parts of the state is indicated by the fact that in East Tennessee the ratio of slaves to whites was about one to twelve, with some counties having not more than one slave to sixty whites, while at the other extreme, in Haywood and Fayette counties in West Tennessee, the slave population outnumbered the whites in both 1850 and 1860.[4] These wide variations mean that for purposes of statistical analysis the state must be examined by sections rather than as a single unit.

Prior to the time that the census schedules gave more than a "counting of noses," Tennessee appears to have followed much the same pattern of development as the other new states: land speculators, groups, and individuals all contributing in one way or another to winning the area for civilization. There were some wealthy planters, many yeomen, numerous squatters, absentee operators, Negro slaveowners, poachers, cheats, and other types of the "forked biped." By 1840 the ever-hungrying group had accumulated 18,251,622 taxable acres valued at $70,708,313 and owned 76,639 slaves of taxable age—twelve to fifty years—worth $43,073,760. More than one fourth of the total population, or 227,739, were engaged in agriculture, while 17,815 were occupied with manufacturing and trade, and 2,217 gained their livelihood from commerce.[5]

By 1850 the Volunteer State passed the million mark in population but the 5,175,173 improved acres in the farms loomed relatively small beside the 13,808,849 still unimproved acres. Ten years later the improved acreage had increased by more than one and a half million while the unimproved was tabulated as only about 65,000 more. The 1860 evaluation of $271,358,985 was almost treble that of 1850.[6]

But the published census materials tell little of the actual economic mosaic and permit only relatively meaningless comparisons and analyses. Who operated this land: the so-called planters, the small slaveowners, the nonslaveowners, the tenants? What relationship, if any, existed between landownership and slaveownership? Were the large slaveowners segregated on the best farming land and the smaller slaveowners and incorrectly termed "poor whites" thrust out into the poorest and least productive areas of all? Or is the house-to-house recording of the census enumerator a chronicle stating in black and white that the wealthy slaveowner lived next door to the yeoman nonslaveowner, the small slaveowner, the renter, or maybe the squatter and that the planters constituted the islands rather than the sea? The pages following will answer these and other questions.

It was stated in the introduction that it was neither possible nor necessary to study every farmer in the state to obtain a reasonably accurate picture of slavery and ante-bellum agriculture in Tennessee, and that fifteen of the sixty counties of the state had been chosen as the sample. That these counties may be considered a representative cross section of the state as a whole is indicated by the fact that they include some counties in which the nonslaveholders formed the major part of the agricultural element, others in which slaveowners and nonslaveowners were about equally divided, and still others in which the slaveholders were the dominant agricultural group. They also include each of the various types of production economy—stock and grain, cotton, tobacco, and diversified farming—on which the majority of the farming class depended in the different parts of the state.

In compiling the data for these counties, attention has been confined to that part of the agricultural population shown by the records to have been definitely engaged in agricultural pursuits, and since the farm is the unit for such enterprise it has seemed reasonable to base the analysis upon the number of farm operators rather than upon the total farm population. The term "heads of agricultural families" is used to designate these operators, and in selecting these heads one specific requirement has been followed. Each one included was a farm operator who produced not less than one hundred dollars' worth of agricultural commodities dur-

Slavery in Tennessee

ing the year previous to the taking of the census. He may or may not have been a slaveholder or a landowner, but he had to be a producer to be counted.[7] For the fifteen sample counties, 18,718 such heads of agricultural families appear in the unpublished schedules for 1850 and 20,558 in those of 1860.[8] Table I presents an analysis of these heads of families as to slaveownership and landownership for each county, and by grouping the counties according to their location a similar analysis is obtained for each of the three grand divisions of the state.

Table I. Heads of Agricultural Families: Percentage of Slaveownership and Landownership in Fifteen Sample Counties

Counties	Heads of Agricultural Families	SLAVEOWNERSHIP		LANDOWNERSHIP	
		Owners	Nonowners	Owners	Nonowners
		EAST TENNESSEE			
Johnson					
1850	350	13.43	86.57	89.71	10.29
1860	399	12.03	87.97	86.47	13.53
Greene					
1850	1,785	11.76	88.24	71.09	28.91
1860	1,895	11.61	88.39	83.22	16.78
Totals					
1850	2,135	12.04	87.96	73.77	26.23
1860	2,294	11.68	88.32	83.78	16.22
		MIDDLE TENNESSEE			
Fentress					
1850	501	8.98	91.02	69.86	30.14
1860	697	7.17	92.83	73.74	26.26
DeKalb					
1850	731	19.70	80.30	78.39	21.61
1860	903	20.27	79.73	84.16	15.84
Lincoln					
1850	1,959	32.36	67.64	73.61	26.39
1860	2,481	28.17	71.83	58.81	41.19
Maury					
1850	1,974	51.62	48.38	70.36	29.64
1860	2,298	50.17	49.83	76.63	23.37

Counties	Heads of Agricultural Families	SLAVEOWNERSHIP		LANDOWNERSHIP	
		Owners	Nonowners	Owners	Nonowners
Davidson					
1850	1,618	54.70	45.30	72.87	27.13
1860	1,148	62.02	37.98	76.74	23.26
Robertson					
1850	1,067	53.80	46.20	96.53	3.47
1860	1,269	48.23	51.77	91.80	8.20
Montgomery					
1850	1,340	56.64	43.36	79.33	20.67
1860	1,156	53.89	46.11	83.30	16.70
Totals					
1850	9,190	44.18	55.82	76.41	23.59
1860	9,952	40.51	59.49	75.37	24.63
		WEST TENNESSEE			
Hardin					
1850	694	15.56	84.44	85.88	14.12
1860	1,034	19.83	80.17	70.99	29.01
Henry					
1850	1,471	33.31	66.69	81.71	18.29
1860	1,732	32.10	67.90	78.52	21.48
Gibson					
1850	2,352	24.70	75.30	67.77	32.23
1860	2,580	33.64	66.36	67.27	32.73
Dyer					
1850	747	30.79	69.21	73.76	26.24
1860	994	33.80	66.20	69.72	30.28
Haywood					
1850	956	62.66	37.34	76.26	23.74
1860	1,011	57.76	42.24	83.38	16.62
Fayette					
1850	1,173	79.45	20.55	85.68	14.32
1860	961	78.77	21.23	86.99	13.01
Totals					
1850	7,393	39.77	60.23	76.80	23.20
1860	8,312	39.77	60.23	74.74	25.26
Grand Totals for the Fifteen Counties					
1850	18,718	38.77	61.23	76.32	23.68
1860	20,558	37.00	63.00	76.01	23.99

The most obvious fact indicated by these figures is that there seems to be little correlation between ownership of slaves and ownership of land. In Fayette County, for example, 78.77 per cent of the heads of agricultural families owned slaves and 86.99 per cent owned land in 1860, while in Johnson County in the same year only 12.03 per cent owned slaves and 86.47 per cent owned land. Likewise the landownership percentages for Greene, Montgomery, and Haywood counties are almost identical for 1860 (83.22, 83.30, 83.38), but the slaveownership percentages were 11.61, 53.89, and 57.76, respectively. It is worthy of note that in Greene County, where the slaveowners were relatively unimportant, the increase of landownership between 1850 and 1860 was far greater than in the two counties with a much larger slave population.[9]

Before the assertion of little correlation between slave- and landownership can be accepted, however, it is necessary to examine thoroughly the percentage of landownership among the slaveholders and the percentage of slaveownership among the landowners. These relationships are shown in Tables II and III.[10]

Table II. Landownership among Slaveholders and Nonslaveholders

| | | SLAVEHOLDERS | | | NONSLAVEHOLDERS | |
Counties	No.	Land-owners	Per Cent	No.	Land-owners	Per Cent
			EAST TENNESSEE			
Johnson						
1850	47	45	95.74	303	269	88.78
1860	48	41	85.42	351	304	86.61
Greene						
1850	210	197	93.81	1,575	1,072	68.83
1860	220	211	95.91	1,675	1,366	81.55
Totals						
1850	257	242	94.16	1,878	1,341	71.41
1860	268	252	94.03	2,026	1,670	82.43
			MIDDLE TENNESSEE			
Fentress						
1850	45	42	93.33	456	308	67.54
1860	50	46	92.00	647	468	72.33
DeKalb						
1850	144	127	88.19	587	446	75.98
1860	183	172	93.99	720	588	81.67

Counties	No.	SLAVEHOLDERS Land-owners	Per Cent	No.	NONSLAVEHOLDERS Land-owners	Per Cent
Lincoln						
1850	634	573	90.38	1,325	869	65.58
1860	699	624	89.27	1,782	835	46.86
Maury						
1850	1,019	880	86.36	955	509	53.30
1860	1,153	1,036	89.85	1,145	725	63.32
Davidson						
1850	885	778	87.91	733	401	54.71
1860	712	632	88.76	436	249	57.11
Robertson						
1850	574	562	97.91	493	468	94.93
1860	612	598	97.71	657	567	86.30
Montgomery						
1850	759	686	90.38	581	377	64.89
1860	623	579	92.94	533	384	72.05
Totals						
1850	4,060	3,648	89.85	5,130	3,378	65.85
1860	4,032	3,687	91.44	5,920	3,816	64.46
WEST TENNESSEE						
Hardin						
1850	108	106	98.15	586	490	83.90
1860	205	196	95.61	829	538	64.90
Henry						
1850	490	459	93.67	981	743	75.74
1860	556	520	93.53	1,176	840	71.43
Gibson						
1850	581	527	90.71	1,771	1,067	64.71
1860	868	783	90.21	1,712	953	55.61
Dyer						
1850	230	217	94.35	517	334	64.60
1860	336	308	91.67	658	385	58.51
Haywood						
1850	599	499	83.31	357	230	64.43
1860	584	546	93.49	427	297	69.56
Fayette						
1850	932	835	89.59	241	170	70.54
1860	757	691	91.28	204	145	71.08
Totals						
1850	2,940	2,643	89.90	4,453	3,034	68.13
1860	3,306	3,044	92.08	5,006	3,158	63.08
Grand Totals for the Fifteen Counties						
1850	7,257	6,533	90.02	11,461	7,753	67.66
1860	7,606	6,983	91.81	12,952	8,644	66.74

Table III. Slaveownership among Landowners and Non-Landowners

Counties	No.	LANDOWNERS Slave-owners	Per Cent	No.	NON-LANDOWNERS Slave-owners	Per Cent
			EAST TENNESSEE			
Johnson						
1850	314	45	14.33	36	2	5.56
1860	345	41	11.88	54	7	12.96
Greene						
1850	1,269	197	15.52	516	13	2.52
1860	1,577	211	13.38	318	9	2.83
Totals						
1850	1,583	242	15.29	552	15	2.72
1860	1,922	252	13.11	372	16	4.30
			MIDDLE TENNESSEE			
Fentress						
1850	350	42	12.00	151	3	1.99
1860	514	46	8.95	183	4	2.19
DeKalb						
1850	573	127	22.16	158	17	10.76
1860	760	172	22.63	143	11	7.69
Lincoln						
1850	1,442	573	39.74	517	61	11.80
1860	1,459	624	42.77	1,022	75	7.34
Maury						
1850	1,389	880	63.23	585	139	23.76
1860	1,761	1,036	58.83	537	117	21.79
Davidson						
1850	1,179	778	65.99	439	107	24.37
1860	881	632	71.74	267	80	29.96
Robertson						
1850	1,030	562	54.56	37	12	32.43
1860	1,165	598	51.33	104	14	13.46
Montgomery						
1850	1,063	686	64.53	277	73	26.35
1860	963	579	60.12	193	44	22.80
Totals						
1850	7,026	3,648	51.92	2,164	412	19.04
1860	7,503	3,687	49.14	2,449	345	14.09

Counties	No.	LANDOWNERS Slave- owners	Per Cent	No.	NON-LANDOWNERS Slave- owners	Per Cent
			WEST TENNESSEE			
Hardin						
1850	596	106	17.79	98	2	2.04
1860	734	196	26.70	300	9	3.00
Henry						
1850	1,202	459	38.19	269	31	11.52
1860	1,360	520	38.24	372	36	9.68
Gibson						
1850	1,594	527	33.06	758	54	7.12
1860	1,735	783	45.13	845	85	10.06
Dyer						
1850	551	217	39.38	196	13	6.63
1860	693	308	44.44	301	28	9.30
Haywood						
1850	729	499	68.45	227	100	44.05
1860	843	546	64.77	168	38	22.62
Fayette						
1850	1,005	835	83.08	168	97	57.74
1860	836	691	82.66	125	66	52.80
Totals						
1850	5,677	2,643	46.56	1,716	297	17.31
1860	6,201	3,044	49.09	2,111	262	12.42
Grand Totals for the Fifteen Counties						
1850	14,286	6,533	45.73	4,432	724	16.34
1860	15,626	6,983	44.69	4,932	623	12.63

These three tables make possible the examination of certain relationships between landowning and slaveowning for the fifteen counties by analyzing the changes which occurred between 1850 and 1860. In that ten-year span the total number of heads of agricultural families increased by 9.83 per cent; the total number of slaveholders by 4.81 per cent; and the total number of landowners by 9.38 per cent. At the same time, however, the ratio of slaveholders to total heads declined from 38.77 per cent in 1850 to 37.00 per cent in 1860, and the ratio of landowners to total heads from 76.32 per cent in 1850 to 76.01 per cent in 1860. The fact that in 1850 only 45.73 per cent of the landowners were slaveowners while 90.02 per cent of the slaveholders were landowners suggests that the dependence of slaveownership on landownership was greater than that of landownership on slaveownership. This suggestion is strengthened by the fact that the ratio of landowning slaveowners to the total slaveowners increased to 91.81 per cent by 1860 while that of the slaveholding landowners to the total landowners declined to 44.69 per cent. Or, to look at it from the obverse, the non-landowning slaveholders decreased in the last ante-bellum decade, while the nonslaveholding landowner increased in relation to the total number of individuals. These changes were small, but the fact that they all point in the same direction may be significant—though not conclusive until further tests have been applied.

Does the above analysis of the fifteen counties as a whole make adequate allowance for the variations which existed in the various parts of the state? A quick examination of the above tables reveals that the percentage of heads of agricultural families owning slaves and the percentage of heads of agricultural families owning land were by no means uniform for the various counties and that the changes between 1850 and 1860 also varied. In East Tennessee, both percentages declined in Johnson County during the decade, while in Greene County slaveownership declined and landownership increased. In Middle Tennessee the percentages for both increased in DeKalb and Davidson counties and declined in Lincoln and Robertson, while in Fentress, Maury, and Montgomery slaveownership declined and landownership increased. In West Tennessee, Henry County showed a decline in both percentages; Hardin, Gibson, and Dyer showed higher percentages in slaveowning in 1860 and lower in landowning, while in Haywood and Fayette the reverse was true.

Certain of the most pronounced changes deserve a word or two: the large increase in landownership in Greene and the large decrease in Lincoln and Hardin. Greene, in the East Tennessee Valley, had long been one of the more prosperous small slaveholding sections of the state, but internal improvements in the 1850's materially aided the farmers in getting their products to market. An increase in prosperity, based on a sound and little-fluctuating stock-grain economy could readily account for the increase in landownership.[11] The non-landowners increased more in Lincoln

County than they decreased in Greene. It is believed that many of the non-landowners in Lincoln in 1850 were squatters and were not entered upon the census records. Then, too, that county underwent a change to diversified farming with internal improvements playing a significant role in making markets accessible. The increase in the number of land operators was far greater in Lincoln than in any other county except Hardin, which showed almost the same decrease in the percentage of landownership. The situation in Hardin may be explained in much the same manner as in Lincoln. In both instances it was the nonslaveowners who augmented the ranks of the landless, but Hardin had a much larger numerical increase among the landowners. No comparable percentage changes are to be found in slaveownership.

Obviously, this lack of a consistent pattern raises doubt as to the validity of a generalization based only on an analysis of the sums of the county figures, and at the same time makes it impossible to generalize on the basis of the statistics for the individual counties. However, by using the three grand divisions of the state, it is possible to take into consideration certain regional similarities and differences which do not become apparent through either of the other two approaches.

The following tabulation shows what proportions of the total (for the fifteen sample counties, that is) number of heads of agricultural families, the total number of landowners, etc., were contained in each of these three grand divisions in 1850 and 1860:

		East Tenn. % of Total	Middle Tenn. % of Total	West Tenn. % of Total
Heads of agricultural families..............	1850	11.40	49.10	39.50
	1860	11.16	48.41	40.43
Landowners............	1850	11.08	49.18	39.74
	1860	12.30	48.02	39.68
Nonslaveowning landowners...........	1850	17.30	43.57	39.13
	1860	19.32	44.15	36.52
Slaveowners.............	1850	3.54	55.95	40.51
	1860	3.52	53.01	43.47
Non-landowning slaveowners	1850	2.07	56.91	41.02
	1860	2.57	55.38	42.06

The very close correlation between the percentages of land-owners and the percentages of heads of agricultural families in each of these groupings is especially striking; and when compared with the relatively wide variations between the percentages of slaveowners and the percentages of heads, it seems to substantiate the conclusion suggested that landownership in Tennessee was by no means dependent upon slaveownership. The conclusion appears to be made more nearly definite by the contrasting percentages of nonslaveowning landowners and non-landowning slaveowners in East Tennessee. On the other hand, those same percentages for Middle Tennessee seem to point in another direction.[12] The percentages for West Tennessee—in all categories—are remarkably close one to the other; worthy of mention only is the decrease between 1850 and 1860 of the nonslaveowning landowner.

Before leaving this particular relationship a few other points are pertinent: in 1850, 1.99 per cent of the non-landowning farmers of Fentress County were slaveowners; in Fayette 57.74 per cent of the landless farmers were slaveholders. By 1860 these percentages were 2.19 and 52.80, respectively. These percentages represent the extremes; for the fifteen counties as a whole, there were fewer landless slaveowners in 1860 than in 1850, although the total number of landless operators had increased during that decade. Also, the landowning nonslaveowners had shown a marked increase in numbers with the result that in 1860 the slave-owners constituted a smaller percentage of both the landless and landowning operators than they had in 1850.

On the other hand, since nine tenths of the slaveholders owned the land which they worked, it is not quite so clear that slave-ownership did not depend, in large degree, upon the ownership of land. Or was there a relationship between the number of slaves held and landownership? Table IV may help to provide an answer.[13]

Table IV. Size of Slaveholdings of Landowners and Non-Landowners

No. of Slaves Owned	1850			1860		
	Land- owners	Non- Land- owners	Per Cent of Slave- owners	Land- owners	Non- Land- owners	Per Cent of Slave- owners
EAST TENNESSEE						
1-4............	162	10	66.93	158	12	63.43
5-9............	54	4	22.57	68	3	26.49
10-14..........	15	1	6.23	15	0	5.60
15-19..........	5	0	1.95	9	1	3.73
20-29..........	4	0	1.56	0	0	.00
30-39..........	2	0	.78	1	0	.37
40-49..........	0	0	.00	1	0	.37
MIDDLE TENNESSEE						
1-4............	1,550	256	44.48	1,430	220	40.92
5-9............	928	93	25.15	993	80	26.61
10-14..........	481	31	12.61	536	32	14.09
15-19..........	267	14	6.92	237	9	6.10
20-29..........	232	11	5.99	269	1	6.70
30-39..........	89	2	2.24	110	1	2.75
40-49..........	39	3	1.03	38	1	.97
50-74..........	46	2	1.18	45	1	1.14
75-99..........	7	0	.17	21	0	.53
100-199........	8	0	.18	7	0	.17
200+..........	1	0	.02	1	0	.02
WEST TENNESSEE						
1-4............	1,088	158	42.38	1,176	158	40.35
5-9............	640	83	24.59	784	66	25.71
10-14..........	334	23	12.14	410	16	12.89
15-19..........	186	13	6.77	213	4	6.56
20-29..........	204	7	7.18	209	10	6.62
30-39..........	93	4	3.30	101	2	3.12
40-49..........	34	3	1.26	62	4	2.00
50-74..........	53	4	1.94	65	1	2.00
75-99..........	8	2	.34	13	1	.42
100-199........	2	0	.07	9	0	.27
200+..........	1	0	.03	2	0	.06

Looking first at the statistics for each of the three grand divisions, it will be noticed that although almost 94 per cent of the slaveholders in East Tennessee were also landowners in both 1850 and 1860, approximately two thirds of them held fewer than five slaves each. It is clear that most of the agricultural activity of that area was conducted on the small-farm basis, and more than likely the owner worked side-by-side with his slaves in the field. Very few of the owners had twenty or more Negroes, and practically none of them could be classed as operators of plantations. The average holding was less than four and one-half slaves for 1850 (4.35) and 1860 (4.46) with only a very slight increase taking place during the decade.

In Middle Tennessee, characterized by a great variety of geographic conditions, the average holding was larger than in the eastern area. But some of the Middle Tennessee counties—notably Fentress and DeKalb—closely resembled those of East Tennessee, while others were very similar to the larger slaveholding regions to the west. For the entire section the largest single group of slaveowners was made up of those owning fewer than five slaves, and they comprised more than two fifths of the total owners. More than two thirds of the owners had fewer than ten slaves each and only five per cent held thirty or more. Practically all of this last group were found in the rich Basin counties of Maury and Davidson and in the large tobacco-producing areas of Robertson and Montgomery counties. There were more landless slaveowners in this section of the state than in the eastern division, but they still constituted only about ten per cent of the slaveowning class. In 1850 this group held six per cent of the total slaves, but by 1860 their holdings amounted to only just over four per cent of the slaves of Middle Tennessee. The average holdings of all slaveowners ranged from just less than three in Fentress to approximately twelve in Maury, Montgomery, and Davidson, but for the entire area the 9.59 average of 1850 had increased to only 9.76 ten years later.

There was not a great difference between the size of slaveholdings in West Tennessee and those in Middle Tennessee—the average holding increased from 10.10 slaves in 1850 to 10.81 in 1860. As in the other areas by far the largest single group had fewer than five slaves each and two thirds of the owners had fewer than ten. However, the large slaveowners of West Tennessee were more numerous than in the other areas: those with thirty or more slaves amounted to 6.94 per cent of the total in 1850; a decade later they constituted 7.87 per cent of the slaveowners. The non-landowning slaveholders were about one tenth of the total slave-owners in 1850 and held 7.4 per cent of the slaves; but this group declined more rapidly than in the other two areas so that by 1860 the 7.92 per cent in this class held only 4.6 per cent of the slaves.

Haywood and Fayette counties deserve especial mention since they may be considered the only two real plantation counties studied and were the only two in which the Negroes outnumbered the whites.[14] Even here, however, more than 31 per cent of the slaveowners had fewer than five slaves in 1850, and 55.3 per cent of them had fewer than ten slaves. The percentage of owners in the one-to-four group declined between 1850 and 1860, but the five-to-nine group retained nearly the same percentage ratio. Although the total number of slaveowners declined in Fayette County in the last prewar decade, the number of owners of fifty or more slaves increased, as it did in Haywood. By 1860, 6.51 per cent of the Haywood slaveowners were in this category and they owned 31.54 per cent of the slaves in the county. The corresponding percentages for Fayette were 4.90 and 22.67. Maury, third in this category in 1850, was replaced the next census year by David-son, but the two West Tennessee counties had a larger fifteen-to-forty-nine owner group than did the Middle Tennessee subdivisions.

The figures for the fifteen sample counties as a whole (see Appendix A) show that during the ten years the number of landless slaveowners decreased from 724 to 623 (13.95 per cent), and that the average number of slaves held by them declined from 6.20 to 5.31. Meanwhile the landed slaveowners increased from 6,533 to 6,983 (6.89 per cent) and their average holding in-

creased from 9.69 to 10.44, thus raising the average for all slaveowners from 9.34 to 10.02. More than two thirds of the owners
held fewer than ten slaves—5,026 (69.26 per cent) in 1850 and
5,148 (67.69 per cent) in 1860—but their holdings amounted
to only 28.19 per cent of the total slaves in 1850 and 26.82 per
cent in 1860. At the other extremity—the fifty-or-more category
—134 (1.85 per cent) held 14.07 per cent of the slaves in 1850[15]
and 166 (2.18 per cent) held 16.26 per cent in 1860. In both
census years more than 40 per cent of the slaves were held by
persons who had from ten to twenty-nine Negroes each. The
larger landless slaveowners had made rapid strides toward becoming landowners by 1860, but the greatest decline in the number of
landless slaveowners came in the group owning from one to four
slaves, many of whom had probably acquired a slave or two before 1850 in anticipation of the acquisition of land within the next
decade.[16]

At the risk of interrupting the land-slave ownership discussion,
it is necessary to say something of the state as a whole. The published Census of 1860 gives the counties studied as having 11,342
owners and 95,882 slaves. These were 30.78 per cent and 34.78
per cent, respectively, of the totals for the entire state, there being
36,884 persons with 275,719 slaves.[17] The average holding for
the fifteen counties was 8.45 slaves; that for the entire state, 7.51.
For the whole state, 19,179 persons, or 52.05 per cent, held less
than five slaves each; their holdings of 40,171 were 14.57 per cent
of the total. There were 9,210 owners, or 25.00 per cent, who had
between five and nine slaves each; they held 61,417 Negroes which
were 22.28 per cent of the total slaves in the state. Thus, 77.05
per cent of the owners in Tennessee in 1860 had fewer than ten
slaves, and, in the aggregate, had 36.85 per cent of the total slaves
in the state.

Of the 46,274 persons in all the South holding twenty or more
slaves each in 1860, 2,932 were in Tennessee. This is approximately the number to which she was "entitled" when the proportion of her slave population to the total slave population of the
South is considered. Tennessee, however, did not have as large a

percentage in the over-fifty bracket as the more southern states. Only one person in Tennessee had between three hundred and five hundred slaves in 1860, and only forty-seven owned one hundred or more. Some of the Tennesseans were definitely planters, but the census applied only the term "farmer" to the agriculturists of the Volunteer State.

It is clear that by far the greater number of the slaveowners in Tennessee held only a small number of slaves and that the ownership of land was not an absolutely essential accompaniment of the ownership of slaves, but it might not be safe to draw conclusions from the foregoing analysis alone with regard to the effect of landownership upon the size of the slaveholdings. The fact that the average slaveholdings of the non-landowners declined while those of the landowners increased may indicate a definite relationship between land and slaves; but it may also be little more than a reflection of the normal conditions in an agricultural society where land was the fundamental requirement and slavery merely formed a part of the labor supply. The landless slaveowners in such a society were usually tenants for the time being, whose first desire was to buy land rather than more slaves. It is probable, therefore, that the decline in the number of the non-landowning slaveholders was due not so much to the fact that they were slaveowners as to the fact that they became economically able to buy land.

The possible relationship between land- and slaveownership is so linked with another question that judgment should be reserved until that, too, has been examined. In making this examination, a distinction must be made between the total acreage owned and the amount of improved acreage actually under cultivation, and since the latter is perhaps more indicative of the real economic status than is the former, only the improved acreage has been included in this analysis.

On the whole, the figures in Table V[18] indicate what one might reasonably expect to find: in an area where the slaveholdings were small, the amount of improved acreage operated was less than in the regions of large slaveholdings. In East Tennessee, where no

Table V. Amount of Improved Acreage Operated by Slaveowners and Non-slaveowners

No. of Acres Operated	1850				1860			
	No. of Slave-owners	% of Total Operators	No. of Non-Slave-owners	% of Total Operators	No. of Slave-owners	% of Total Operators	No. of Non-Slave-owners	% of Total Operators
				EAST TENNESSEE				
1-24.........	5	.32	164	10.46	0	.00	185	9.91
25-49.........	19	1.21	289	18.43	12	.64	345	18.49
50-99.........	58	3.70	525	33.48	67	3.59	632	33.87
100-199......	88	5.61	295	18.81	101	5.41	385	20.63
200-299......	39	2.49	46	2.93	41	2.20	54	2.89
300-499......	25	1.59	6	.38	23	1.23	11	.59
500-999......	8	.51	1	.06	8	.43	2	.11
1000+.......	0	.00	0	.00	0	.00	0	.00
				MIDDLE TENNESSEE				
1-24.........	236	3.51	885	13.16	159	2.16	845	11.46
25-49.........	515	7.66	1,081	16.07	323	4.38	1,161	15.74
50-99.........	1,104	16.41	917	13.63	933	12.65	1,206	16.35
100-199......	1,103	16.40	227	3.37	1,267	17.18	372	5.04
200-299......	340	5.06	19	.28	510	6.91	102	1.38
300-499......	201	2.99	7	.10	321	4.35	22	.30
500-999......	82	1.22	0	.00	126	1.71	6	.08
1000+.......	9	.13	0	.00	20	.27	0	.00
				WEST TENNESSEE				
1-24.........	149	2.71	904	16.42	128	2.15	680	11.44
25-49.........	478	8.68	1,232	22.38	434	7.30	1,174	19.75
50-99.........	848	15.40	596	10.82	795	13.37	927	15.59
100-199......	700	12.71	130	2.36	782	13.15	246	4.14
200-299......	229	4.16	13	.24	327	5.50	25	.42
300-499......	162	2.94	4	.07	232	3.90	12	.20
500-999......	54	.98	1	.02	152	2.56	6	.10
1000+.......	6	.11	0	.00	25	.42	0	.00

individual operated as many as one thousand improved acres either in 1850 or 1860 and where the slaveholdings were relatively small, the largest single group consisted of those farmers who operated between 50 and 99 acres each. More than 37 per cent of the total operators for the region were in this group in both census years, and in both years approximately nine tenths of them were nonslaveowners. The largest group of slaveowners operated between 100 and 199 improved acres each, but they formed only about one twentieth of the total farmers.

In Middle Tennessee, also, the operators of from 50 to 99 acres formed the largest single group, amounting to 30 per cent of the total heads in 1850 and 29 per cent in 1860; but here the proportion of slaveowners was much higher than in East Tennessee—54.63 per cent in 1850 and 43.68 per cent in 1860. In 1850 slightly less than 21 per cent of the slaveholding farmers of the region operated less than 50 acres each and nearly 18 per cent operated over 200 acres each, while 63 per cent of the nonslaveholding farmers operated less than 50 acres and only .82 per cent more than 200 acres. By 1860, however, the proportions of both types of operators had declined in the smaller acreage group and had risen among the larger operators. Especially noteworthy was the increase from 19 to 102 in the number of nonslaveowners who operated between 200 and 299 improved acres each.

In West Tennessee, the largest group of operators in both census years consisted of those heads of agricultural families cultivating between 25 and 49 acres each, and in both years the nonslaveholders in that group outnumbered the slaveholders by almost three to one. In both years, the largest single group of slaveowners operated between 50 and 99 acres each, although even in that group they were outnumbered by the nonslaveowners in 1860. On the other hand, 451 slaveowners and only 18 nonslaveowners operated more than 200 acres each in 1850; the corresponding numbers in 1860 were 736 and 43. In view of the fact that West Tennessee was supposed to be the plantation area of the state, it is interesting to note that in 1850 it had only 61 operators of more than 500 acres each, while Middle Tennessee had 91. By 1860, however, it had established a small lead, with

183 such operators—exactly three times the 1850 number—against 152 for Middle Tennessee.

While this breakdown is significant, it does not reveal certain facts relevant to the comparative positions of the slaveowners and nonslaveowners. For the fifteen counties as a whole, 68.31 per cent of the nonslaveowners in 1850 operated less than fifty improved acres; only 23.35 per cent of the slaveowners were in that group. In 1860 the corresponding percentages were 69.37 and 16.68—a small increase for the nonslaveowners and a significantly large decrease among the slaveowners. At the other extreme, 8 of every 100 slaveowners in 1850 and 13 of every 100 in 1860 operated 300 or more acres each, while among the nonslaveowners, only 1 in every 250 in 1850 and 1 in every 167 in 1860 operated comparable tracts. In this class there were only 2 with more than 500 acres in 1850 and only 14 in 1860. Slaveholders farming more than 500 improved acres in 1850 numbered 159; in 1860 they had increased to 331, with 45 operating more than 1,000 acres each. The slaveholders constituted less than 50 per cent of the farmers in the three smallest acreage divisions; in the five largest divisions they formed from two thirds to 97 of every 100 operators. It must be borne in mind, however, that less than one fourth in 1850 and less than three tenths in 1860 of all the farmers were owners of the labor they used.

Further still, the comparative amount of land controlled by the slaveowners has not been revealed by the acreage distribution table. In 1850 slaveowners operated from 19.71 per cent of the land in Fentress to 92.45 per cent in Fayette. For the fifteen counties as a whole they operated 66.46 per cent of the improved acreage and their farms averaged 119.49 acres as compared with the 42.68 acres of the nonslaveowner—bringing the average for all to 74.51 acres. Somewhat surprisingly, the largest average slaveowner's farm was in Greene County (169.58 acres), as was the largest average nonslaveowner's farm. A greater number of large farms, however, gave to Fayette the largest average for all farms.

By 1860 the high and low percentages operated by slaveowners were still in Fentress and Fayette, and the latter county had the largest average for slaveowners', nonslaveowners', and all types of farms. The slaveowners had increased, in proportion to the total, in Davidson, Hardin, Henry, Gibson, and Dyer counties, and in all of these except Davidson they operated a larger percentage of the land than they did ten years earlier. In Johnson, Greene, Fentress, Maury, Davidson, and Fayette the slaveowners operated a smaller percentage of the total acreage in 1860 than in 1850, but increases in the other counties resulted in a net increase of the fifteen counties, raising the percentage operated in 1860 to 68.07. The slaveowners, however, had declined from 41.44 per cent to 40.60 per cent of the operators. The farms of this group had increased to an average of 156.73 acres (31.17 per cent), while the farms of the nonslaveowners had increased to 50.24 acres (17.71 per cent). Practically all of the increase occurred among the landowning groups; the landless slaveowners increased their average acreage by only .01 per cent while the landless nonslaveowners increased their average acreage 3.78 per cent. The average for the 18,122 farms was 93.47 improved acres. The total number of acres tended by the nonslaveholders had increased 27.96 per cent during the decade, while those of the slaveholders showed an increment of 37.67 per cent.

The taxable land of the entire state had increased 20 per cent during this decade (Table VI). It will be noted that Middle Tennessee led in every year both in the amount and value of the tax-

Table VI.* Taxable Land and Slaves in East, Middle, and West Tennessee

Year	Section	Acres	Value	Slaves	Value
1839	East	3,119,869	$ 14,752,438	7,878	$ 3,712,033
	Middle	5,100,909	35,948,660	46,067	27,084,515
	West	3,763,007	16,077,236	24,073	13,646,664
	Total	11,983,783	66,778,334	78,018	44,443,212
1849	East	7,255,028	14,700,029	9,660	3,911,680
	Middle	9,532,661	36,016,386	55,697	25,844,385
	West	4,949,620	15,698,356	34,637	16,984,764
	Total	21,737,509	66,414,771	99,994	46,740,829
1859	East	8,970,292	41,529,758	12,546	9,309,025
	Middle	10,453,588	92,303,542	64,201	48,696,295
	West	6,686,623	50,028,135	45,506	38,847,699
	Total	26,110,503	185,861,435	122,253	96,853,019

*Report of the Comptroller of the Treasury of the State of Tennessee, 1839; ibid., 1849, pp. 26-31; ibid., 1859, pp. 18-23. Slaves between the ages of twelve and fifty years were taxable.

able land and slaves and that the land of Middle Tennessee, although not as much in area as that of the other two sections combined, was valued at more than all the rest of the land of the state. Her slaves, likewise, were valued at more (except in 1859) than all the others; they, however, constituted more than half of the state's slaves. This table tells much of the agricultural "progress" of the state in the two decades before the Civil War. From 1839 to 1849 the taxable acres nearly doubled, but the value per acre was scarcely more than half as much in the latter year as in the former. The increase in acreage in the next decade was less than 25 per cent; the value almost trebled. There was also a substantial increase in the value of the slaves. The fifties were a decade of prosperity, the prices of slaves and agricultural products were high, and land value increased proportionately.[19]

While much doubt has been cast on the possibility of a close correlation between slaveowning and landowning, there seems to be no question that a definite relationship existed between the

Table VII.* Value of, and Taxes on, Land and Slaves in Tennessee, 1836–1859

Year	Value of Land per Acre	Average Value of Slaves	State Tax on $100 Evalua-tion	Poll Tax
1836	$4.00	$584.00	$0.05	$0.125
1838	3.82	540.00	.05	.125
1840	3.84	543.00	.05	.125
1842	3.56	509.00	.05	.125
1844	3.35	420.00	.075	.125
1846	3.03	413.72	.075	.125
1848	3.06	467.44	.115	.15
1850	3.25	506.93	.115	.15
1852	3.84	547.26	.115	.15
1854	4.60	605.52	.14	.40
1856	5.49	689.00	.14	.40
1858	7.04	792.23	.13166	.50
1859	8.19	854.65	.13166	.50

*Report of the Comptroller of the Treasury of the State of Tennessee, 1857, p. 37; ibid., 1859, p. 17.

value of slaves and the value of land (Table VII). Whether the increase—or decrease—in land value was the cause or effect of the changes in slave value cannot be said; perhaps both changes were the result of a common cause. Be that as it may, it should be noted that land and slave values decreased *pari passu* from 1836 to 1846. The next four years the value of slaves increased at a more rapid rate than the value of land; but in the last decade before the war the increase of land values far outstripped the substantial increases in the value of slaves. It is worthy of note that in every instance both values moved in the same direction.

A state as varied in topography and economic modes as Tennessee naturally showed a wide range in its property evaluation. Land values, in 1859, ranged from 86¢ per acre in Fentress County to $48.50 in Davidson—considering only the fifteen counties used as a sample. (The low was 71¢ in Scott County, and Davidson was high for the state.) This value in Davidson, however, should probably be excluded from consideration when examining the agricultural land of the state. The comptroller noted that the tax collector had included some of the Nashville lots in his computation, and thus it is not a fair value of the land in the unincorporated areas. Evidently, these values are for the rural sections—the acreage—of the state, which would be practically all-inclusive at that time. The land in Maury County was valued at $19.34 per acre, in Robertson at $14.78, in Montgomery at $14.55, and in Haywood and Fayette at $10.96 and $9.68, respectively.

In the fifteen counties studied slave values in 1859 ranged from $563 in Johnson to $981 in Haywood. Values of $700 and $711 per slave were given for Greene and Davidson counties, respectively, but only in Hardin ($795) and in Henry ($781) of the remaining counties were slaves valued at less than $800 each. The low for the state was in Johnson; the high was the $1,100 evaluation in Dickson.[20]

By way of summary to this point, it is possible to observe certain general facts concerning the relationship between land- and slaveownership. In the first place, the wide variations in the figures for the different grand divisions show clearly that no uniform pattern can be assumed for the state as a whole. Secondly, although a great majority of the slaveholders—both landowners and non-landowners—held fewer than ten slaves each, the fact that only twenty non-landowners held more than thirty slaves each in 1850 and that this number dropped to eleven in 1860 seems to indicate that the size of the individual slaveholding had a direct bearing on the matter of ownership of land. Further, this relationship seems to be borne out by the fact that the number of landowning holders of more than thirty slaves increased from 383 in 1850 to 476 in 1860. In the third place, it is apparent that although landownership did not depend upon slaveownership, the owners as a group operated considerably larger tracts of improved land than did the nonslaveowners. This point might be considered almost axiomatic to the system, but heretofore no analysis of landholdings and operation has been made. In this connection it might also be noted that the increase in the number of nonslaveowning landowners between 1850 and 1860, together with the upward trend in the number of acres they operated—as well as their location in the various counties—contradicts the oft-repeated and ill-supported contention that the slaveowners were driving the nonslaveowners from the good lands and reducing them to a position of economic and political vassalage.

On the basis of materials presented thus far, it seems safe to conclude that neither landownership nor slaveownership made any real difference so far as the small farmers of the state were concerned—and that group was the great majority—but that among the "larger" farmers the landowners seemed to have the advantage in sizes of slaveholdings and the slaveholders to have a similar advantage in amounts of improved acreage operated. What proportion of the heads of agricultural families were in this "favored" group? What proportion of the land did they operate? Did they constitute a dominant planter class?

While many factors must be recognized in trying to differentiate between planters and farmers, it seems clear that the basic requirements for a plantation would be a large enough number of slaves to cultivate whatever amount of land was necessary to enable concentration on the growing of a staple crop for market rather than for home consumption and enough domestics and artisans to maintain a way of life that has come to be traditionally associated with the planter group. It is, of course, impossible to designate an exact number of slaves and/or an exact amount of land as the point of transition from farmer to planter, but in general the operator with fewer than thirty slaves and less than five hundred acres of improved land found it extremely difficult to depend upon the returns from a single crop for a living. Planters' records indicate that thirty slaves often would not furnish more than fifteen to twenty field hands; such a force could not, of course, operate a plantation in the then existing state of technological advance. Nevertheless, using thirty slaves as a minimum, Table VIII shows the amounts of improved lands operated by heads of agricultural families in the fifteen sample counties who owned at least that many slaves.

These figures suggest that a considerable stretch of the imagi-

Table VIII. Improved Acreage Operated by Heads of Families with 30 or More Slaves

	1850			1860		
Counties	No. of Operators	Total Acreage	Average Acreage	No. of Operators	Total Acreage	Average Acreage
EAST TENNESSEE						
Greene............	2	750	375.0	2	650	325.0
MIDDLE TENNESSEE						
Lincoln..........	16	8,845	552.8	23	29,490	1,282.2
Maury............	78	33,571	430.4	89	38,820	436.2
Davidson.........	61	29,356	481.2	51	25,852	506.9
Robertson........	9	6,400	711.1	9	9,275*	1,030.6
Montgomery.....	33	10,370	314.2	52	24,511	471.4
Totals.........	197	88,542	449.5	224	127,948	572.0
WEST TENNESSEE						
Hardin..........	0	0	0	7	2,450	350.0
Henry...........	22	7,405	336.6	23	10,100	439.1
Gibson..........	6	1,700	283.3	20†	11,240	562.0
Dyer............	3	675	225.0	9	3,220	357.8
Haywood........	68	28,084	413.0	80	50,700	633.8
Fayette..........	104	47,394	455.7	120	74,308	619.2
Totals.........	203	85,258	420.0	259	152,018	586.9
Grand Totals.....	402	174,550	434.2	485	280,618	578.6

*This includes one plantation of 5,000 improved acres operated by George A. Washington.

†This does not include one owner of more than thirty slaves for whom the census enumerator neglected to record the amount of improved acreage operated.

nation would be required to find a great planter aristocracy in Tennessee which held a dominating position in the affairs of the state. Of the 18,718 heads of families studied for 1850 only 402 had thirty or more slaves. Ten years later only 486 of the 20,558 heads of families were found in that category. This is only one out of every forty-five heads, and at their point of greatest concentration—Fayette County in 1860—only one of every eight could possibly be called a planter. The improved acreage operated by each of these individuals was several times larger than that of many of their neighbors; but in spite of the fact that they operated slightly more than one sixth of the total improved acreage of the fifteen counties, the average of their acreage in 1850 was below the acceptable margin for planters in 1850 and was only a few acres above it in 1860. This group was increasing its improved acreage at a more rapid rate than the small slaveowners and the nonslaveowners—but he had more controlled labor with which to operate. If the other groups had not also been increasing their improved acreage, then there might be some basis for asserting that there was a dominant planter group. As it was, however, the planters were few in number, they did not prosper at the expense of their fellow farmers, and they were definitely the islands rather than the ocean.

As has been indicated above, this analysis of the relationship between landowning and slaveowning in Tennessee presents only a part of the picture which cannot be considered complete without an examination of their possible relationship to agricultural production. In the following chapter this agricultural production will be analyzed; for purposes of comparison and contrast information will be given for both slaveowners and nonslaveowners.

SIX

Agricultural Production, 1850 and 1860

As MIGHT be expected because of the wide variety of geographic conditions within the state, the agricultural interests of Tennessee as a whole reflected diversity of activity rather than concentration on a single crop. At the end of the decade covered by this study Tennessee ranked third in the nation in the production of tobacco, fifth in corn production, third in number of swine, seventh in value of livestock, eighth in cotton production, and thirteenth in amount of wheat grown.[1] Of these, the production of cotton, tobacco, and corn not only came nearest to attaining the proportions of great staple crops but also depended more heavily on slave labor than did the others. They may properly be used, therefore, as a basis for studying the relationship between slavery and agricultural production; but in using them it must be recognized that the interest in each of them was largely regional rather than statewide. Cotton, for example, was definitely the outstanding money crop in Hardin, Gibson, Haywood, Fayette, and parts of Dyer County. Tobacco was the chief crop for parts of Dyer County and for Henry, Robertson, and Montgomery counties. In the remaining seven counties studied, corn constituted the major crop, although cotton represented an important secondary interest in Maury and Lincoln counties, and tobacco in Davidson.

COTTON

The first cotton crop west of the mountains was raised by John Donelson in Davidson County, Tennessee, in 1780, but for many years cotton made slow headway in the Volunteer State. In 1801 Tennesseans produced only 2,500 bales, but the opening up of West Tennessee in the latter part of the second decade of the century greatly increased the amount of good cotton-producing soil, and in 1820 the state raised 50,000 bales. Twenty years later Tennessee ranked seventh; in 1850 her production of 194,532 bales was exceeded only by that of Alabama, Georgia, Mississippi, and South Carolina.[2] She did not keep pace with the other states, however, and 296,464 bales could command no better than eighth position in 1860.[3]

The greatest portion of the Tennessee cotton was produced, after the 1840's, in the western part of the state, and all five of the counties here analyzed for that production are located in West Tennessee. In 1850 they produced 49,530 bales, or slightly more than one fourth of the total crop of the state. Their yield of 70,087 bales in 1860 was only a little less than one fourth of the state production.

Table IX shows the amount of cotton produced in those five counties by the slaveowners and nonslaveowners, the relative sizes of their crops, and the average production; Table X gives production information on the owners of thirty or more slaves.

Table IX.* Cotton Production by Slaveowners and Nonslaveowners

1850

County	Type Grower	No.	% of Total	Bales (400 lbs.)	% of Total	Average Production
Hardin	Slaveowner	39	16.67	162	23.79	4.15
	Nonslaveowner	195	83.33	519	76.21	2.66
Gibson	Slaveowner	317	30.45	2,798	57.34	8.83
	Nonslaveowner	724	69.55	2,082	42.66	2.88
Dyer	Slaveowner	68	37.36	172	46.36	2.53
	Nonslaveowner	114	62.64	199	53.64	1.75
Haywood	Slaveowner	525	66.79	14,030	91.99	26.72
	Nonslaveowner	261	33.21	1,221	8.01	4.68
Fayette	Slaveowner	918	80.39	26,775	94.45	29.17
	Nonslaveowner	224	19.61	1,572	5.55	7.01
Totals	Slaveowner	1,867	55.16	43,937	88.71	23.53
	Nonslaveowner	1,518	44.84	5,593	11.29	3.68
Grand Totals		3,385		49,530		14.63

1860

Hardin	Slaveowner	65	20.06	370	37.41	5.69
	Nonslaveowner	259	79.94	619	62.59	2.39
Gibson	Slaveowner	416	47.27	5,477	76.46	13.17
	Nonslaveowner	464	52.73	1,686	23.54	3.63
Dyer	Slaveowner	56	33.94	551	59.63	9.84
	Nonslaveowner	109	66.06	373	40.37	3.42
Haywood	Slaveowner	529	59.77	23,740	89.77	44.88
	Nonslaveowner	356	40.23	2,705	10.23	7.60
Fayette	Slaveowner	686	80.42	32,016	92.62	46.67
	Nonslaveowner	167	19.58	2,550	7.38	15.27
Totals	Slaveowner	1,752	56.39	62,154	88.68	35.48
	Nonslaveowner	1,355	43.61	7,933	11.32	5.85
Grand Totals		3,107		70,087		22.56

*Compiled from Schedules I, II, and IV, Censuses of 1850 and 1860 (unpublished). Only Districts 1, 2, 3, 13, and 14 of Dyer County are included in the 1860 count. See Table XI.

Table X.* Cotton Production by Heads of Families with 30 or More Slaves

1850

County	No.	% of Slave-holding Pro-ducers	% of Total Pro-ducers	Bales	% of Slave-owners' Crop	% of Total Crop	Average
Hardin	..	..	..	..	..	..	..
Gibson	5	1.58	.48	200	7.15	4.47	40.00
Dyer	..	..	..	..	..	..	..
Haywood	67	12.76	8.53	5,625	40.09	36.88	83.95
Fayette	104	11.33	9.11	10,229	38.20	36.09	98.36
Totals	176	9.43	5.20	16,054	36.54	32.41	91.22

1860

Hardin	4	6.15	1.24	81	21.89	8.19	20.25
Gibson	18	4.33	2.05	872	15.92	12.17	48.44
Dyer	..	..	..	..	..	..	..
Haywood	80	15.12	9.04	11,452	48.24	43.30	143.15
Fayette	120	17.49	14.07	15,083	47.11	43.64	125.69
Totals	222	12.56	7.15	27,488	44.23	39.22	123.82

*Compiled from Schedules II and IV, Censuses of 1850 and 1860 (unpublished).

As a main staple, cotton production was confined to the West Tennessee region, but the variations were so great there that each county should be treated briefly. Hardin County, perhaps the poorest in the area, more nearly fits into the diversified farming category than in the staple economy niche. In 1840 the farmers of that county had produced 52,564 pounds of tobacco, but ten years later the crop had fallen to relative insignificance and only 6,098 pounds were raised.[4] During the same period the production of cotton had risen from 97 to 681 bales. Slaveholders were relatively few in 1850, and their holdings were small—but they produced almost one fourth of the cotton. The nonslaveholders outnumbered the slaveholders five to one, but their average production was much lower than that of the slaveowners and showed a decline between 1850 and 1860. Among the nonslaveowners the landless group in 1850 had a higher average production than the landowners—an unusual situation, two other instances of which will be mentioned later.

By 1860 the slaveowners had become more important in the economy of Hardin; they were more numerous and their average yield had increased while that of the nonslaveowners declined. Hardin, however, was by no means dependent on cotton: corn production was 546,114 bushels and wheat 27,169 bushels— both well above the 1850 figures which had shown a sharp decline from the production of 1840. In many other indices the county showed vast improvements in the last pre-Civil War decade.[5]

Gibson County had more cotton producers than any of the other counties studied, except Fayette in 1850 and Haywood in 1860. Probably the most striking change between 1850 and 1860 was the singularly large decrease in the nonslaveowning cotton producers resulting in a rather nice numerical balance between that group and the slaveowning producers. Among the slaveowners the greatest increase came in the landed group, while the largest decrease among the nonslaveowners appeared in the landless category. The Gibson cotton economy was by no means an all-absorbing one; the county already bore witness to its later claim as the center of diversified farming.

The picture for Dyer County is much the same as that for Hardin, except that the slaveowners formed a much larger percentage of the total producers. In the 1850's a split cotton-tobacco economy developed with cotton culture concentrated in five districts of the county. The 924 bales shown in the table account for all but twenty-two bales of the 1860 crop. In Dyer the slaveowners increased their average yields much more rapidly than in any of the other counties.

Haywood and Fayette were the two great cotton producing counties studied,[6] and the slaveowners produced nine or more of every ten bales. The eighty-six landless slaveowners in Haywood had a higher average production in 1850 than the 439 landed slaveowners. It is suspected that many of these eighty-six were hiring slaves and were in the process of acquiring land in 1850, for in 1860 there were only thirty-one landless slaveowning cotton producers and their average yield was less than half that of the landed group. There is not sufficient evidence to convert this suspicion into fact, but it is worth noting that the increase in the landed slaveowners is almost identical with the decrease in the landless group.

In Fayette the number of producers decreased markedly, 1,142 to 853, but the ratio of slaveowners and nonslaveowners remained almost exactly the same. In Fayette, as well as in Haywood, the nonslaveowner increased his yield more rapidly than did the slaveowner and was producing a higher percentage of the crop in 1860 than in 1850, even though in Fayette he had shown a slight numerical percentage decrease. The difference between the average production of the slaveowners and norslaveowners was not as great as in Haywood County. In Fayette in 1850 the former group averaged four times as much as the latter, but ten years later the ratio was little more than three to one, while in Haywood for both census years the ratio was approximately six to one.

For the five counties as a whole the total cotton producers decreased 8.21 per cent between 1850 and 1860, with the nonslaveowners showing a more rapid decrease than the slaveowners—10.74 per cent to 6.16 per cent. In spite of the decreased number

of producers the yield was up 41.48 per cent, and the nonslaveholder's average production (or production per operator) showed
an increase of 58.97 per cent (3.68 to 5.85 bales) as compared
with 50.79 per cent (23.53 to 35.48 bales) for his slaveholding
neighbor. Does this indicate the superiority of free labor? Does it
point to greater efficiency of operation of the smaller units? Nothing seems conclusive except the cold, bare percentages and the
fact that only in Fayette County does there appear to have been
land consolidation of a considerable degree and an accompanying concentrated cotton economy. And it was in Fayette that the
nonslaveowner increased his production most rapidly in the last
pre-Civil War decade!

Table X gives the cotton production of those who for this study
have been designated as "planters." It shows that in the counties
of greatest concentration the owners of thirty or more slaves
constituted from one twelfth (Haywood, 1850) to one seventh
(Fayette, 1860) of the cotton growers and that they produced
approximately two fifths of the total crop. It shows further that in
Haywood this group increased its average yield by 70.52 per cent
over the 1850 production, but in Fayette the average yield of the
thirty-or-more group increased only 27.79 per cent. Also, for all
the counties involved this group increased its average yield by
only 35.77 per cent as compared with a 50.79 per cent increase
for all the slaveowners. If the "planter" group is excluded, the
average production increase of the slaveowners is 60.46 per cent.
This group, then, was not increasing its production per operator
as rapidly as the smaller producer, but the numerical increase in
the group resulted in its producing a larger percentage of the
slaveowners' crop and of the total crop in 1860 than it did in
1850. The growth of the "planter" was less rapid than that of the
other producers, but he was such a sturdy youth by comparison
that it would have required many years for the others to overtake
him.

The early dream of Tennessee farmers had been of a great
money crop which would ensure the prosperity of the agricultural
population of the entire state. Though the output of cotton in-

creased steadily after 1840—with an ever growing concentration in West Tennessee—many farmers agitated against a single-crop economy, and some of the counties in Tennessee never raised any cotton. This was true of five counties in East Tennessee, and between 1840 and 1860 there were twenty-one more counties added to the non-cotton producing list. Twenty-one other counties showed a decrease in the number of bales produced between 1840 and 1860. Thirty-seven counties listed an increase in cotton production; fourteen of these were in West Tennessee. The others were divided between Middle and East Tennessee, but the crops of the latter section were small and primarily for home consumption.

The five counties studied above did not confine themselves to production of cotton alone, but more and more of the land was used for that crop in Haywood and Fayette counties. (It is worth-while to mention again that Haywood and Fayette were the only two of the sample counties in which the slaves outnumbered the white population.) The improved acreage in each of the five counties increased substantially between 1850 and 1860. The rate of increase in the value of the farms far exceeded the rate of increase of the improved land. If 1.00 is used as the value of the farms in each county for 1850, the values in 1860 were (approximately): Fayette, 1.33; Hardin and Gibson, 3.00; and Haywood and Dyer, 4.00. All the counties, except Fayette, had a larger total number of livestock in 1860 than in 1850, but frequently the 1860 holdings did not equal those of 1840. The value of livestock increased from two- to threefold in all the counties except Fayette, where approximately the same number of livestock were valued at one and one-third times as much in 1860 as they were in 1850. Farmers of Fayette were centering their interest on cotton; other aspects of farming suffered accordingly.

The most notable decrease occurred in the amount of oats produced. In none of these counties were as many oats grown in 1860 as in 1850. Gibson had 93,734 bushels in 1850 but only 5,210 bushels in 1860; the corresponding figures for Fayette were 113,595 and 2,678; while the crop in Haywood declined from 67,275 to 3,605 bushels. All the counties raised more wheat in 1860 than in 1850, but Hardin and Haywood were still under their 1840 yield. The year 1849 must have been a bad one for wheat; practically every county in the state showed a smaller yield by the Census of 1850 than in the Census of 1840. The 1860 Census listed large increases over the 1850 production, but not in all the counties did this increase bring the crop up to the 1840 yield. The tobacco crop, between 1850 and 1860, nearly quintupled in Dyer, quadrupled in Gibson, but declined in Haywood and Fayette. Hardin produced more than in 1850, but the 6,995 pounds were only one eighth of the 1840 crop.

The West Tennesseans, particularly those in Haywood and Fayette counties, were devoting more and more of their improved acreage to cotton culture. Most of the additional cotton land, however, was not acquired by decreasing the production of corn, wheat, potatoes, and peas, but by lessening the amount of land planted to tobacco and oats. The number of livestock per person was not as large as in the non-cotton counties, but the plantation economy was fairly well balanced. Very few essentials had to be obtained from other areas.

TOBACCO

Tobacco was the second largest money crop of the Volunteer State, and her production of 29,550,432 pounds in 1840 was exceeded only by the yields of Virginia and Kentucky. Production decreased by 1850 to 20,148,932 pounds, and Tennessee dropped below Maryland to fourth place. She retained, however, her third position in the number of farms—2,215—raising 20,000 pounds or more.[7] By 1860 Tennessee had again surpassed Maryland, and then raised 43,448,097 pounds.[8] In that year every county of the state grew some tobacco, and ten years earlier only nine had not produced tobacco. The chief tobacco producing areas were in the northern parts of Middle and West Tennessee.

Table XI shows the tobacco production for Robertson, Montgomery, and Henry counties for 1850, and for Robertson, Mont-

Table XI.* Tobacco Production by Slaveowners and Nonslaveowners

1850

County	Type of Grower	No.	% of Total	Pounds	% of Total	Average
Robertson	Slaveowner	261	54.83	979,700	68.32	3,754
	Nonslaveowner	215	45.17	454,370	31.68	2,113
Montgomery	Slaveowner	346	67.32	2,946,655	87.63	8,516
	Nonslaveowner	168	32.68	416,100	12.37	2,477
Henry	Slaveowner	245	31.53	967,947	48.24	3,951
	Nonslaveowner	532	68.47	1,038,698	51.76	1,952
Dyer	Slaveowner	..	..	..	..	..
	Nonslaveowner	..	..	..	..	..
Totals	Slaveowner	852	48.22	4,894,302	71.94	5,744
	Nonslaveowner	915	51.78	1,909,168	28.06	2,087
Grand Total		1,767		6,803,470		3,850

1860

County	Type of Grower	No.	% of Total	Pounds	% of Total	Average
Robertson	Slaveowner	353	56.12	1,973,400	76.96	5,590
	Nonslaveowner	276	43.88	590,656	23.04	2,140
Montgomery	Slaveowner	400	61.44	4,592,530	86.36	11,481
	Nonslaveowner	251	38.56	752,526	13.64	2,891
Henry	Slaveowner	440	31.38	2,594,033	52.64	5,896
	Nonslaveowner	962	68.62	2,333,532	47.36	2,426
Dyer	Slaveowner	177	44.03	1,668,949	71.99	9,429
	Nonslaveowner	225	55.97	649,499	28.01	2,887
Totals	Slaveowner	1,370	44.42	10,828,912	71.58	7,904
	Nonslaveowner	1,714	55.58	4,299,213	28.42	2,508
Grand Total		3,084		15,128,125		4,905

*Compiled from Schedules I, II, and IV, Censuses of 1850 and 1860 (unpublished). Dyer was a cotton county in 1850; there was a split cotton-tobacco economy in 1860. The tobacco count includes all except Districts 1, 2, 3, 13, and 14. See Table IX.

gomery, Henry, and Dyer counties in 1860. These counties produced more than one third of the total tobacco of the state in 1850 and 1860. As in the case of cotton production, there is considerable variation among the counties, but one of the first things that attracts attention is that the slaveowners constituted a smaller percentage of the producers in 1860 than in 1850, produced less of the total crop, and formed less than fifty per cent of the growers in each of the census years.

Robertson County, it is to be remembered, was primarily an

area of small farms and small slaveowners, with very widespread
landownership. There, it was found that the landless nonslaveowner had a higher average production in 1850 than his landowning counterpart or the landless slaveowner.[9] The difference
in production between the slaveowner and nonslaveowner was
not as great as in the other counties in 1850 and only slightly
greater than the difference in Henry County in 1860. Between
1850 and 1860 the slaveowning producers increased more rapidly
than those who did not own slaves. Their average production increased almost fifty per cent, while the nonslaveowner increased
his yield only twenty-seven pounds or a little more than one per
cent.

Montgomery County, on the other hand, had a higher percentage of slaveowners than Robertson, but by 1860 this group formed
a smaller part of the total producers than they had in 1850. Average production increased more than twice as much as among the
nonslaveowners—34.82 per cent to 16.71 per cent—with the
result that the slaveowners accounted for only 1.27 per cent less
of the total crop in 1860 than in 1850. Unlike the other tobacco
counties, fewer landless farmers were producing in Montgomery
in 1860 than in 1850. It was also discovered that in Montgomery
the disparity between the production of the landed slaveowner
and the landless slaveowner was far greater than between the
landed nonslaveowner and the landless nonslaveowner. The
average yield for all types of growers was more than double that
of Robertson and Henry for 1850 and 1860, and one and one-
half times that of Dyer in 1860.

Henry County in 1850 produced only 2,006,645 pounds of
the leaf, less than one fourth of the 1840 production of 9,479,065
pounds—nearly one third of the state's total.[10] In Henry, the
slaveowners formed a smaller percentage of the producers than
in any other county, but in spite of their slight relative decline
they produced a larger percentage of the crop in 1860 than in
1850. Henry had more landless nonslaveowning producers than
the other counties combined—112 of 184 in 1850 and 262 of
435 in 1860—and her total producers approached fifty per cent

of the total in 1860. As a matter of fact, the most marked increase of the tobacco-growing population took place in Henry County.

Dyer was rapidly becoming a tobacco county between 1850 and 1860; her production in the latter year was almost five times that of the former. Certain sections, however, still clung to cotton. The inclusion of parts of Dyer in the 1860 count had very little effect on the percentage which the slaveowners formed of the total producers of all the counties and the percentage of the total crop produced by them. Dyer was, so to speak, the "average" tobacco county in respect to distribution of type of grower and proportionate amounts of crop produced. As in the case of Henry, however, there were more landless nonslaveowning producers than in Montgomery and Robertson. The relative newness of settlement of Dyer may have had some bearing on this development.

All of the tobacco counties had a larger number of producers in 1860 than in 1850 in contrast to the cotton counties. Also, the slaveowners constituted 3.80 per cent less of the producers in 1860 than in 1850 but grew only 0.36 per cent less of the tobacco; in the cotton counties they were 1.23 per cent more of the total and grew 0.03 per cent less of the crop in 1860 than in 1850. Though he did not come as near to monopolizing the tobacco production as he did the cotton production, the slaveowner more nearly "held his own" against the nonslaveowner in the former than in the latter field.

Table XII reveals the scattering of large slaveowning producers: one in forty-four in 1850 and one in thirty-nine in 1860. This group of forty, however, produced one eighth of the tobacco in 1850 and one sixth in 1860. They declined in proportion to the total producers only in Robertson County, where their percentage of production showed the sharpest increase. This county, however, had as a resident George A. Washington, who produced a quarter million pounds of tobacco in 1860 and was a millionaire.[11] In Henry County, the thirty-or-more group remained practically stable in relation to the total producers, but their importance in the production picture lessened.

Table XII.* Tobacco Production by Heads of Families with 30 or More Slaves

1850

County	No.	% of Slave-owning Pro-ducers	% of Total Pro-ducers	Pounds	% of Slave-owners' Crop	% of Total Crop	Average
Robertson....	7	2.68	1.47	93,600	9.55	6.53	13,371
Montgomery..	22	6.36	4.28	584,000	19.82	17.37	26,545
Henry........	11	4.49	1.22	172,840	17.86	8.61	15,713
Dyer.........	..	..	..	..	..	..	..
Totals........	40	4.69	2.26	850,440	17.38	12.50	21,261

1860

County	No.	% of Slave-owning Pro-ducers	% of Total Pro-ducers	Pounds	% of Slave-owners' Crop	% of Total Crop	Average
Robertson....	7	1.98	1.11	416,500†	21.11	16.24	59,500
Montgomery..	43	13.25	6.61	1,411,500	30.77	26.54	32,826
Henry........	20	4.55	1.43	348,400	13.47	7.07	17,420
Dyer.........	9	5.08	2.24	284,000	17.02	12.25	31,556
Totals........	79	5.77	2.56	2,460,400	22.72	16.26	31,144

*Compiled from Schedules II and IV, Censuses of 1850 and 1860 (unpublished).
†250,000 pounds, more than half of this total, were grown by George A. Washington.

While Henry had approximately half of the total producers and raised nearly as much tobacco as Montgomery in 1860, the influence of the large producer was much more pronounced in the latter county. More than half of the "planter" group was in Montgomery and by 1860 forty-three individuals—one fifteenth of the total—accounted for more than one fourth of the production. Altogether, the large slaveowner had become a more significant cog in tobacco production in 1860 than in 1850, though the role of the entire slaveowning class had been reduced in the last pre-Civil War decade.

As was the case in the cotton counties, these tobacco areas did not attempt to subsist on one crop alone. Montgomery, Robertson, and Henry counties[12] increased their improved acreages between 1850 and 1860 and the value of the farms was nearly four times as great in the latter as in the former year. Important crop shifts, however, were occurring.

The amount of wheat raised in these tobacco counties showed a marked increase between 1850 and 1860; the quintupling of production in Robertson was most noticeable. Oat production declined more rapidly than wheat increased—but fewer oats were being produced everywhere in the state. Corn production increased in Robertson and Henry, but declined in Montgomery between 1850 and 1860. Livestock decreased in Montgomery and Robertson, but the smaller number were valued at nearly twice as much. Henry was stationary in respect to livestock; the value of such was twice as great in 1860 as in 1850. The breed of the cattle seems to have been improved at the expense of numbers.

From the above comparisons—and from many others that were made from the census schedules—the economy of Robertson County stands out as the most evenly balanced. It was prosperous, but it did not exhibit as rapid increases or decreases as did the other counties. The large percentage of landownership was, perhaps, responsible for its agricultural soundness and stability.

CORN

Corn was the chief crop of the counties which depended on a stock-grain economy, although a considerable amount of cotton was produced in Maury and Lincoln counties. Tennessee raised more corn, 44,986,188 bushels, than any state in the Union in 1840. After that year the other states began to outstrip the Volunteer State, and she fell to fifth place in 1850; her production was 52,276,223 bushels, or a total of fifty-two bushels per person. Ten years later only 52,089,926 bushels, or forty-two bushels per person, were raised in Tennessee, and the state ranked sixth nationally.[13] Tennessee supplied some of the states of the lower South with corn and meat, but the decline in the number of livestock accompanied the decrease per person of the corn production.

Every county for which there were agricultural returns in 1850 and 1860 showed corn production of some importance. The soil of Middle Tennessee is the best in the state for that crop, and the land of East Tennessee is better suited to corn production than that of West Tennessee. Corn was chosen as the crop for comparative study in seven of the fifteen counties because it was the most essential farm product—since none of the seven relied mainly on cotton or tobacco as a money crop. Table XIII shows corn production by slaveowners and nonslaveowners for Johnson, Greene, Fentress, DeKalb, Lincoln, Maury, and Davidson counties, while

Table XIV gives production in those counties by owners of thirty or more slaves.

Table XIII.* Corn Production by Slaveowners and Nonslaveowners

1850

County	Type of Grower	No.	% of Total	Bushels	% of Total	Average
Johnson..........	Slaveowner..........	46	13.57	25,810	29.20	561
	Nonslaveowner......	293	86.43	62,576	70.80	213
Greene..........	Slaveowner..........	206	12.18	201,800	25.73	980
	Nonslaveowner......	1,485	87.82	582,496	74.27	392
Fentress..........	Slaveowner..........	44	8.89	35,240	19.92	801
	Nonslaveowner......	451	91.11	141,669	80.08	314
DeKalb..........	Slaveowner..........	139	19.66	110,916	29.33	798
	Nonslaveowner......	568	80.34	267,313	70.67	471
Lincoln..........	Slaveowner..........	633	32.51	954,206	52.14	1,507
	Nonslaveowner......	1,314	67.49	875,993	47.86	667
Maury..........	Slaveowner..........	1,004	52.16	1,481,475	74.45	1,476
	Nonslaveowner......	921	47.84	508,470	25.55	552
Davidson........	Slaveowner..........	797	57.30	1,196,458	78.43	1,501
	Nonslaveowner......	594	42.70	329,106	21.57	554
Totals...........	Slaveowner..........	2,869	33.77	4,005,905	59.14	1,396
	Nonslaveowner......	5,626	66.23	2,767,623	40.86	492
Grand Totals........		8,495		6,773,528		797

1860

County	Type of Grower	No.	% of Total	Bushels	% of Total	Average
Johnson..........	Slaveowner..........	47	12.08	15,400	17.52	328
	Nonslaveowner......	342	87.92	72,519	82.48	212
Greene..........	Slaveowner..........	213	11.72	201,311	26.55	945
	Nonslaveowner......	1,604	88.28	556,968	73.45	347
Fentress..........	Slaveowner..........	43	8.02	30,568	18.09	711
	Nonslaveowner......	493	91.98	138,367	81.91	281
DeKalb..........	Slaveowner..........	183	20.27	171,285	33.20	936
	Nonslaveowner......	720	79.73	344,705	66.80	479
Lincoln..........	Slaveowner..........	646	30.49	824,558	55.92	1,276
	Nonslaveowner......	1,473	69.51	649,920	44.08	441
Maury..........	Slaveowner..........	1,070	53.10	1,663,968	77.21	1,555
	Nonslaveowner......	945	46.90	491,190	22.79	520
Davidson........	Slaveowner..........	685	61.82	891,636	80.47	1,302
	Nonslaveowner......	423	38.18	216,390	19.53	512
Totals..........	Slaveowner..........	2,887	32.49	3,798,726	60.60	1,316
	Nonslaveowner......	6,000	67.51	2,470,059	39.40	412
Grand Totals........		8,887		6,268,785		705

*Compiled from Schedules I, II, and IV, Censuses of 1850 and 1860 (unpublished).

Table XIV.* Corn Production by Heads of Families with 30 or More Slaves

1850

County	No.	% of Slave-owning Pro-ducers	% of Total Pro-ducers	Bushels	% of Slave-owners' Crop	% of Total Crop	Average
Greene........	2	.97	.12	7,900	3.91	1.01	3,850
Lincoln.......	16	2.53	1.22	75,000	7.86	4.10	4,688
Maury........	76	7.57	3.95	342,800	23.14	17.23	4,511
Davidson.....	56	7.02	4.03	275,080	22.99	18.03	4,912
Totals........	150	5.23	1.77	700,780	17.49	10.35	4,672

1860

County	No.	% of Slave-owning Pro-ducers	% of Total Pro-ducers	Bushels	% of Slave-owners' Crop	% of Total Crop	Average
Greene.......	1	.42	.06	7,000	3.48	.92	7,000
Lincoln.......	23	3.56	1.09	99,750	12.10	6.77	4,337
Maury........	89	8.32	4.42	329,315	19.18	15.28	3,700
Davidson.....	51	7.44	4.60	198,105	22.22	17.88	3,884
Totals........	164	5.68	1.85	634,170	16.69	10.12	3,867

*Compiled from Schedules II and IV, Censuses of 1850 and 1860 (unpublished).

Table XIII shows that the slaveowners formed from slightly less than one twelfth (Fentress, 1860) to slightly more than three fifths (Davidson, 1860) of the corn producers and that they produced from 17.52 per cent (Johnson, 1860) to 80.47 per cent (Davidson, 1860) of the corn. On the average, the slaveowner produced slightly less than three times the amount of the non-slaveowner in 1850 and slightly more than three times as much in 1860. The schedules revealed that the landed slaveowners averaged 1,446 bushels for 1850; the landless slaveowners, 971 bushels; the landed nonslaveowners, 508 bushels; and the landless nonslaveowners, 462 bushels. This relative production indicates, at least, a concern of the slaveowner regarding production of one of the more important items in the diet of the slave. The larger slaveholding counties were by far the larger corn producers.

In the last pre-Civil War decade there was a decided decline in the average production in the seven counties, and the number of producers did not increase as much as might have been expected. Among the slaveowners the small numerical increase did not allow that class to keep relative pace with the nonslaveowners, with the result that they formed 1.28 per cent less of the producers in 1860 than in 1850. Their production had not decreased as rapidly as that of the nonslaveowners so that in 1860 they produced 1.46 per cent more of the crop than they had ten years earlier.[14] Only in Maury among the slaveowners and in both groups in DeKalb was there a higher average production in 1860 than in 1850.

The "planter" group among the corn producers raised approximately three times as much of the slaveowners' production and six times as much of the total crop as mere numbers entitled them to. Interestingly enough, while the large slaveowners had increased numerically and percentage-wise between 1850 and 1860, they produced a smaller percentage of the total crop. The average production of the thirty-or-more group decreased 17.23 per cent in ten years; the nonslaveowners' declined 16.26 per cent; while the over-all decrease was only 11.54 per cent. This means, of course, that it was the smaller slaveowner who kept corn production from slipping farther than it did in Tennessee. The cultivation of corn did not require as much of the slave's time as did the cultivation of cotton or tobacco; consequently, it was less profitable to use slave labor in the growing of corn than in the raising of the other staples. If the slave could be engaged in some other remunerative occupation in between the times when the corn needed attention, the labor costs of producing cotton, corn, and tobacco were more nearly equalized. Such, however, was not always possible.

Farmers of these counties did not depend entirely on corn for their well-being. They had to produce other crops, and were more nearly self-sufficient than the cotton and tobacco farmers. The improved acreage increased between 1850 and 1860 in each of these seven corn counties, with the largest increases occurring in Lincoln and Maury. The farms were valued at from two to four times the evaluation of 1850, although the acreage had not increased by any such amount. Only in Johnson County did the livestock increase, and there they were worth one and one-half times as much in 1860 as in 1850. In the other counties, which showed a decrease in the number of livestock, the livestock were worth double, or more than double, the amount of 1850. The number of swine declined more than any other kind of livestock, and the decrease from 79,209 to 36,590 head in Davidson County was the largest.

Every county increased the amount of its wheat production between 1850 and 1860, but Maury and Davidson did not reach their 1840 yield. Greene raised four times, and Lincoln seven times, as much wheat in 1860 as in 1850. The oat crop declined in every county, but less in Johnson than in the others. Tobacco production increased in all the counties except Johnson, which raised a very small amount. Maury Countians grew five times as much of that crop in 1860 as in 1850.

Greene and Johnson were the only counties producing more potatoes, sweet and Irish combined, in 1860 than in 1850, but all the counties showed substantial increases in the amount of beeswax and honey made. The large slaveowning counties—Davidson, Greene, Lincoln, and Maury—decreased in the value of home manufactures, but the other three exhibited gains in this respect.[15]

In summarizing the agricultural productions for these fifteen sample counties, it should be noted that in the cotton counties there were fewer producers in 1860 than in 1850, but the average yield was about fifty per cent larger for all the farmers. Cotton, which has been called "king" for parts of Tennessee, ". . . like a sponge . . . absorbed the land, absorbed the planter, in fact cleaned up most everything except the darkey and the mule."[16] Land was consolidated into fewer hands in the cotton counties, particularly in Fayette. In 1860 the owners of thirty or more slaves formed a larger percentage of the slaveowning cotton growers and a larger percentage of all the cotton growers, and raised a larger amount of the crop than in 1850. All the slaveowners were a larger percentage of the total growers in 1860 than in 1850, but they produced a slightly smaller percentage of the total crop than they had in 1850. Thus, the nonslaveowner, although his average yield was much less than that of the slaveowner, increased his annual crop more rapidly than did the slaveowner.

The tobacco growers increased more rapidly than the producers of any other one crop. The owners of thirty or more slaves formed a larger percentage of the slaveowning tobacco farmers in 1860 than in 1850, and were a larger percentage of the total tobacco raisers. They produced a larger amount of the slaveowners' and total crop in 1860 than in 1850. The total slaveowners, however, were less numerous, proportionately, in 1860 than in 1850 and produced a smaller amount of tobacco. As was the case with the cotton farmers, the nonslaveowners raised a much smaller average crop than the slaveowners, but their annual percentage increase was greater than that of the slaveowners. The thirty-plus slaveowners, however, increased their yield more rapidly than any other one class of the agricultural population.

The situation in the corn counties was similar, except that the average production of all farmers was less in 1860 than in 1850. The owners of thirty or more slaves increased in number, but their average production declined more rapidly than that of all the farmers. Corn raising seems not to have been considered as profitable—by the larger slaveholders—as the production of the "money" crops. The total slaveholders, however, formed a smaller percentage of the farmers in 1860 than in 1850, but they produced more of the crop. Their average yield did not decline as rapidly as that of the nonslaveowners.

Tennessee did not have as high a standing in the national agricultural picture in 1860 as in the two preceding decades. The new states outstripped her in many respects in those twenty years. In 1840 and 1850 she was the fifth most populous state in the country; she was seventh in cotton production in 1840, fifth in 1850, and eighth in 1860. Tennessee was third in the amount of tobacco grown in 1840, fell to fourth in 1850, but regained her earlier standing in 1860.

The Volunteer State ranked first in corn production in 1840, by 1850 she was in fifth place, and ten years later had slipped one more notch. In milch cows Tennessee ranked second in the South in 1850 and fourth in 1860, but was in ninth place in 1850 and seventh in 1860 in the number of "other cattle." For the southern states, Tennessee was second to Virginia in number of sheep in

1850 and 1860, but in the former year had more swine than any state in the Union. In 1860 she still had more swine than any of the other southern states, but Indiana and Illinois were in first and second place, respectively, for the entire country. The total value, $29,978,016, of Tennessee livestock was the largest in the South in 1850, but was fourth nationally. The total number of livestock increased only slightly between 1850 and 1860, but in the latter year they were valued at $50,211,425. This was high for the South, but seventh for the nation. Tennessee was first for all the states in the value of home manufactures in 1850; the small increase to a value of $3,174,977 by 1860 did not allow her to retain that rank. The Volunteer State was thirteenth in the country for the amount of wheat produced in 1850 and 1860, though the crop was 5,459,268 bushels in the latter year and only 1,619,386 bushels in 1850.[17]

On the basis of the analyses of this and the preceding chapter at least two general conclusions seem to be justified. First, the wide variations between the conditions of slavery and agricultural interests in different parts of the state would seem to raise a very serious question as to the validity of any generalization based on the assumption of a more or less uniform pattern for the South as a whole. Second, these figures definitely show that the traditional picture of a white population divided into two broad categories of planters and poor whites certainly should never again be accepted as portraying conditions in ante-bellum Tennessee. There the ownership of land and slaves was fairly widespread. A few large planters lived lives of relative ease and comfort; some poor whites were unable to sustain themselves by their own efforts; tenants and sharecroppers did exist; but there was—and it constituted a great majority of the population—a large middle class who had few or no slaves, operated medium-sized tracts of land, and approached as near to self-sufficiency as did the large slaveowners. Even in the production of the staple crops, where he apparently had the greatest advantage over the other producers, the large slaveowner could hardly be said to have dominated the enterprise. It was as a result of the efforts of slaveowners and nonslaveowners, landowners and non-landowners, that Tennessee was gradually increasing her improved acreage and rapidly augmenting the value of her land during the last pre-Civil War decade. The war practically arrested this upward trend of agriculture in West Tennessee and seriously retarded it in Middle Tennessee, but the effects were little felt in the eastern part of the state.

SEVEN

Some Tennessee Planters

THE MATERIALS on individual planters in Tennessee are practically nonexistent; many of the records were accidentally destroyed by fire, while others were disposed of because of a lack of knowledge of their historical significance. Material from the records that were located is given below in the hope that a description of their activities may reveal, in a measure, the life of the larger Tennessee slaveowners. The records do not portray the full lives of the individuals concerned, but what was recorded seems to show that slavery, to the owners, was not all ease and comfort.

HARROD CLOPTON ANDERSON

Harrod Clopton Anderson of "Sherwood Forrest," Haywood County, was what one might consider the "average" planter of West Tennessee. He was born at Culpeper Court House, Virginia, about 1830, and went to medical school in Philadelphia in 1847 or 1848, or both. The boy's health was not too good; he studied medicine a "year or two," and then moved to Gibson Wells, Tennessee, to drink the water for his dyspepsia. There he met his future wife, Almira Asenith Cherry, who owned a considerable amount of land which had been given to her father for his services as a surveyor. Anderson married Miss Cherry in 1849 or 1850 and received a farm and a few slaves as a wedding gift.[1]

Although his granddaughter says that Anderson received a farm as a wedding gift, the population schedule of the 1850 Census lists him as not owning any land. The farm, 600 improved and 2,200 unimproved acres valued at $8,400, was listed as belonging to his wife. Anderson, however, was credited with the following possessions and productions: fifty-one slaves; farm implements valued at $500; livestock—seven horses, five asses and mules, six milch cows, eight work oxen, twenty-seven other cattle, fifty sheep, and 120 swine—valued at $1,305; seventy-five bushels of wheat, 3,500 bushels of corn, 400 bushels of oats, sixty-two bales of cotton, 100 pounds of wool, twenty bushels of Irish potatoes, 100 bushels of sweet potatoes, 200 pounds of butter, $225 worth of home manufactures, and $240 worth of slaughtered animals.[2]

The diary does not begin until January 2, 1854, when he recorded that no streams were running; his cotton had not been hauled to the gin; the hogs had ceased to die of swelled throat and other diseases; and the twenty-five-acre field "has been fired and the trees cut."[3]

Clearing the new land was the big task, and when that work for the year was finished on about forty-five acres, Anderson was not satisfied with his life in Tennessee. He wrote, "I am completely broken down heaving and setting at logs & at the end of the year we make nothing. I must see Texas. I want prarie [*sic*] land."[4] He had been working in the field with only seven hands, for Abram was "laid up" with a hurt leg. During the early part of 1854 the entries in the diary were rather infrequent, but on April 12 the birds had begun to pull up the corn so badly that he was forced to keep "a boy constantly in the field guarding." Six days later he was "quite in the notion for Texas" because a heavy frost had taken toll of his early crops. He advised everyone never to plant cotton before April 25 or May 1.[5]

The year 1854 was not a good one for Anderson. He could not keep the crops clean because of excessive rain during the early part of the season, and the weeds were "thicker than the wheat" which made only three bushels to the acre.[6] Measles kept four hands out of the crop for some time, and five smaller Negroes were afflicted with the same disease. Only one slave had scarlet fever, and Anderson thanked God that there were no more.[7] There was no rain from July 9 to September 16, but when it did come on the latter date, it was too late to bring production up to the normal amount. Only eighteen 500-pound bales of cotton and 217 barrels of corn were made on fifty-three and "over 50" acres, respectively.[8]

The winter months were the time for rail splitting, clearing ground, and building fences. During January, February, and the early part of March, 1855, Anderson and his hands split 4,470 rails, cleared eight acres of new ground, and partially fenced a forty-acre field. He did not make many entries for this year, but did note on April 26 that the servants' patches had been plowed. As did most of the slaveowners who had farming land, Anderson gave his slaves small plots on which to raise vegetables to supplement their rations from the "big house."

As September approached, the West Tennessean was despondent. On the 5th of that month he wrote:

I fear we will not make enough cotton to pay current expenses—besides them I owe Mrs. Holman $100. Mr. Graves 52$ & upwards—Cousin Matt Abatit 400$ Mr Ira Johnson $200 & upwards Mr Joyner $110 & upwards & Mr Lindsey $200. & Mr. Partee 200. with int—2 years—

The cotton, however, grew to "6 and 8 feet," and the first picking started on September 17. The hands were getting only 148 pounds —the highest—on October 19; two weeks later they had increased on the average of twenty-five to fifty pounds. Three of the Negroes were sick—Jane for the entire picking season—and the last cotton was not picked until March 15, 1856. Anderson had estimated the crop at thirty bales, but made thirty-three.[9] This pleased him greatly, and he turned back to the entry of September 5 to record, in joyous mood, that the "cotton crop sold for upwards of $1300.00—Oh man." If his numerous "upwards" were not too much, he could just about pay his debts with the proceeds from the "white gold."

In addition to the cotton, the West Tennessean made 130 bushels of wheat,[10] 378 barrels of corn on sixty acres[11]—much better than the year before—and sold thirty-seven hogs to Dr. R. H. Oldham for $300 "cash at the pen."[12] On November 9 he anticipated killing sixty-nine hogs, but only twenty-six were butchered on December 10. These weighed 4,701 pounds, and fifty-three hogs were left in the "bottom." The "bottom" was a sort of commons where several of the planters allowed their hogs, after they had been branded, to roam at large and feed on the mast.

The winter of 1855-1856 was inclement, for, as stated above, the cotton was not completely harvested until March 15, 1856, and on January 26, Anderson noted that "we have a tremendous snow on the ground Raining & snowing this morning a perfect '*slosh*'—Every thing of the stock order are in a *woful pickle*— What awful! awful!!! weather!!!" Anderson was a religious man and seldom complained about the course of events. He wished to be neither rich nor poor: "How truly & from my heart can I say Oh Lord! my God! give me neither *poverty* nor *riches*—This world is a curious anomaly What noble hearts some of our people have, what craven selfish ones others have."[13]

Again his hands were sick, but cotton picking began on September 1 when it was "Bony Dry—Cool dry—Dusty dry." The yield was only twenty-one bales, but he does not say how many acres were planted to that crop; the proceeds, $1,227, were less than the year before.[14] The gin had been completed on October 10, and the ginning was done on the plantation. The wheat crop of thirty-one bushels was considerably below expectations,[15] and only 251 barrels of corn were produced.[16]

Although his pumpkin crop failed, and it was too dry for the two-and-one-half-acre turnip patch which he always sowed, he bought twenty-three hogs from J. L. Page for $20 and killed thirty-four, averaging 156 pounds. When Anderson took "inventory" on January 19, 1857, he had 200 barrels of corn, six horses, two jennets, and eighty hogs. He does not state how many sheep he owned, but three weeks later he had thirteen lambs and had lost two. Also, by this time twenty-five of the "bottom" hogs had died.

Farm life and troubles did not prevent Anderson from making his political observations. He considered the election of 1856 the most important one in which he had ever voted, and "unless the Democracy prevail the days of this union are numbered—Mr.

Fillmore if elected would have no party in Congress to carry out his measures." Fremont and Dayton were referred to as the "North Abolition Blk Republican" candidates. Nine days later, November 13, 1856, he had heard of Buchanan's election and wrote ". . . how thankful I am that the country is saved from dissolution; oh what a curse will rest upon the men that dissolve this Union." Then, a later penciled entry reads "In 1861—Jeff Davis with South Carolina to back him & the Abolitionists of the north did this work."[17]

Again, the spare time of the winter months was spent in "splitting rails, grubbing & cleaning out the place." The twenty-seven acres of new ground, the greater portion of which had been belted for three years, Anderson considered "entirely too much" for his force. His slaves, however, were increasing both through birth and purchase. Maria had a child on March 19, 1855, and another on February 27, 1857. Three days previous to the latter date Anderson had paid $1,200—"too much!"—for Martha who gave birth to a child on March 15 of the following year. Abram, however, ran off on May 20, 1857, and was not recovered until July 14. On September 22, 1858, Anderson went to Memphis where he purchased "two boys," aged eighteen and twenty-two, for $1,100 and $1,250, respectively.

Farming operations were slow in getting under way in 1857, but this was fortunate as many of the early planters had to turn under their crops and replant. The army worm got in the wheat, lice on the cotton, and mosquitoes "upon us." The cotton was "smaller" on June 22 than it had been four days earlier, and the disheartened planter would be "thankful to make an abundance to eat this year." Twelve days later plantation affairs were in a more satisfactory state "oweing to all hands pulling at the same end of the rope, getting to work early & doing something before the middle of the day & evening."

In August some of the plows were stopped so that the hands might notch logs for new cabins. Three hands worked regularly on these, until they were almost finished on September 26. The only unfinished carpentry work was the laying of the floor and hanging the door on one cabin. These little tasks were postponed for want of lumber. Meanwhile, the other slaves performed the yearly chore of stripping fodder.

Corn pulling, cotton picking, and hog killing followed. This year Anderson made 427 barrels of corn on sixty-eight acres, twenty-five bales of cotton on seventy-five acres—a very poor yield—and killed twenty-two hogs averaging 170 pounds.[18] He also made 190 bushels of wheat and seventy-seven of rye,[19] but was dissatisfied. He said "my overseer must work I did after Nathan Reed left he can to." Anderson's first entry concerning an overseer was on August 27, 1857, when he hired a Mr. Edwards of Dyer County for "another year." At the expiration of that contract year, Edwards was released, and John P. Ward of the same county obtained to replace him. Ward came on Christmas Eve in one of Anderson's wagons, and on December 29 the task of getting logs for the new overseer's house was begun.

In the spring of 1858 Anderson had in forty acres of wheat and rye on which he turned his six yearlings, five jennets, one mule, three colts, forty-seven ewes and lambs,[20] and seven or eight calves.[21] The blue jennet and the youngest jack were sold on May 10 for $200.

Frost came late this spring, for on April 27 some cotton, corn, and a "great many vegetables paid the Death penalty the peaches are not killed." Damage to the cotton was slight, however, and on that same day Anderson finished planting eighty-eight acres. The weather was not the only trouble with the planter's corn. He had put it too close together for the best results, and rather disgustedly asks himself "will I ever learn to give corn distance?"

Daniel McCarty and John Dundan, Irishmen, were hired in the early days of July to dig an icehouse 16½ feet square at the top, 10½ feet deep, and sloping to 10½ feet square at the bottom. They finished this job in 3½ days and began to build a dam across the ravine to the north of the house. Anderson paid $30 for the construction of the dam, and evidently wanted it to back up the water in order that he might more easily supply his own ice. The icehouse was not lined until the following month when shingles were rived for the sheds.

The year 1858 was a "tolerable good year for cotton," and

Anderson made fifty-eight bales, seventeen of which he sold for $899.55 on October 30. He killed forty-one hogs weighing 6,280 pounds, made 292 barrels of corn, had increased his horses and mules to twelve and his jacks and jennets to seven.[22]

It was unfortunate, in a way, for Anderson that the cotton crop of 1858 brought such good returns. The next year some of the corn land was put in cotton. All told, he had 120 acres of cotton on which he made seventy-seven bales, but the corn crop amounted to only 220 barrels. The result was that corn had to be purchased, much to the displeasure of the proprietor of "Sherwood Forrest." Some of his remarks during the time of hog feeding were: "This thing of not making corn enough for the plantation is a very bad as well as a very annoying business."[23] "Corn Corn Corn!!!! is wanted Let me never get in such another fix!!!!!!"[24] He complained that he had to kill his thirty hogs while they were still too small, and that they could almost have been bought for what they ate in corn.[25]

Sickness claimed three hands during the fodder pulling season, and the driver left; thus there were only six good hands in the field the last two weeks of August. Where were the remainder of Anderson's fifty-one slaves? At no time does he mention working as many as ten Negroes, and the crops he produced seem very small for a plantation the size he held. Also, it does not seem likely that he would have hired an overseer for as few slaves as he says were "in the crops." It is quite probable that Anderson was hiring out some of his slaves and renting a large portion of his land. This would account for some of the income he received, that, according to the amount of produce he listed, could not well have been derived from farming operations. Another possibility—noted above —is that the slaves should also have been credited to his wife in the 1850 Census. She may have carried on farming activities entirely separate from those of her husband, but he made no note of this. At any rate, there should have been more than eight or nine working hands out of fifty or more Negroes.

In addition to sickness among the Negroes, the overseer was no longer satisfied with his position. On September 1, 1859, Anderson recorded the following:

Mr. Ward becoming dissatisfied or rather I think his wife has left my services Monday & gone to get a home his wages will go on for two weeks & he is making me some gates—I will move his family through favor as he cannot get any one to move him. Shall charge him nothing.

Seven weeks later a Mr. Smith was hired as overseer at the rate of $16 per month. Apparently, he henceforth hired his overseers by the month rather than by the year as most planters did. The above item relative to Smith is the last entry mentioning any overseer, and Anderson seems to have had no difficulty with any of them concerning treatment of slaves. If he did, he refrained from leaving any recorded statement of it.

In spite of the scarcity of corn, "Sherwood Forrest" enjoyed a prosperous year in 1859. Between June 29 and July 7 Anderson made a trip to Cincinnati where he purchased two brood mares. These mares were sent by steamer as far as Fulton, Kentucky, and were received on August 10. They cost $125 each plus delivery charges of $72.68 for the two. The following day the stables—all but the floors—were finished. There were seven stalls, six by eight feet, with one shallow and one deep trough in each. The Cincinnati mares, however, were not the first fine horses that Anderson owned.[26] On August 2, 1858, he had driven Bill, his Kentucky horse, the thirteen miles to Brownsville in one hour and forty-five minutes. "That was most excellent trotting." Indeed, it was!

Another evidence of prosperity was the purchase of two male slaves for $1,450 and $1,200, aged twenty-three and twelve years, respectively. They were "likely boys but an enormous price."[27] Later in the same year, December 23, 1859, Anderson bought 846½ acres of land in "Lauderdale in the Fulton neck," for which he paid $2,075 cash. The balance of $3,000 was payable, with interest, on February 1, 1861. As most of the planters, Anderson acquired more land as soon as he felt financially able to incur the new obligation necessary to expansion of activities.

The late spring and early summer of 1859 had been very dry, and when the rains came in June, they did "untold damage" by washing gullies in Anderson's fields. He realized that something should be done to prevent a repetition of such loss of soil, and asserted "I must endeavour to circle my land next year, then disastrous floods will [not] soon deprive me of the *'upper crust title of my land'*." His hoped-for "circling" evidently was not done; the next June his lands were "badly washed" by the hard rains.

Anderson's diary is rather incomplete for 1860, is still more meager in 1861, and is discontinued on July 20, 1862. In 1860 he began to spend more time with his horses, and about all one gets of the farming operations are the summary results of the year's work. The acreage planted in cotton had increased to 130 and that in corn to ninety-five; he now had "17 hands tho two of them have young children."[28] The turnip patch that year was five acres instead of the usual two and one-half or three acres, but he still pulled the fodder in August and made baskets about one week before cotton picking time, which, in 1860, began on August 28. The scarcity of corn that had so vexed him the year before was remedied by the production of 598 barrels in 1860. Seventy-six bales of cotton, slightly more than one-half bale to the acre, were picked off the 130 acres; the pumpkins produced to the amount of six loads; and Anderson had ninety-six hogs in "good condition."[29] The only recorded misfortune of the year, other than the June rains, was the temporary escape of one of his Negroes. Hubbard ran away on October 26, but was taken up in Moscow, Kentucky, and jailed at Clinton. Anderson, after a three-day trip and expenditures of $115, returned with him on December 31.

The diary of the proprietor of "Sherwood Forrest" does not furnish, at any one time, a complete picture of the plantation. A more nearly complete picture of the productions, value of the property, and amount and value of livestock is obtainable from the unpublished census schedules. By June 1, 1860, the end of the census year, Anderson was the owner of 250 acres of improved and 757 acres of unimproved land valued at $20,500.[30] He was also credited with the following: $350 worth of farm implements; $5,170 worth of livestock which included sixteen horses, thirteen asses and mules, fifteen milch cows, four oxen, thirty-five other cattle, twenty-five sheep, and eighty-five swine; forty-five bushels of wheat, twenty bushels of rye, 1,500 bushels of corn, eighty-five bales of cotton, eighty pounds of wool, seven bushels of peas and beans, one hundred bushels of Irish potatoes, 250 bushels of sweet potatoes, $90 worth of orchard products, 312 pounds of butter, home manufactures to the extent of $30, and $492 worth of slaughtered animals. His slaveholdings had decreased to thirty-three, but there were six slave houses on the plantation.[31] If one compares Anderson's status in 1860 with that of 1850, he will find that some definite changes had taken place during ten years. He now had 1,007 acres of land of his own, and it was valued at almost three times as much as the 2,800 acres of his wife in 1850. His work animals had increased over fifty per cent, and all the live-stock were valued at nearly four times the amount of 1850. Certain crops show a remarkably smaller production, but Anderson seemed to have experimented until he could raise a sufficient amount of each crop to keep the plantation supplied. The amount of corn listed, 1,500 bushels, is 400 bushels more than Anderson said he made, for this is the production of his "bad" year, 1859. The census taker could not record the yield of 1860, 2,490 bushels, because the census year closed on June 1.

Some of the fifty-one slaves credited to Anderson in 1850 must have belonged to his wife. He makes no note of having disposed of any Negroes between 1854 and 1860, and he did purchase several, to say nothing of the natural increase. Anderson, like most of the other planters, was not a one-crop agriculturist. He raised cotton as his money crop, but did not neglect the others. It will be re-called that he was provoked when he had to buy corn. One item, hay, is conspicuously absent from the census schedules, and Anderson never once mentions it. Apparently fodder, which was stripped every year, was the only forage.

The prosperity of the farm did not quiet the owner's political misgivings. On October 24, 1860, he returned from Jackson where he had heard Stephen A. Douglas speak. He considered the "little giant" the "greatest living statesman of the age" and said "he utterly demolished the southern *secessionists* & the Northern Black Republicans showing the tendency of those parties to be the *overthrow* of the government . . . Unless we follow his advice we are nationally lost." Four years and five months later he added to the above, "was ever a prediction more fully vindicated."

December 31, 1860, found the planter still more worried over the course events had taken. He wrote:

Mr. Lincoln having been elected by the foolish management of the Democratic party not centering on the Hon Stephen A. Douglas of Ill,[32] the negroes are expecting to be made free & they are not far from being right about it—There is a class of men in the south, ambitious to set up a separate government or Confederacy they call it—These men backed by the fanatical abolition party of the north (but for a different object) are doing all they can to dissolve this Union—
Wo betide! the south when they succeed, the whole civilized world is against us & we will be literally without sympathy & perhaps help from any quarter—I fear my prophecy of Nov 4th 1856 & Oct 24th 1860 will be fulfilled—Dark and ominous clouds are overwhelming this southern land—But if calamity does come may a just God so direct the affairs of this country that events will redound to *his honor & glory*— M[a]y the south be never tinged with infidel notions of the north & their many isms.

As stated above, the diary for 1861 contains very little information. One learns from it, though, that Anderson made 230 bushels of wheat, had fifty "gentle hogs" to kill and fifteen in the "bottom tho very doubtful whether we get them," sowed sixteen acres in wheat and clover, wondering if it would grow, made 535 barrels of corn, and sixty-five bales of cotton which he bound with "white oak and hickory ties."[33]

The last entry, July 20, 1862, reads as follows: "Our national troubles coming on now thick & fast this Journal was discontinued —I see trouble ahead, endless trouble." Anderson mounted his horse from a stump—he was too short and fat to pull himself up from the ground—and rode off to join Forrest's cavalry. He served throughout the war and returned home "a thin emaciated wreck of a man."[34] On February 6, 1868, he moved to Ripley, and slightly over four years later to Brownsville,[35] where he died on October 26, 1888.[36]

Anderson, according to his granddaughter, was "very stern with his (grandma's) slaves, and whipped them when they were lazy or disobedient." This sternness, however, does not seem to have been harshness, and though he records the escape and return of two of his slaves, he never states anywhere that either was punished. Mrs. Smith's statement implies that he whipped them only in instances where punishment was warranted. In a letter of December 11, 1938, to the writer, Mrs. Smith further states that her grandfather was "fair but worked them hard," and "had no compunction about separating a male slave & his 'wife.' " Also, Anderson's wife resented his punishing the slaves, and when she heard the news of emancipation, she "jumped up and down and cracked her heels together for joy."

There was nothing very exceptional about Anderson as a prewar planter, not even the fact that he was the father of ten children. Perhaps a majority of the other planters had "compunctions" about separating man and wife, but, like many others, he was increasing his amount of land, and centered the plantation economy around one money crop. Unlike many others, however, he learned that it would be disastrous to sacrifice corn acreage to cotton, and he worked in the fields with the slaves, thus conducting himself more as a small proprietor. There was no moonlight, mockingbird, magnolia, and mint julep atmosphere hovering about the life of Harrod Clopton Anderson of "Sherwood Forrest," Haywood County, Tennessee.

Anderson was a prosperous planter when he left to go to the war, but between 1854 and 1860 the amount of farm produce was small for the size of his plantation and the number of slaves he owned. As mentioned above, some of these slaves should possibly have been listed as belonging to his wife; she may have carried on independent farming operations, and he may have rented out some of his slaves and land.

THE POLKS

The Polks of Maury County, Tennessee, were larger planters than Anderson. Lucius, son of Colonel William Polk of Raleigh, North Carolina, looked after his own and his father's plantation affairs in the Volunteer State. Farming operations were going on in 1823, but did not assume large-scale proportions until a few years later.

Lucius wrote to his father on July 4, 1823,[37] telling him of the general conditions on the farm. He said that the library kept him company while he was in the house, but "without I am *overseeing my overseer* and hands." Only six hands were able to work at the time, for Jacob had not recovered from his sickness. The forty-two acres of cotton and twenty-eight of corn were "good," and since cotton was such a "fine price" last year, the son thought he would "go the Whole Amount this year."

An unmarried tenant by the name of Batts was cultivating part of one of Polk's farms of 2,500 acres. Lucius described him as a man of "fortune, industry, and economy and . . . upon the whole is one of the most desirable tenants we have." The plot which Batts was tilling would make fifteen barrels of corn to the acre.[38] Two years later Lucius had entirely changed his mind about tenants. He said that they "may be a benefit but generally speaking they are a *curse.*"[39]

The tenants, whether satisfactory or not, were soon to be replaced by slaves brought from North Carolina. William had been buying slaves around Raleigh, and thought that Lucius paid too much for the ones he purchased in Tennessee.[40] The Colonel told his son that he would send eighty or ninety slaves, including about thirty working hands, and suggested that they be used at "Rattle and Snap" since that was the only place where enough open land was available.[41] Nearly two months later, September 15, 1826, William wrote Lucius that the Negroes were not yet on their way, but that those from Wake County should get started on the road within two weeks. It would require seven or eight days to reach Rockland, and at that place preparations for the long trek would take another week. It was not until October 4, however, that thirty-nine Negroes, with two wagons, left for Charlotte, and the entire coffle did not leave Rockland until twenty-two days later.[42] William did not give the exact number he was sending, but the contents of the letter indicate that it was between eighty and ninety, as he had previously stated.

A Mr. Blailock, who had been hired to deliver the slaves to Lucius, received $1 per day from October 15 or 16 until his arrival in Maury County, and the same for each day he would be returning home. The overseer, also, was brought from North Carolina. He received $100 per year, $60 of which William gave him before he left North Carolina.

The Negroes arrived at "Rattle and Snap" on November 28. Some trouble occurred *en route,* but no more than one would expect from such a large group. Bob was missed at Murfreesboro, but Blailock did not think he had deliberately run away. The "manager" attributed the Negro's waywardness to getting drunk and taking the Nashville instead of the Columbia road. Lucius sent his overseer in pursuit of Bob, but Lucius said that he "flattered" himself to think that news of the missing one would be brought back. Harry, the blacksmith, had caused more immediate trouble. He had thrown a bundle of clothes into a heavily loaded wagon; and when the bundle was thrown out, he pitched it into the wagon again. Thereupon the overseer and Harry exchanged blows, and then the Negro was "severely chastised." Blailock—not to be confused with the overseer whose name was Harrison—felt that the punishment was just and justifiable, but the Negroes started a report that Harry had been murdered by five hundred lashes. Though this was not true, Lucius was rather skeptical about the overseer his father had sent. The Negroes did not like him, and Lucius wrote that he was "rather fond of his grog and if I am to believe the tales of the negroes I would say he was a trifling fellow; I am told he has been caught in crinn-con [criminal connection?] with one of the negroes." He would, however, be given a trial.[43]

The Colonel was all questions in his next letter of February 6, 1827. Had Lucius been able to house them *all in families?* Had they received the necessary cooking utensils? Had they been provided with hoes, iron, and smith tools for a crop? Had the overseer provided pad or shuck collars to save the leather ones? What had been done with boy Humphrey? Did Lucius have a "parcel of saws," so that Old Dick might be "put to his promised vocation"? He then advised Lucius to do as he saw fit with Harrison, the overseer, and suggested that he fatten his hogs in Maury County and then drive them to Raleigh. "In that way," he said, "you can use corn for which there is no advantageous market."

William later restricted Lucius' action in regard to Harrison. The Colonel was sorry to learn that the overseer was "such a numscull; he came highly recommended to me by several persons with whom he had lived . . . but, he is not to quit my service untill he remunirates me for money advanced; provision found & for taking him to Tennessee."[44] Shortly before this letter was written Lucius had attempted to remedy the unfortunate situation by bringing Harrison to his place and sending his overseer, Wilson, to his father's farm. Some change was imperative, for the "negroes . . . had such an unconquerable hatrid for the man, that I believe they would have done better without any."[45]

A hemp project was started that year, 1827, and William advised Lucius to take exceedingly good care of it, as he, William, hoped to get a greater income from farming than just the returns from cotton. In the same letter, the father admonished Lucius not to abandon the blacksmith shop entirely.[46] Lucius, in his letter of May 8, had recommended the purchase of Mendenhall's vertical grist mill that was attachable to the running gears of the cotton gin. William, however, did not have "much confidence" in that mill, and said there were two others on the market.[47]

Lucius was disheartened by the "dryest summer known to oldest inhabitants," and could not "find much" in farming. He requested his father to send $6,000 (secured) so that he might enter the iron business with Judge John Catron and a "professional iron-master." Mitchell—who was, perhaps, hiring his own time—was living with his wife, and, Lucius said, "treats her well; but more from fear of me than love for her I presume." Lucius wanted to know what Mitchell was allowed for the year's work, and, if he stayed, what he would be given for next year. Lucius said he had been told that Mitchell "would not work under Wilson (the overseer) for all *your estate* another year—There has been one death and six births since their arrival."[48]

The next year, 1828, Leonidas, the future "Fighting Bishop," wrote his brother, Lucius, that he intended to dispose of his eighteen Negroes in North Carolina, and would like for Lucius to buy them. Leonidas wanted the slaves kept in the family, and described several of them as "family negroes." He had taken the trouble to purchase a wife to please her husband, a child to please the mother, and done other deeds of this type.[49] A bill of sale, dated March 6, 1830, shows that Lucius bought Leonidas' twenty slaves for $3,847.50. This small sum indicates that the North Carolinian made a sacrifice rather than sell the Negroes outside the family.

More Negroes were evidently brought to "Rattle and Snap" before 1830. Lucius, in reply to his father's question, wrote on November 1, 1828, that he had engaged Henry Briggs of Maury County to go to North Carolina for "the negroes." No further letters concerning these Negroes were found, but it can probably be assumed that they arrived in much the same fashion as the earlier group.

Wilson, the overseer whom Lucius had transferred from his own to his father's plantation, was dismissed in the late summer of 1828. He had refused to send Lucius two sawyers that had been requested, and embodied his refusal in an insulting message. Lucius, in communicating the circumtances to his father, said that he went *"well armed* determined to kill him [Wilson] if he made the least advance to anything like violence." Wilson denied having sent the message, humbled himself, and Lucius, contrary to his "first determination," retained him a few days longer.[50]

Very few of the letters from Lucius to his father tell anything of the productions of the plantation, but a letter of January 4, 1829, informed the Colonel that his fifty bales of cotton were on the boat at Columbia, and would be sent off with the first rise of the river. Lucius had made seventeen bales for himself, and expected to get 12½ ¢ per pound for all the cotton. Four cribs had been filled with corn, and about 350 barrels were still in the field. Lucius was preparing to build new hewn-log cabins for his Negroes, and wanted to know what his father wished done for his.[51]

The last letter containing important plantation news from Lucius to his father was written on August 27, 1829. The Colonel's cotton crop was estimated at 150 or 160 bales, or about 375 pounds to the acre. Three of the slave boys had died from dysentery, but the others who had been "down" were well again.[52]

Information on the Polk plantation affairs is even more meager after 1829. A plantation record, very inadequately covering the years 1821 to 1839, gives a little insight as to the status of "Rattle and Snap." In 1829 the cotton yield was 111 bales, and in July, 1830, there were twenty families of 132 Negroes on the place. Analysis of this list of slaves shows that practically all of them were under middle age. Only seven of them were forty or over, to wit: Sam, forty; Hannibal and Jenny, forty; Jim, sr., forty-two; Olive, forty-four; Bob, forty-eight; and Sylvia, seventy. At the end of the list of families the names of fourteen children, from one to six years old, were written in pencil. These 146 Negroes must have been worth $55,000, and the cotton crop must have sold for as much as $6,000.

William died in 1834, and after that year Lucius wrote the plantation news to his mother, Mrs. Sarah Polk.[53] Letters were not as frequent, however, and it was not until December 10, 1835, that he wrote concerning the West Tennessee plantation, "Fayette Park," near Somerville. There, the farm was very well equipped. This plot of land, already under cultivation, was being prepared for more extensive operations. There was an overseer's house of four rooms, an excellent gin and press, three cribs, two wagon sheds, and "excellent negro houses." Eighteen of the anticipated seventy bales of cotton had been sent to Randolph, and next year 400 acres, now in corn and cotton, would be planted to cotton.[54]

The next month, January, 1836, Lucius took eighty-three Negroes—evidently from "Rattle and Snap"—to this Fayette County plantation. He did not take the exact list which he had previously communicated to his mother, but made some changes "because of marriages." He had 1,000 barrels of corn and two hundred shoats and pigs on the place. The overseer, Colburn, was to be kept until Leonidas could make arrangements to employ "Booker[55] old overseer," Bigam. Bigam was considered to be the "best in the state," but Lucius added, "I have such confidence in *my*

own ability as a manager that I dont fear the result—hem!"[56]
Weather conditions did not even permit grubbing, and Lucius dis-
liked having to feed the Negroes and *"get nothing for it."*

Still another tract, known as "Hamilton Place," was located at
Ashwood in Maury County. From here Lucius wrote his mother
on March 16, 1839, that he had recently received a letter from
Mr. White stating that seventy-four bales of cotton had been sold
for 11½ ¢ per pound. Lucius was highly displeased, and rather
suspected dishonest dealings. He said it was

a most outrageous sale considering that the article was worth when I
left Orleans 12¾ I cant account for it in no other way than that there
is a system of stealing among the merchants there and they cant get
along without it he has not sent a dollar.[57]

The crop in Fayette was very promising for 1839, but Lucius
thought that the overseer for the place should be changed. No
dishonesty had been discovered, but Lucius felt that he was just
"wearing out."[58] M. D. Cooper and Company of New Orleans
wrote Lucius on December 24, 1839, that 102 bales of his cotton
had brought 8½ ¢ per pound, or $3,801.19. The charges—freight,
drayage, storage, weighing, river and fire insurance, and the 2½
per cent commission—on this shipment totalled $449.34, so that
Lucius received only $3,351.85.[59] In a later letter the merchants
informed Lucius that his fourteen bales had brought from 6¾ ¢
to 8¼ ¢ per pound, or $417.69 after expenses had been paid.[60]
That fall, 1840, Lucius sold thirty-two bales through Cooper and
Company. The prices ranged from 8¢ to 8¾ ¢, and the planter
received only $795.27.[61] The 1841–1842 shipment of forty-seven
bales brought from 8⅛ ¢ to 8½ ¢, or net proceeds of $1,542.15.[62]

Little further information on these Polk plantations in Tennessee is available from personal correspondence. It may have been
that Mrs. Polk died about 1840, and that some of Lucius' brothers
took over the management of their share of the estate. At least,
three of his brothers, William, Andrew, and George, were operating tracts in Tennessee in 1850.

The census records show that William Polk was the owner and

operator of a Fayette County farm in 1850 and 1860. This may
not have been the same place that Lucius had been managing; if
it was, much of the four hundred acres in cotton and corn in 1835
had been sold. William's holdings and productions in 1850 were:
two slaves; ninety improved and 240 unimproved acres valued at
only $1,500; $80 worth of farm implements; $555 worth of live-
stock which included three horses, two asses and mules, eight
milch cows, four oxen, eight other cattle, fifteen sheep, and forty
swine; forty-five bushels of wheat, 1,100 bushels of corn, twelve
bales of cotton, thirty pounds of wool, one hundred bushels of
peas and beans, fifteen bushels of Irish potatoes, 150 bushels of
sweet potatoes, $10 worth of home manufactures, and $210 worth
of slaughtered animals.[63] Ten years later, William was more prosperous and his farming activities were more varied. He was then
credited with: eleven slaves; 150 improved and 200 unimproved
acres valued at $3,000; $40 worth of farm implements; $2,000
worth of livestock which included ten horses, four asses and mules,
four oxen, four milch cows, fifteen other cattle, eighteen sheep,
and twenty-five swine; 650 bushels of corn, thirty-five bales of
cotton, twenty-three pounds of wool, 200 bushels of peas and
beans, twenty bushels of Irish potatoes, 100 bushels of sweet potatoes, $20 worth of orchard products, 100 pounds of butter, five
tons of hay, 210 pounds of honey, $10 worth of home manufac-
tures, and $212 worth of slaughtered animals.[64] Rather than call
William a planter, it would be more fitting to say that he was a
successful farmer.

There were in 1850 three Polks, Lucius and his brothers Andrew J. and George W., in Maury County, who can well be classed
as true planters. None depended entirely on one crop, and only
Andrew produced much cotton. Lucius' census record follows:
sixty-one slaves; 900 improved acres valued at $45,000; $700
worth of farm implements; the livestock of fifty horses, nine asses
and mules, twenty-one milch cows, six oxen, fifty other cattle,
200 sheep, and 500 swine were valued at $8,000; 200 bushels of
wheat, 10,000 bushels of corn, 300 bushels of oats, 800 pounds
of tobacco, three bales of cotton, 600 pounds of wool, 150 bushels
of Irish potatoes, 300 bushels of sweet potatoes, 1,000 pounds of

butter, ninety tons of hay, $200 worth of home manufactures, and $800 worth of slaughtered animals.[65] Andrew lived next to Lucius and was more prosperous than his brother. Andrew's holdings and productions were: 168 slaves; 1,800 improved acres valued at $100,000; $1,500 worth of farm implements; livestock, including 110 horses, twenty asses and mules, six milch cows, sixty oxen, sixty other cattle, 200 sheep, and 400 swine, valued at $11,535; 12,500 bushels of corn, 1,000 bushels of oats, 230 bales of cotton, 400 pounds of wool, twenty-five bushels of peas and beans, 800 pounds of butter, fifteen tons of hay, $250 worth of home manufactures, and $1,000 worth of slaughtered animals.[66]

The other brother, George W., lived in the eleventh civil district of Maury County. His holdings and farm produce follow: 67 slaves; 770 improved and 790 unimproved acres valued at $47,-000; $1,560 worth of farm implements; fifteen horses, 100 asses and mules, fourteen milch cows, six oxen, 101 other cattle, 200 sheep, and 350 swine valued at $9,445; 200 bushels of wheat, eighty bushels of rye, 10,000 bushels of corn, 600 bushels of oats, 400 pounds of wool, 100 bushels of peas and beans, sixty bushels of Irish potatoes, 200 bushels of sweet potatoes, 500 pounds of butter, forty tons of hay, 800 pounds of beeswax and honey, $400 worth of home manufactures, and $800 worth of slaughtered animals.[67] This was probably the plantation known as "Hamilton Place."

A careful examination of the records of these three brothers will show that Andrew was the only one raising cotton as a money crop, and that his farming operations were less diversified than those of the other two. The plantations of Lucius and George seem to have been self-sufficient, but it would have been impossible for Andrew to have fed his large number of livestock on the amount of hay which he produced. In making such a statement, though, one should always bear in mind that the census taker was too often careless, that serious omissions sometimes occurred in the records of individuals, and that many of the planters stripped fodder for forage.

Lucius and Andrew were listed in the tenth district in 1860. Lucius' holdings and productions follow: thirteen houses for eighty-three slaves; 350 improved and 231 unimproved acres valued at $58,100; $1,310 worth of farm implements; livestock—twenty-one horses, fourteen asses and mules, fifteen milch cows, six work oxen, thirty other cattle, thirty sheep, 225 swine—valued at $13,885; 200 bushels of wheat, 9,200 bushels of corn, 15,400 pounds of tobacco, thirty-seven bales of cotton, 100 pounds of wool, seventy-five bushels of Irish potatoes, sixty bushels of sweet potatoes, 1,095 pounds of butter, 200 tons of hay, and $1,550 worth of slaughtered animals.[68] Lucius was operating a much smaller tract than he was ten years earlier; perhaps he had disposed of some of it to raise money to purchase his Mississippi plantation.

Andrew did not have as many slaves as in 1850, but he had more land. It is probable that he bought part of Lucius' farm. Andrew's record follows: 95 slaves (no slave houses listed); 2,400 improved and 1,200 unimproved acres valued at $250,000; $4,000 worth of farm implements; livestock—twenty-five horses, twenty asses and mules, twenty milch cows, four work oxen, twenty-four other cattle, 200 sheep, 600 swine—valued at $15,-890; ninety-six bushels of rye, 7,500 bushels of corn, 225 bushels of oats, 150 pounds of wool, twenty-five bushels of peas and beans, 300 bushels of Irish potatoes, 300 bushels of sweet potatoes, 500 pounds of butter, fifty tons of hay, fifty pounds of beeswax, 500 pounds of honey, and $5,000 worth of slaughtered animals.[69] Andrew's record appears incomplete; his productions are scarcely as large as those of Lucius, and he is credited with no tobacco and no cotton. He must have been hiring out many of his slaves and renting much of his land.

George was still in the eleventh district, and another kinsman, S. M. Polk, was living on the adjoining tract. George's holdings and productions in 1860 were: 15 slave houses, 81 slaves; 600 improved and 1,100 unimproved acres valued at $76,200; $1,036 worth of farm implements; fifty-five horses, thirty-four asses and mules, sixteen milch cows, seventy other cattle, 165 sheep, and 225 swine valued at $15,095; 160 bushels of wheat, 100 bushels of rye, 500 bushels of corn, 600 pounds of wool, 100 bushels of Irish potatoes, ten tons of hay, and $1,485 worth of slaughtered animals.[70] George's slaves had increased by fourteen since 1850, and the value of his land and livestock was much greater in 1860 than it had been ten years before. The number of his horses had increased, but a large decrease in the number of his asses and mules and in bushels of corn produced—sixty-six and 9,500, respectively—should be noticed. George appears to have been on the decline as a successful planter.

His kinsman, S. M. Polk, had a more well-rounded plantation. His census record reads as follows: sixteen houses for 87 slaves; 670 improved and 743 unimproved acres valued at $56,520; $940 worth of farm implements; six horses, twenty asses and mules, twelve milch cows, two oxen, nineteen other cattle, 113 sheep, and 254 swine valued at $3,250; 240 bushels of wheat, sixty bushels of rye, 8,750 bushels of corn, 800 bushels of oats, 16,000 pounds of tobacco, sixty bales of cotton, 318 pounds of wool, sixty bushels of Irish potatoes, 600 pounds of butter, twenty-three tons of hay, and $1,640 worth of slaughtered animals.[71]

The last bit of prewar evidence—from personal papers—bearing on any of these Polk plantations is found in the farm ledger for 1859. On November 15 of that year 11,642 pounds of pork were butchered at Ashwood.[72] This was the tract known as "Hamilton Place," and, as stated above, was probably the plantation operated by George.

Lucius, some time before 1855, acquired a large Mississippi plantation. His nephew, Niles, wrote him to the effect that "with a fair fall" he (Lucius) would make from 300 to 350 bales of cotton on this tract. Lucius had never raised anywhere near that amount in Tennessee, and 300 bales was more than his slaves in Mississippi could "possibly pick out."[73]

The letters of Ephraim Beanland, overseer for James K. Polk and his brother-in-law, Dr. Silas M. Caldwell, throw much light on the essential figure of every smooth-working plantation. It was the overseer who had to bring into co-ordination the brains of the planter and the brawn of the slaves; it was he who had to absorb the bitterness the slaves felt for their enslavers; and it was he, as the inflicter of punishment, who became the symbol of the hardest features of bondage. Bassett pictures the overseer as receiving slight respect from the master—much less from the slaves —and "it was not even his fortune to be esteemed for what he did."[74] The overseer was not loved, "as a rule he was not lovable," and his life was "hearty rather than gentle."

Polk and Caldwell operated a tract in Maury County and one in Fayette County, but attention here will be centered on the plantation in Fayette where Beanland was located. This place, known as "Pleasant Grove,"[75] was not large. The first evidence of the amount of production on this farm is found in a letter from Cooper, Caruthers and Company of New Orleans to James K. Polk on December 29, 1832. The commission merchants acknowledged receipt of ten bales of cotton from the Western District, and said they would account to Walker and Harris for the proceeds. Prices were low at the time; Cooper, Caruthers and Company attributed the condition of the market to an "apprehension among dealers that the Belgian question will involve Europe in a general war." This condition was not expected to exist long, and soon holders "will be enabled to realize former prices."[76]

In 1833 the Fayette farm produced twenty-five bales of cotton and so little corn that the 4,000 pounds of hogs had to be butchered before they were as fat as they should have been. When the place was sold in 1834, there were thirteen plows, twenty-nine sheep and goats, nine cows, and twenty-two calves and young cattle. The acreage is not known, but Bassett estimates the number of slaves at twenty-five.[77]

Beanland, a young, unmarried, untutored man, became the overseer in 1833. He received $350 per year—a rather large amount for the time and his location—in addition to the usual perquisites of a house, cook, manservant, and feed for one horse. Dr. Caldwell owned a plantation of his own in Haywood County, and supervised[78] the overseers of the Maury and Fayette plantations by infrequent visits. Though Beanland "conducted the place with fair efficiency," he did not have the confidence of his supervisor who was a "temperamental man and hard to please."[79] Other brothers-in-law, A. O. Harris and James Walker, also interfered in plantation affairs, but Polk generally sustained Beanland. The slaves were in a state of disorganization in late 1833, but the overseer worked them hard, talked plainly, and did not seem "to have tried to rule by stimulating the pride or good will of his subjects. . . . He gave his orders and enforced them in the manner most familiar to him."[80] Beanland, however, had trouble keeping all the Negroes at home.

Three of the slaves ran away on November 28, 1833. The overseer wrote Polk on December 22, telling him the condition of plantation affairs and describing the circumstances that prompted the Negroes to run away. The winter work was progressing well, and Elizabeth and Mariah had "fine living children." Jack, Beanland said, "went alf and broke into a grocery which he was caught and when I was thoroly convinced that it was him I corected." Part of the punishment was administered for telling "5 or 6 positif lyes." While Beanland was eating dinner, Jack and Ben left the field. They had not been heard from since, but the overseer wanted them back as an example to the other slaves. The trouble did not lie, according to Beanland, in any method of plantation discipline, but in the white people of the neighborhood. He continued: "sir your negroes has traded with white people and bin let run at so loce rained that I must be verry cloce with them   they is a set of white people that lives cloce hear that would spoile any set of negroes."[81] Polk is then informed of the low corn supply, the early killing of the hogs, and the weight of each and every bale of cotton that had been sent to Memphis.

Ben and Jim (the third runaway) went to Columbia where they got in touch with A. O. Harris. Harris wrote to Polk on December 30, 1833, that, although he had approved of hiring Beanland, he was afraid the Negroes were not being treated properly. Ben and Jim said that Jack had been badly whipped, and had been salted "four or five times" during the inflicting of the punishment. Ben was determined not to go back, so he (Harris) had hired him to the Iron Works for $100 per year. Four days later Harris wrote Polk that he had written Beanland to hire another hand to replace Ben.[82]

Caldwell, writing from Fayette County on June 4, 1834, informed Polk that Jack had been recovered by Hughes (or Hues) on the bank of the Mississippi River. He was taken from the company of two men whom Jack said had stolen him in Memphis.[83] The charges for apprehension were approximately $140. Caldwell thought if Beanland were "more mild with the negroes he would get along with them better," but he said, "I don't know this from observation."[84]

The overseer was not at all pleased that Ben had been hired out by Harris. A hand to replace him would cost $130 a year, so none had been hired. In addition to losing the services of Ben, Beanland reiterated his contention that the policy of not returning a runaway made it more difficult for him to discipline the remaining ones:

now if I correct any of the others they are shore to leave me thinking that if they can get back to that will do for they must be youmered to as well as ben and sir I do not think any such foolishness as this is write for I caime her to make a crop and I am determined on doing of it.[85]

The Negroes' shoes were in bad condition, but Beanland had patched them to make them last as long as possible. The overseer also had the misfortune of not being able to clear any new land, and now so much timber had fallen that he had to start moving the dead logs from the old land.

On February 13, 1834, Beanland again wrote Polk relative to Ben. The slaves, he said, seemed to be becoming more and more unruly, and he was about ready to quit trying to control any of them. He wrote:

if he [Ben] is not sent heare maide stay all the rest of the fellows had better be sent to Maury for I will be damde if I can do anythinge with them and they all ways in the mads and if you do anythinge in this matter I want you to do it as soon as poseable and you will oblige your friend.[86]

Three other Negroes, including Hardy and Jim, had run away. None of them, so Beanland said, had been punished or "insulted any way," and Hardy had been so trusted that he hauled cotton to Memphis.

Polk sustained the overseer; Ben was ordered back to the Fayette plantation; and the other runaways were soon recovered. The effect of Ben's return is best described by the words of the overseer:

. . . since I have brought ben back the all appear satisfied ande Squire Walker rote me a letter which I redit to all of them which he sayes that they shall stay heare or he will sell them to negro trader and by otheres in there plases which they do not like . . . I thinke they ar all verry well aweare that if they go to runninge away that it will not do for I am determined to break it aup this set of white people that they had so much corispondance with I have broke it aup entirely and they are verry well satisfied and crop time is now heare and if Jim goes to Maury he must be sent back to me for I have not time to go after him but I want his servisis verry much indeade.[87]

The letter of the same date, March 7, 1834, said that forty acres of cotton land had been broken, the ten acres of oats looked "verry fine," there were nine lambs, and "every thinge is moovinge on verry well at this time which I am glad to say so."

Trouble, however, was by no means over. The latter part of March Beanland felt that Jack should be corrected. When the overseer attempted to do such, Jack cursed him "verry much" and "run alf." Whereupon, Beanland caught him in about two hundred yards, but was greeted by three raps over the head with a stick. The stick broke when the Negro hit Beanland the third time, and the overseer stabbed the Negro twice. Jack was brought back in chains—and kept chained for a while—but, the overseer wrote, he "swares he will never stay with the Polk family any more I can worke him and I intend to do it."[88]

The prospect of a good crop in 1834 was darkened by a late frost, and on April 17 a storm blew down many of the "deaded" trees, killing some of the corn and cotton. Beanland soon had most of the logs out of the way of the plows, and the Negroes were behaving for the time being. He wrote to Polk on May 1 saying, "my negroes all of them stayes with me and they appear like they are very well satisfied I make the moste buter and the moste butermilke that I ever saw and I have got the finest oats that I ever sawe in my life."[89] On June 1 fifty acres of the cotton crop were described to Polk as "only tolerable good," and the "rest of the crop is very indifferent."

Four months later, August 2, 1834, Beanland again wrote Polk about prospects for the cotton crop. The overseer was uncertain as to exactly what the prospects were, and the result is an interesting commentary: "I have sum good and sum indifferent and to take the crop all to gether I am afraide it is two fine   it is the rite stage to make a firste rate crop or to make a sorry wan if we have a good dry season crops will be fine and mine is good." Beanland said he would not "give a dam" for the running gears of the old gin, and if the new ones were as "indifferent," he would not leave them in the gin house.[90]

Jack, though, could not be made to stay on the plantation. He ran away again the first week of September, and went to Shawnee Town, Arkansas Territory. Beanland said he had been advised not to go there in an effort to recover the Negro. He described the place as a "den of thieves," and told Polk that "I donte think you will ever git him." Undaunted by tales that the place was dangerous, Beanland went and brought Jack back, but decided that he had better give up the idea of trying to work him. He wrote Polk on October 10, 1834, that "I want you to sell Jack and never let him come here no more for they is a greate many of the neighbors is afraid from him to come hear."[91]

Beanland's struggles with cotton, fallen trees, and Negroes in Tennessee soon came to an end. Polk sold the Fayette plantation in September to a Mr. Booker for $6,000. The future president said that the crop might bring $2,500, and he thought that "Beanland has done well, considering the trouble he has had with the negroes." Plans were being made for a move to Mississippi, but the Negroes did not know about them. This was as Polk wished.[92]

The acquiring of slaves for the new plantation was probably the largest item of preparation, and Polk showed his confidence in Beanland by authorizing him to purchase wherever he could obtain good bargains. Polk met G. T. Greenfield, a large planter of Maury County, in Washington, and, since Greenfield was about to purchase some slaves, Polk asked that he also buy some for him. Greenfield made the effort, but without success.[93] Finally, thirty-six slaves, valued at $16,050,[94] were taken to the 800-acre tract in Yalobusha County, Mississippi, and Beanland was retained as overseer for one year. He did a creditable job, but was released on January 1, 1836. The now ex-overseer went to La Grange, Tennessee, acquired some land and more slaves, and farmed for himself until his death in 1855 or 1856.[95]

The success or failure of the plantation depended on Beanland's efforts, and he certainly strove, with a large degree of success, to make the venture profitable. Bassett thinks "there is no reason to believe that he did not have ability in husbandry, as in planting, cultivating, and harvesting the crops."[96] Also, Beanland had "many sterling qualities. He was a man of his word, he had good judgment in the conduct of the affairs of the plantation and he met opposition with a stout heart. . . . He made it known that he was master, and having taken that position he stood ready to make his assertion effective."[97] He may have been too harsh, but the situation may have justified all his actions. The only witness against him, besides the slaves, was Dr. Caldwell, "who was apt to form his opinions quickly and without taking all things into consideration."

Bassett reaches the conclusion that "slavery was just slavery. It was neither the thing of horror the abolitionists thought nor the benign institution its defenders depicted."[98] Beanland, who had no "delusions about slavery," seemed not to realize—at least, not in 1833 or 1834—that it was an institution, but dealt with it as the daily problems of Jack, Ben, Willy, or Hardy. Be that as it may, he utilized the occupation of overseer as a steppingstone to becoming a slaveholder himself.

SAMUEL HENDERSON

Samuel Henderson was born in Knox County, Tennessee, on October 8, 1804, and was taken to the upper portion of the Louisiana Territory by his father, then to Maury County in 1811 or 1812, and finally settled in Williamson County in the fall of 1813. There he worked with his father until the latter's death in the late 1820's, and then Samuel became a planter in his own name. His journal does not begin until 1834, generally contains nothing more than the bare outline or briefest summary of the day's events, and has very few entries prior to the 1840's that are of importance to the student of plantation life.

Henderson was a smaller planter than the Polks or Anderson, and misfortune seemed to beset him at every turn. Work on the plantation proceeded in a seemingly ceaseless round of planting corn, plowing corn, stripping fodder, cutting millet, pulling corn, sowing wheat, and killing hogs. The only unusual recorded event for 1847 was the height of the Harpeth River, which carried away a "great deal" of his fencing.[99] The following March 20 the river had gone on another rampage. This time it spoiled 1,200 or 1,500 pounds of Henderson's flour, 100 bushels of "corn and other things," and washed away 200 or 300 panels of his fences.

On January 8, 1849, Henderson sold his town (Franklin) property to a Dr. Morton, and began moving to his new place on Five Mile Creek. At this time—and before—he was grinding his own flour, and noted that his new Hotchkiss cast wheel ran well in the mill.[100] The number of hands on the place must have been rather large, for between December 7 and December 18, 1849, he killed upwards of 100 hogs, weighing 20,497 pounds. After allowing the meat to take salt, Henderson stored some of it in ashes and cobs, some was coated with lime, and some with black pepper.[101]

In 1850 Henderson employed Jo Andrews to be his overseer. Andrews received $130 for the year, 500 pounds of pork and corn meal,[102] and, supposedly, the usual house and cook. It is not known whether Henderson had an overseer previous to, or after, this year, for that was the only entry he ever made on the subject. He must not have allowed his overseer to punish his slaves; on April 29, 1850, Henderson whipped Bill and I. F. Hughes' boy, Marsh, for fighting.

The first cotton crop that Henderson raised was in 1850. It was planted between April 15 and 18, and the Williamson Countian received $450.03 for the 15,103 pounds of seed cotton produced.[103] Again, the Harpeth flooded; this time it destroyed practically all the early corn. Henderson did not record the amount of money he made on the farm in any one year, but one notes that he was careful to alternate cotton and clover so as not to bleed the soil of its fertility. Rye was likewise used as a soil restorer. Different kinds of wheat—"May," "bearded," and "Mediterranean" —were raised. In 1851 he made 335 bushels of wheat and seventy bushels of rye, but the following year these productions fell off to 275 and thirty-five bushels, respectively.[104]

The "heavy frost and hard freeze" of May 2, 1851, destroyed much of the corn, killed the fruit, and "even the leaves of some trees," but, fortunately, did not injure Henderson's cotton. If it was not the river, it was the unusual and variable weather. The cotton crop for that year amounted to only nine bales after the toll was paid,[105] and no other entry relative to cotton was found until the end of the war.

The journal after 1852 gives practically no information concerning farm productions. From that date until 1865 it is scarcely more than a catalogue of plowing, planting, clearing, births, deaths, misfortunes, and the number and weight of hogs killed.

For the light that they may throw on the number of people who had to be fed on the plantation the hog killing records are given in summary form for the years 1851–1864, inclusive: sixty-one hogs, 9,994 pounds; seventy hogs, 12,757 pounds; eighty-four hogs, 15,146 pounds; sixty-two hogs, 9,310 pounds; sixty hogs, 10,995 pounds; fifty-one hogs, 10,503 pounds; sixty-six hogs, 11,820 pounds; fifty-seven hogs, 9,857 pounds; fifty-three hogs, not weighed; forty-one hogs, 5,769 pounds; thirty-eight hogs, 5,301 pounds; forty-one hogs, 6,220 pounds; twenty-three hogs, 3,730 pounds; and twenty-six hogs, 3,612 pounds. It will be noted that even before the beginning of the war the amount of meat slaughtered shows a definite decrease, with the low in weight being reached in 1864. By that time Henderson did not have so many slaves to feed, as death and the Federals had taken their tolls. Births on the plantation scarcely more than offset the deaths.

Many of the children died in early infancy, so many, in fact, that one is led to believe that some of Henderson's Negroes might have been diseased. Of the twenty children born to Chainey, Mary,

Peggy, Fanny, and Amanda from 1849 to 1863, five died soon after birth. Their span of life ranged from one week to one year. Peggy, the most prolific, lost three out of eight, Mary one out of seven, and Chainey, deaf and dumb, her only one. Peggy gave birth to a boy of "quite yellow color" on June 6, 1850, and Amanda's only child was yellow.

Deaths from various causes and sickness were rather frequent at Henderson's place. Bill drowned on June 15, 1846, and measles and dysentery struck at the same time in July and August, 1853. Twenty Negroes had the former malady and two died of the latter. Two years later Henry, nearly nineteen years old, died of "Hemorhage and Disease of the lungs," and on November 27, 1856, Lewis, aged fourteen years, died of "Titanic occassioned [sic] by a burn which he had from falling into the fire when he had an epilectic fit." Henderson became concerned over the three deaths of 1857. Old Tom[106] died on May 7; Nancy, seventeen or eighteen, on May 18; and Jim, twenty, on September 17.[107] On the last date Henderson recorded: "It appears like I am under the frown of Providence for I am losing all my negroes and becoming poor. Lord help me to bear the misfortune without a murmur."

The only death of 1859 was that of Harriet, who fell down in a fit of apoplexy or "disease of the heart" while repairing fences. She was forty or forty-five years old and in seemingly good health.[108] Man, about twenty years old, died of pneumonia the following February 28.

Henderson was reasonably well situated in 1860. The unpublished agricultural schedule for Williamson County for that year credits him with the following holdings and productions: 300 improved and 175 unimproved acres valued at $31,000; $200 worth of farm implements; the livestock of four horses, two asses and mules, four milch cows, two oxen, ten other cattle, twenty-five sheep, and one hundred swine, were valued at $900; 2,500 bushels of corn, 200 bushels of wheat, 300 bushels of rye, and fifty pounds of wool.[109] This enumeration does not look complete; Henderson would certainly have objected to the omission of the value of the slaughtered animals, and from his later remarks one is led to believe that he surely had more horses than are listed above. Henderson may have been completely overlooked in the 1850 census, for his name could not be located on the schedule.

If Henderson thought he was getting poor in 1859, he must have felt poverty-stricken after 1862 and early 1863. In September and October of the former year three of his slaves ran off to join the Federals at Nashville. On March 31, 1863, the Federals took his bay filly and had "frequently" taken his bacon. In addition to this "awful state of things," Henderson said that recently Mrs. Hughes' Negroes had attempted to poison her. By April 13 the Union soldiers had taken all the horses and mules except "two little work mules and two mule colts . . . all my hams . . . good deal of my corn and all my hay and near all my fodder . . . I will certainly go crazy." Then, two more Negro men left, and the women would not remain with persons to whom they had been hired.

Henderson was broken in spirit by the theft of his property, and he left on April 11, 1864, to visit his daughter in Hayesville, Ohio. Depredations continued in the community, and he records, under the above date, that during his absence Mr. Chadwell's Negroes "and others" had been robbed and one of Mr. Williams' Negroes had been killed. Six months later two robbers came to his house, but his Negroes notified him of their presence. Henderson attacked them with "shot gun in hand and drove them off."

Henderson again turned to cotton in 1865, and in July of that year bought 640 acres near Trenton, Gibson County, for $5,000. He had lost heavily by the war, and his journal for late 1865 and 1866 contains the record of the purchases of many articles, animals, and pieces of machinery to replace those that had been taken, stolen, or destroyed during the previous four years.

ROBERT H. CARTMELL

Robert H. Cartmell, of near Jackson, Tennessee, began farming operations in 1849 when he was twenty-one years of age, and during the next four years he produced 307 bales from the 598 acres planted to cotton.[110] By 1853 the young planter was lamenting the fact that a great many of the farmers neglected the small things such as stock, plows, and tools, and was decrying earth butchery. Systematic rotation, manuring, deep plowing, and clovering must be "attended to," he said, in order to reclaim the old fields.

It appears that Cartmell worked his father's slaves—thirteen of them—in 1849, and that his slaves and his father's "hands" worked together in 1851 and 1852. His independent operations began in 1853 when he bought 600 acres from his father for $4,000 and worked twelve hands which included one girl and four small boys. He counted them nine hands and concluded that "they will barely make that much."[111] In June of that year he added 250 acres of bottom land to his holdings at the cost of $10.40 per acre.[112] This first year was a good one: the first child to survive was born on September 27; he paid more than $1,200 on the river bottom, and had paid his father $2,500.

Cartmell had his problems, however, as John, Ned, and Dave, all under fifteen years of age, ran away for the first of several times. John had been chastised; they all ran away; and upon return all were punished on August 13. Two months later, the master said that whipping "does but little good, as negroes, especially young ones, *will not* work unless there be some one to see them and *make* them do." Shortly thereafter he again recorded his feelings that "negroes are unpleasant . . . requiring constant watching . . . feel an interest in nothing—*only punctual* in coming *regularly* when their meat gives out."[113] To remedy the situation he employed the "young and inexperienced" Deberry as overseer for $12.50 per month. Cartmell thought Deberry's presence "with the chaps" would keep them from cutting up too much cotton and would keep them working.[114] Plans were made to move the cabins which were described as "very indifferent," located in a muddy place, and dangerous for the children because the stock moved about them at liberty.

The presence of Deberry did not detain Dave—he was off again in June of 1854. Word from Cartmell's cook that a free Negro woman was connected with his flight apparently prompted Cartmell to state that "I *would like very* much to catch that *wench* or any other free negro about my premises—there is no doubt that they are an injury to our Negroes making them dissatisfied & causing stricter discipline to be exercised." There is no entry regarding the punishment of the runaway.[115] Four months later the flight of Dave prompted his owner to the conclusion that he should whip him severely or sell him to the *"southern* country" if he were lucky enough to recover the slave. Dave was suspected of being involved in housebreaking and of having a pass. Dave was recovered in Ballard County, Kentucky—the jail fee alone amounting to $95.33. The troublesome one must have been whipped "severely" for in August, 1855, Cartmell still had him.[116]

In the fall of 1855 Cartmell complained that his area was "no cotton country," but since the region was shut off from the world except by wagon communication cotton was the only crop that would bear the transportation. "Sorry crops" and *"heavy taxes"* made farming an "uphill business." He seemed, however, to be doing very well: his fifty bales (from ninety acres) brought only 7¢ per pound but the "clear profits" of $1,178.29 were "near enough for all practical purposes." He paid the balance on the river bottom land and gave "Pa" the cotton notes that were due on December 25, 1856.[117] In 1858 expenses on the cotton crop amounted to $948.59, leaving a profit of $1,647.27.[118] Good fortune had not always smiled on him, but only in one of the years under study did he suffer a loss—$10.87 in 1854. His highest profit before 1858 had been the $1,367.04 for 1856.

The Madison County operator did not always fulfill his desire to go into Jackson on January 1 or 2, but at times he did get there for the selling and hiring of slaves. He indicated that there was always a big crowd on hand for purposes of business and celebration. Negro traders also passed through the countryside, for on September 24, 1857, Cartmell bought a sixteen-year-old girl for $1,250—"high." The girl was to replace—according to the wishes of his wife, Mary Jane—little Mary "who is not house *girl to hurt."*

The number of entries on punishments and the comments on discipline indicate that young Cartmell may have been rather stern when dealing with a shirker or a fugitive. However, he very definitely had a softer streak in his nature. On January 30, 1857, he recorded that Dick, who had been sick for four days and attended by Dr. Fenner, died of pneumonia. This was the first death among Cartmell's slaves since he began independent operations. Dick was a *"good and* faithful servant—well disposed, entirely peaceable, attentive to his business—in fine Dick was a *correct man."* After Dick's burial the next day, Cartmell said he had been a "great help" and "I hope he is better off and in a better world." Four months later young Dick, aged eleven, died of the same disease and was buried by "his daddy."

These few gleanings from the diary of this young farmer do not by any means give a good picture of his operations. They do indicate that he was a rather perceptive young man, that he was conscious of some of the major problems that confronted the farmer and the nation, that he wanted his work performed with efficiency and punctuality, and, as his production shows, that he was fairly successful in his farming activities.

The study of the above planters does not give a complete picture of any of them, but taken on the whole, it does show the life of the larger slaveholder in the Volunteer State. All was not easy; Anderson and Cartmell found it difficult to keep their slaves working; the Polks had a great deal of difficulty with the overseers and runaway slaves; Henderson was pestered by disease among his Negroes, and then much of his life earnings was destroyed or lured away by the Federal troops. It is true that none[119] of these was a really big planter, but they belonged to the group that held from twenty to fifty slaves, and that group owned a large majority of the slaves that were held by the farmers of Tennessee. None of the group studied above grew rich rapidly, nor did any of them seem to lead lives of leisure and self-satisfaction. Some of the planters in Tennessee probably lived as the large planters have been pictured, but they were doubtless very few in number. Slavery in Tennessee had neither the grandeur nor the harshness that it did in some of the more southern states.

Précis

Parts of this study are new only in that they are applicable to the state of Tennessee for which no previous monograph on slavery has appeared. In this area of investigation no material startlingly different from that found in older studies for other states was discovered.

Legislation concerning slavery and slaves in Tennessee so combined the civil and common law that the slave had characteristics, rights, and privileges of a person as well as a chattel. The laws were not as restrictive as those of some of the states of the lower South, but they did become noticeably more severe after the radical abolition movement and the Nat Turner insurrection. It should be borne in mind, however, that many of the post-1831 laws were precautionary in nature—they were ready to be put into operation should the occasion demand. There is no discernible difference in the life and activity of the slaves in the later period of the institution: owners still sent them "abroad" without passes; they continued to teach them to read and to write and to give them religious instruction; the courts thought it universally accepted that the slave was the agent of the master whether he had written instructions or not; some masters continued to let their slaves live as free or quasi-free persons. Slaveowners made it a practice to violate the code whenever violation was to their advantage or inclination. Slavery was more a government of men than of laws.

As was to be expected, there were people who hired and bought slaves as well as slaves who attempted to escape their bondage—either because of their own desires or because of the intervention of others. The practice of hiring in Tennessee seems to have provided a small, mobile slave labor force to supplement the free laborer and appears to have been accompanied by a minimum of difficulties. Sale of slaves naturally occurred from the beginning of the institution in Tennessee, but many individuals would not sell unless the slaves were to be kept in families or at least close to the area to which they were accustomed. In spite of the legal prohibition of interstate trading, it was carried on by Tennesseans; this trade, however—even after re-legalization—never assumed the proportions it did in some of the other states. Fugitive slaves and "emissaries of abolitionism" were problems of more significance than they were in the lower South, but they might better be termed vexations than serious difficulties.

There was a strong antislavery sentiment in Tennessee in the second and third decades of the nineteenth century, but various factors combined to lessen, and virtually to dry up, this attitude by 1840. It should be noted that the shift to a defense of slavery did not come as soon as has often been stated, and that in the 1834 constitutional convention there was a strong minority in favor of emancipation. Even when the turn to defense was more nearly completed, practically all who spoke for slavery saw it as the only feasible solution to the race problem. The institution was not supported as a "positive good"; it remained the "necessary evil."

Antislavery sentiment probably had the effect of ameliorating the condition of some of the slaves, but evidence on this point is rather intangible. There were some harsh masters in Tennessee, but in the main the holdings were small, the owners worked side by side with their slaves, and the severity of the regime found in the rice and sugar areas was not present in the Volunteer State.

The statistical portion of this study does represent a radical departure from previous analyses of slavery, and it is by use of this material that an insight may be gained into the population structure of the state, that the production of the slaveholder and nonslaveholder can be studied, and that the relationship of landownership and slaveownership to each other and to production may be examined. As a result, the validity of a number of earlier generalizations on the "peculiar institution" are laid open to serious question. Only a few of the salient points will be restated or reiterated here, and it should be remembered that these are based on analyses of data for 18,718 heads of agricultural families in 1850 and 20,558 in 1860.

In the first place, it should be noted that landownership was rather widespread: 76.32 per cent in 1850 and 76.01 per cent in 1860. Slaveownership was 38.77 per cent in 1850 and 37.00 per cent ten years later. The Middle Tennessee counties showed a higher percentage of ownership than did the other areas, but also experienced a greater decrease of ownership in the last prewar decade. West Tennessee remained exactly constant in the percentage of individuals holding slaves. For the entire sample, the slaveholders increased only 4.81 per cent, while the landowners increased 9.38 per cent, or approximately the same as the increase (9.83 per cent) in the total heads of agricultural families. However, slightly more than nine out of every ten of the slaveowners were landowners; this category increased between 1850 and 1860 even though they constituted a smaller percentage of the total landowners in the latter year. To put it a little differently, the non-landowning slaveholder decreased in the last ante-bellum decade and the nonslaveholding landowner increased in relation to the total heads.[1]

More than two thirds of the slaveowners held fewer than ten slaves both in 1850 and 1860, and their total holdings amounted to a little more than one fourth of the slaves—28.19 per cent in 1850 and 26.82 per cent in 1860. At the other extremity, the approximately two per cent who had fifty or more slaves owned 14.07 per cent of the slaves in 1850 and 16.26 per cent in 1860. More than forty per cent of the slaves were held by persons who had from ten to twenty-nine each. The fact that the average slave-holdings of the non-landowners declined while those of the land-owners increased may indicate a definite relationship between slaves and land, but it may also be little more than the reflection of the normal conditions in an agricultural society where land was the fundamental requirement and slavery merely formed a part of the labor supply.

The percentage of the improved acreage operated by slave-owners varied greatly in the state, but altogether it amounted to 66.46 per cent of the total in 1850 and the slaveholders' farms averaged 119.49 acres. Ten years later the figures were 68.07 and 156.73. The average farm of the nonslaveowners increased from 42.68 acres to 50.24 acres. The total number of acres tended by nonslaveowners had increased 27.96 per cent in the ten years, while that of the slaveholders showed an increment of 37.67 per cent. Especially, it should be emphasized that the increase in the number of nonslaveholding landowners between 1850 and 1860, together with the upward trend in the number of acres they oper-ated—as well as their location in the various counties—contra-dicts the oft-repeated contention that the slaveowners were driving the nonslaveowners from the good lands and reducing them to a position of economic and political vassalage.

This contradiction is further sustained by an analysis of pro-duction figures of the various groups. In cotton production—where the slaveowner supposedly enjoyed his greatest advantage —the nonslaveowner increased his average yield (or yield per operator) by 58.97 per cent in ten years, while that of the slave-owner increased by only 50.79 per cent. In addition, the average yield of the owners of thirty or more slaves—the island of "plant-ers" in the sea of Tennessee farmers—increased by only 35.77 per cent, but the numerical increase in that group resulted in its producing a larger percentage of the slaveowners' and of the total crop in 1860 than in 1850. There were fewer total producers in 1860 than in 1850; production was up by 41.48 per cent.

In the tobacco counties, total producers increased remarkably in the years under survey and even though the slaveowners formed 3.80 per cent less of the total in 1860 they produced only 0.36 per cent less of the total crop. Here, however, the production of the nonslaveowner was about one third that of the slaveowner; in the cotton counties it was approximately one fifth. The slave-owners did not produce as high a percentage of the tobacco crop as they did of the cotton, but they more nearly "held their own" against the nonslaveowner. The owners of thirty or more slaves were relatively less important in tobacco than in cotton production.

The average yield of all producers of cotton and tobacco increased between 1850 and 1860, but average corn production declined 11.54 per cent; the numerical decrease (80 bushels) was identical, but the percentage was 16.26 for the nonslaveowners and 5.73 for the slaveowners. The average yield of the former was about one third that of the latter. Quite contrary to the accepted idea, the slaveowners produced *less* of the cotton and tobacco but *more* of the corn in 1860 than in 1850. However, the average production of the owners of thirty or more slaves decreased 17.23 per cent, far more than the average decline. It was, then, the smaller slaveowner who kept corn production from slipping farther than it did in Tennessee.

Tennessee's standing in the national agricultural picture was not as high in 1860 as in 1850, but her economy was not dominated by any one crop or any one group. Slaveowners and nonslaveowners, landowners and non-landowners, all contributed to the gradual increase of the improved acreage and the rapid augmentation of land values between 1850 and 1860. Ownership of land and slaves was rather widespread; there were a few planters in the traditional sense; some poor whites were unable to sustain themselves by their own efforts; tenants and sharecroppers did exist; but the great majority of the farmers had few or no slaves, operated a medium-sized tract of land, and approached as near to self-sufficiency as did the large slaveowners. The great mass of the population were the plain folk, the yeomen.

APPENDIX A

Landowning Slaveowners, 1850*

County			1-4 Slaves	5-9 Slaves	10-14 Slaves	15-19 Slaves	20-29 Slaves	30-39 Slaves	40-49 Slaves	50-74 Slaves	75-99 Slaves	100-199 Slaves	200+ Slaves	Total	Average Holding
Johnson	Owners	Number	29	10	4		2							45	4.71
		% of Total	64.44	22.22	8.89		4.44								
	Slaves	Number	61	66	44		41							212	
		% of Total	28.77	31.13	20.75		19.34								
Greene	Owners	Number	133	44	11	5	2	2						197	4.49
		% of Total	67.51	22.34	5.58	2.54	1.02	1.02							
	Slaves	Number	283	286	126	85	43	61						884	
		% of Total	32.01	32.33	14.25	9.62	4.86	6.90							
Fentress	Owners	Number	36	5	1									42	2.93
		% of Total	85.71	11.90	2.38										
	Slaves	Number	72	38	13									123	
		% of Total	58.54	30.89	10.57										
DeKalb	Owners	Number	86	34	6		1							127	3.74
		% of Total	67.72	26.77	4.72		0.79								
	Slaves	Number	167	216	67		25							475	
		% of Total	35.16	45.47	14.11		5.26								
Lincoln	Owners	Number	268	166	64	37	23	7	4	4				573	7.31
		% of Total	46.77	28.97	11.17	6.46	4.01	1.22	0.70	0.70					
	Slaves	Number	546	1134	740	619	523	243	168	213				4186	
		% of Total	13.04	27.09	17.68	14.79	12.49	5.81	4.01	5.09					
Maury	Owners	Number	328	220	114	72	71	29	15	23	4	4		880	11.68
		% of Total	37.27	25.00	12.95	8.18	8.07	3.30	1.70	2.61	0.45	0.45			
	Slaves	Number	740	1518	1311	1200	1670	972	660	1346	335	522		10274	
		% of Total	7.20	14.78	12.76	11.68	16.25	9.46	6.42	13.10	3.26	5.08			
Davidson	Owners	Number	276	207	117	67	53	30	10	12	3	2	1	778	11.32
		% of Total	35.48	26.61	15.04	8.61	6.81	3.86	1.29	1.54	0.39	0.26	0.13		
	Slaves	Number	589	1413	1362	1130	1256	1013	425	730	271	289	332	8810	
		% of Total	6.69	16.04	15.46	12.83	14.26	11.50	4.82	8.29	3.08	3.28	3.77		
Robertson	Owners	Number	294	123	79	29	28	7		1		1		562	7.06
		% of Total	52.31	21.89	14.06	5.16	4.98	1.25		0.18		0.18			
	Slaves	Number	616	842	926	487	666	237		50		143		3967	
		% of Total	15.53	21.23	23.34	12.28	16.79	5.97		1.26		3.60			

188

County														Total	% of Total
Montgomery	Owners	Number	262	173	100	62	56	16	10	6		1		686	9.99
		% of Total	38.19	25.22	14.58	9.04	8.16	2.33	1.46	0.87		0.15			
	Slaves	Number	581	1185	1174	1036	1356	528	450	357		189		6856	
		% of Total	8.47	17.28	17.12	15.11	19.78	7.70	6.56	5.21		2.76			
Hardin	Owners	Number	64	24	13	4	1							106	5.13
		% of Total	60.38	22.64	12.26	3.77	0.94								
	Slaves	Number	146	156	150	67	25							544	
		% of Total	26.84	28.68	27.57	12.32	4.60								
Henry	Owners	Number	224	127	50	21	16	12	5	3		1		459	7.65
		% of Total	48.80	27.67	10.89	4.58	3.49	2.61	1.09	0.65		0.22			
	Slaves	Number	493	835	563	350	376	419	211	158		105		3510	
		% of Total	14.05	23.79	16.04	9.97	10.71	11.94	6.01	4.50		2.99			
Gibson	Owners	Number	273	145	40	42	21	2		4				527	6.70
		% of Total	51.80	27.51	7.59	7.97	3.98	0.38		0.76					
	Slaves	Number	582	1002	475	691	485	71		226				3532	
		% of Total	16.48	28.37	13.45	19.56	13.73	2.01		6.40					
Dyer	Owners	Number	125	46	23	7	13	2	1					217	6.32
		% of Total	57.60	21.20	10.60	3.23	5.99	0.92	0.46						
	Slaves	Number	265	304	271	110	311	67	43					1371	
		% of Total	19.33	22.17	19.77	8.02	22.68	4.89	3.14						
Haywood	Owners	Number	163	106	72	50	50	27	9	19	2	1		499	13.27
		% of Total	32.67	21.24	14.43	10.02	10.02	5.41	1.80	3.81	0.40	0.20			
	Slaves	Number	344	732	862	846	1195	894	397	1068	171	114		6623	
		% of Total	5.19	11.05	13.02	12.77	18.04	13.50	5.99	16.13	2.58	1.72			
Fayette	Owners	Number	239	192	136	62	103	50	19	27	6		1	835	14.27
		% of Total	28.62	22.99	16.29	7.43	12.34	5.99	2.23	3.23	0.72		0.13		
	Slaves	Number	544	1328	1572	1036	2481	1717	831	1655	520		235	11919	
		% of Total	4.56	11.14	13.19	8.69	20.82	14.41	6.97	13.89	4.36		1.97		
Totals	Owners	Number	2800	1622	830	458	440	184	73	99	15	10	2	6533	9.69
		% of Total	42.86	24.83	12.70	7.01	6.74	2.82	1.12	1.52	0.23	0.15	0.03		
	Slaves	Number	6029	11055	9656	7657	10453	6222	3185	5803	1297	1362	567	63286	
		% of Total	9.53	17.47	15.26	12.10	16.52	9.83	5.03	9.17	2.05	2.15	0.90		

*Compiled from Schedules I, II and IV, Census of 1850 (unpublished).

189

Non-Landowning Slaveowners, 1850*

County		1-4 Slaves	5-9 Slaves	10-14 Slaves	15-19 Slaves	20-29 Slaves	30-39 Slaves	40-49 Slaves	50-74 Slaves	75-99 Slaves	100-199 Slaves	200+ Slaves	Total	Average Holding
Johnson	Owners Number	2											2	2.00
	% of Total	100.00												
	Slaves Number	4											4	
	% of Total	100.00												
Greene	Owners Number	8	4	1									13	3.92
	% of Total	61.54	30.77	7.69										
	Slaves Number	12	29	10									51	
	% of Total	23.53	56.86	19.61										
Fentress	Owners Number	2	1										3	2.33
	% of Total	66.67	33.33											
	Slaves Number	2	5										7	
	% of Total	28.57	71.43											
DeKalb	Owners Number	14	2		1								17	3.53
	% of Total	82.35	11.76		5.88									
	Slaves Number	34	11		15								60	
	% of Total	56.67	18.33		25.00									
Lincoln	Owners Number	43	14	3				1					61	4.16
	% of Total	70.49	22.95	4.92				1.64						
	Slaves Number	89	85	35				45					254	
	% of Total	35.04	33.36	13.78				17.72						
Maury	Owners Number	79	32	13	7	5		1	2				139	6.57
	% of Total	56.83	23.02	9.35	5.04	3.60		0.72	1.44					
	Slaves Number	151	206	159	117	112		42	126				913	
	% of Total	16.54	22.56	17.42	12.81	12.27		4.60	13.80					
Davidson	Owners Number	64	22	11	3	4	2	1					107	5.85
	% of Total	59.81	20.56	10.28	2.80	3.74	1.87	0.93						
	Slaves Number	114	135	126	53	87	65	46					626	
	% of Total	18.21	21.57	20.13	8.47	13.80	10.38	7.35						
Robertson	Owners Number	12											12	2.00
	% of Total	100.00												
	Slaves Number	24											24	
	% of Total	100.00												

		1	2	3	4	5	6	7	8	9	Number	% of Total
Montgomery	Owners	Number	42	22	4	3	2					73	
		% of Total	57.53	30.14	5.48	4.11	2.74						5.11
	Slaves	Number	73	157	45	52	46					373	
		% of Total	19.57	42.09	12.06	13.94	12.33						
Hardin	Owners	Number	2									2	
		% of Total	100.00										2.00
	Slaves	Number	4									4	
		% of Total	100.00										
Henry	Owners	Number	21	6	2					2		31	
		% of Total	67.74	19.35	6.45					6.45			7.03
	Slaves	Number	44	38	26					110		218	
		% of Total	20.18	17.43	11.93					50.46			
Gibson	Owners	Number	46	8								54	
		% of Total	85.19	14.81									2.65
	Slaves	Number	89	54								143	
		% of Total	62.24	37.76									
Dyer	Owners	Number	10	2			1					13	
		% of Total	76.92	15.38			7.69						3.62
	Slaves	Number	14	13			20					47	
		% of Total	29.79	27.66			42.55						
Haywood	Owners	Number	41	33	7	7	2	3	3	2	2	100	
		% of Total	41.00	33.00	7.00	7.00	2.00	3.00	3.00	2.00	2.00		10.59
	Slaves	Number	89	229	80	114	47	97	131	102	170	1059	
		% of Total	8.40	21.62	7.55	10.76	4.44	9.16	12.37	9.63	16.05		
Fayette	Owners	Number	38	34	14	6	4	1				97	
		% of Total	39.18	35.05	14.43	6.19	4.12	1.03					7.27
	Slaves	Number	88	230	165	98	92	32				707	
		% of Total	12.48	32.62	23.40	13.90	13.05	4.54					
Totals	Owners	Number	424	180	55	27	18	6	6	6	2	724	
		% of Total	58.56	24.86	7.60	3.73	2.49	0.83	0.83	0.83	0.28		6.20
	Slaves	Number	831	1192	646	449	404	194	264	338	170	4488	
		% of Total	18.52	26.56	14.39	10.00	9.00	4.32	5.88	7.53	3.79		

*Compiled from Schedules I, II, and IV, Census of 1850 (unpublished).

Landowning Slaveowners, 1860*

County		1-4 Slaves	5-9 Slaves	10-14 Slaves	15-19 Slaves	20-29 Slaves	30-39 Slaves	40-49 Slaves	50-74 Slaves	75-99 Slaves	100-199 Slaves	200+ Slaves	Total	Average Holding
Johnson	Owners Number	21	18	2									41	4.59
	% of Total	51.22	43.90	4.88										
	Slaves Number	42	122	24									188	
	% of Total	22.34	68.89	12.77										
Greene	Owners Number	137	50	13	9		1	1					211	4.71
	% of Total	64.93	23.70	6.16	4.27		0.47	0.47						
	Slaves Number	280	324	158	151		39	41					993	
	% of Total	28.20	32.63	15.91	15.21		3.93	4.13						
Fentress	Owners Number	33	8	5									46	3.76
	% of Total	71.74	17.39	10.87										
	Slaves Number	62	51	60									173	
	% of Total	35.84	29.48	34.64										
DeKalb	Owners Number	99	54	14	1	4							172	4.93
	% of Total	57.56	31.40	8.14	0.58	2.33								
	Slaves Number	216	374	155	17	86							848	
	% of Total	25.47	44.10	18.28	2.00	10.14								
Lincoln	Owners Number	280	178	90	23	30	7	7	5	3	1		624	8.22
	% of Total	44.87	28.53	14.42	3.69	4.81	1.12	1.12	0.80	0.48	0.16			
	Slaves Number	618	1177	1041	369	709	235	294	322	260	105		5130	
	% of Total	12.05	22.94	20.29	7.19	13.82	4.58	5.73	6.28	5.07	2.05			
Maury	Owners Number	362	249	163	85	88	50	14	12	11	2		1036	11.80
	% of Total	34.94	24.03	15.73	8.20	8.49	4.83	1.35	1.16	1.06	0.19			
	Slaves Number	848	1757	1918	1416	2072	1671	635	753	937	221		12228	
	% of Total	6.93	14.37	15.69	11.58	16.94	13.67	5.19	6.16	7.66	1.81			
Davidson	Owners Number	191	180	109	43	60	20	7	15	5	2		632	12.04
	% of Total	30.22	28.48	17.25	6.80	9.49	3.16	1.11	2.37	0.79	0.32			
	Slaves Number	418	1205	1292	710	1460	671	314	875	417	247		7609	
	% of Total	5.49	15.84	16.98	9.33	19.19	8.82	4.13	11.50	5.48	3.25			
Robertson	Owners Number	290	174	65	39	21	4	1	2		1	1	598	7.41
	% of Total	48.49	29.10	10.87	6.52	3.51	0.67	0.17	0.33		0.17	0.17		
	Slaves Number	644	1165	788	656	491	133	43	132		104	274	4430	
	% of Total	14.54	26.30	17.79	14.81	11.08	3.00	0.97	2.98		2.35	6.19		

County			1	2	3	4	5	6	7	8	9	10	11	Total	Slaves per Owner
Montgomery	Owners	Number	175	150	90	46	66	29	9	11	2	1		579	12.45
		% of Total	30.22	25.91	15.54	7.94	11.40	5.01	1.55	1.90	0.35	0.17			
	Slaves	Number	425	1020	1072	786	1587	980	405	671	158	105		7209	
		% of Total	5.90	14.15	14.87	10.90	22.01	13.59	5.62	9.31	2.19	1.46			
Hardin	Owners	Number	107	47	18	10	7	4	1	2				196	7.00
		% of Total	54.59	23.98	9.18	5.10	3.57	2.04	0.51	1.02					
	Slaves	Number	225	317	208	170	161	136	45	110				1372	
		% of Total	16.40	23.10	15.16	12.39	11.73	9.91	3.28	8.02					
Henry	Owners	Number	206	159	74	29	29	9	7	5	2			520	8.95
		% of Total	39.62	30.58	14.23	5.58	5.58	1.73	1.35	0.96	0.38				
	Slaves	Number	451	1046	868	493	668	331	319	317	183			4656	
		% of Total	9.69	22.47	18.64	10.59	14.35	6.68	6.85	6.81	3.93				
Gibson	Owners	Number	394	219	90	35	24	15	2	4				783	6.88
		% of Total	50.32	27.97	11.49	4.47	3.07	1.92	0.26	0.51					
	Slaves	Number	869	1502	1060	577	530	496	85	270				5389	
		% of Total	16.13	27.87	19.67	10.71	9.83	9.20	1.58	5.01					
Dyer	Owners	Number	164	73	29	17	16	4	2	3				308	7.24
		% of Total	53.25	23.70	9.42	5.52	5.19	1.30	0.65	0.97					
	Slaves	Number	337	496	334	286	383	144	90	160				2230	
		% of Total	15.11	22.24	14.98	12.83	17.17	6.46	4.04	7.17					
Haywood	Owners	Number	150	128	73	53	65	23	17	27	5	3	2	546	16.49
		% of Total	27.47	23.44	13.37	9.71	11.90	4.21	3.11	4.95	0.92	0.55	0.37		
	Slaves	Number	331	891	855	898	1587	792	754	1643	418	410	423	9002	
		% of Total	3.68	9.90	9.50	9.98	17.63	8.80	8.38	18.25	4.64	4.55	4.70		
Fayette	Owners	Number	155	158	126	69	68	46	33	24	6	6		691	16.58
		% of Total	22.43	22.87	18.23	9.99	9.84	6.66	4.78	3.47	0.87	0.87			
	Slaves	Number	381	1109	1492	1163	1615	1582	1446	1443	516	712		11459	
		% of Total	3.32	9.68	13.02	10.15	14.09	13.81	12.62	12.59	4.50	6.21			
Totals	Owners	Number	2764	1845	961	459	478	212	101	110	34	16	3	6983	10.44
		% of Total	39.58	26.42	13.76	6.57	6.85	3.04	1.45	1.58	0.49	0.23	0.04		
	Slaves	Number	6147	12556	11325	7692	11349	7190	4471	6696	2889	1904	697	72916	
		% of Total	8.43	17.22	15.53	10.55	15.56	9.86	6.13	9.18	3.96	2.61	0.96		

*Compiled from Schedules I, II, and IV, Census of 1860 (unpublished).

193

Non-Landowning Slaveowners, 1860*

County			1-4 Slaves	5-9 Slaves	10-14 Slaves	15-19 Slaves	20-29 Slaves	30-39 Slaves	40-49 Slaves	50-74 Slaves	75-99 Slaves	100-199 Slaves	200+ Slaves	Total	Average Holding
Johnson	Owners	Number	5	1		1								7	4.43
		% of Total	71.43	14.29		14.29									
	Slaves	Number	9	6		16								31	
		% of Total	29.03	19.35		51.61									
Greene	Owners	Number	7	2										9	3.11
		% of Total	77.78	22.22											
	Slaves	Number	13	15										28	
		% of Total	46.43	53.57											
Fentress	Owners	Number	4											4	2.00
		% of Total	100.00												
	Slaves	Number	8											8	
		% of Total	100.00												
DeKalb	Owners	Number	9	2										11	2.64
		% of Total	81.82	18.18											
	Slaves	Number	17	12										29	
		% of Total	58.62	41.38											
Lincoln	Owners	Number	54	14	5	2								75	3.53
		% of Total	72.00	18.67	6.67	2.67									
	Slaves	Number	100	77	56	32								265	
		% of Total	37.74	29.06	21.13	12.08									
Maury	Owners	Number	72	28	13	4								117	4.65
		% of Total	61.54	23.93	11.11	3.42									
	Slaves	Number	142	181	151	70								544	
		% of Total	26.10	33.27	27.76	12.87									
Davidson	Owners	Number	50	20	5	2	1	1	1					80	5.23
		% of Total	62.50	25.00	6.25	2.50	1.25	1.25	1.25						
	Slaves	Number	88	137	60	31	25	34	43					418	
		% of Total	21.05	32.78	14.35	7.42	5.98	8.13	10.29						
Robertson	Owners	Number	8	4	2									14	4.64
		% of Total	57.14	28.57	14.29										
	Slaves	Number	16	26	23									65	
		% of Total	24.62	40.00	35.38										

194

County	Measure	1		2		3		4		5		6		7		8		9		Total	Avg
Montgomery	Owners — Number	23		12		7		1								1				44	6.64
	Owners — % of Total	52.27		27.27		15.91		2.27								2.27					
	Slaves — Number	52		79		78		17								66				292	
	Slaves — % of Total	17.81		27.05		26.71		5.82								22.60					
Hardin	Owners — Number	5		2		2														9	4.89
	Owners — % of Total	55.56		22.22		22.22															
	Slaves — Number	11		11		22														44	
	Slaves — % of Total	25.00		22.22		50.00															
Henry	Owners — Number	29		5		1		1												36	3.86
	Owners — % of Total	80.56		13.89		2.78		2.78													
	Slaves — Number	72		34		11		22												139	
	Slaves — % of Total	51.80		24.46		7.91		15.83													
Gibson	Owners — Number	61		19		4		1												85	3.69
	Owners — % of Total	71.76		22.35		4.71		1.18													
	Slaves — Number	130		115		44		25												314	
	Slaves — % of Total	41.40		36.62		14.01		7.96													
Dyer	Owners — Number	23		2		1		1		1										28	3.54
	Owners — % of Total	82.14		7.14		3.57		3.57		3.57											
	Slaves — Number	41		10		18		20		10										99	
	Slaves — % of Total	41.41		10.10		18.18		20.20		10.10											
Haywood	Owners — Number	15		11		5		2		2		1		1		1				38	10.08
	Owners — % of Total	39.47		28.95		13.16		5.26		5.26		2.63		2.63		2.63					
	Slaves — Number	31		66		57		37		51		30		45		66				383	
	Slaves — % of Total	8.09		17.23		14.88		9.66		13.32		7.83		11.75		17.23					
Fayette	Owners — Number	25		27		3		5		1		1		3				1		66	9.88
	Owners — % of Total	37.88		40.91		4.55		7.58		1.52		1.52		4.55				1.52			
	Slaves — Number	60		181		38		116		17		35		130				75		652	
	Slaves — % of Total	9.20		27.76		5.83		17.79		2.61		5.37		19.94				11.50			
Totals	Owners — Number	390		149		48		14		11		3		5		2		1		623	5.31
	Owners — % of Total	62.60		23.92		7.70		2.25		1.77		0.48		0.80		0.32		0.16			
	Slaves — Number	790		950		550		238		259		99		218		132		75		3311	
	Slaves — % of Total	23.86		28.69		16.61		7.19		7.82		2.99		6.58		3.99		2.27			

*Compiled from Schedules I, II, and IV, Census of 1860 (unpublished).

195

APPENDIX B

Some Large Slaveowners and Planters from Several of the Sample Counties*

County and Name	Year	Slaves	Im-proved Acres	Unim-proved Acres	Value of Farm	Value of Farm Imple-ments	Value of Live-stock	Bu. of Wheat	Bu. of Corn	Bu. of Oats	Pounds of To-bacco	Bales of Cotton	Bu. of Irish Pota-toes	Bu. of Sweet Pota-toes	Value of Slaugh-tered Animals
Greene															
William D. Nelson......	1860	41	500	300	$ 35,000	$ 1000	$ 5680	800	7000	300			20	15	$ 220
Lincoln															
John Clark...........	1850	56	800	600	20,000	700	3115		6000	500		149	20	50	425
William Bonner†.....	1850	44	1165	140	17,660	525	8572		5500	1000		125		25	543
Moses Bonner........	1850	44	500	500	20,000	600	2277		5000	300		118	30	75	537
Moses Bonner........	1860	84	1100	700	39,400	800	4000		1500	50		160	150	150	600
R. A. McDonald......	1860	105	2000	200	100,000	2000	22,000	300	9000	1000		296	50	100	2500
Maury															
Evan Young..........	1850	102	1400	400	40,000	900	10,000		12,500	900		130	70	75	470
Constantine Perkins...	1850	106	375	25	12,000	700	2510		3000	60		20			50
Frederick H. Watkins..	1850	94	600	50	16,250	300	4000	100	4000	200		150	500	400	425
Frederick H. Watkins..	1860	109	800	550	101,250	1500	17,412	125	7500	600	500	200	100	500	2200
J. T. Laurence.......	1850	85	600	600	36,000	1000	11,000		9000	1000		155	30	30	500
Jane H. Y. Greenfield.	1850	146	800	300	16,500	700	3125	60	5000	200		124	100	50	400
Gideon J. Pillow......	1850	75	1100	907	101,870	1500	23,780		15,000	4000			300	60	1500
Gideon J. Pillow......	1860	81	3500	10,870	571,000	10,000	25,000	500	12,500	200			100	500	4124
F. A. Thompson......	1860	97	568	482	55,000	660	7749	300	4500		32,000		60	100	1515
A. Thompson.........	1860	112	660	798	72,900	810	7218	200	4500	300	115,000	112	350	350	2365
Davidson															
William G. Harding...	1850	93	2000	2000	100,000	1500	17,000	300	17,630	2400			100	3000	287
William G. Harding...	1860	136	2500	1000	175,000	3500	35,000	1600	12,500	1500			100	200	4000
Willoughby Williams..	1850	111	800	1000	54,000	1000	9420	50	9000	1500		2	300	600	1050
Willoughby Williams..	1860	76	900	800	93,500	1300	15,000	1000	5000	1000			300	50	1440
Mark Cockrill‡.......	1850	28	2000	3000	150,000	300	43,600						200	200	350

198

*Production figures given here include only the amounts of the most important crops raised. The data were compiled from Schedules I, II, and IV, Censuses of 1850 and 1860 (unpublished).

Name	Year														
Mark Cockrill.........	1860	99	3000	3500	600,000	5000	30,000	200	10,000	1500			200	200	4000
Montgomery Bell§.....	1850	332	3615	24,800	314,150	700	6117	1200	15,000				100	300	500
S. Donelson..........	1850	95	800	700	30,000	1000	4600	100	6000	400		18	75	75	550
A. Jackson...........	1850	137	700	300	20,000	2000	4000	112	9000	2000		94			600
Robertson															
G. A. Washington....	1850	143	2000	2700	20,000	1000	5000	1000	5000	1000	15,000		500	800	2500
G. A. Washington....	1860	274	5000	8000	250,000	2000	30,000	50,000	22,000	4000	250,000		200	600	8000
Elias A. Fort........	1850	51	550	450	11,000	900	3500	450	4500	2000	18,000		50	100	600
Elias A. Fort........	1860	104	800	550	35,000	600	4335	1200	5000	1000	35,000		100	200	1155
Mary A. Baird........	1860	65	500	600	40,000	500	4405	300	6000	600	33,000		75	200	1300
Montgomery															
Robert Baxter, Jr. ǁ ...	1850	189	300	500	5,500	300	6500	1000	5000	1000	55,000		100	300	4000
John W. Barker.......	1850	68	650	3500	13,000	2000	4200	2000	4000	1200	90,000		100	250	1500
John W. Barker.......	1860	82	1460	1600	124,000	2000	6930	1400	11,000	1500	50,000			500	2164
James Clark..........	1850	57	425	350	10,000	600	1000	2000	8500	1200	77,000		500	100	900
James Clark..........	1860	91	800	500	52,000	500	3090	2000	4000	500	80,000		100	25	1500
W. K. Davie..........	1860	76	1000	16,000	178,000	1500	10,000	2000	7500	250		23	100		1500
Hardin															
John J. Williams.....	1860	55	250	5400	20,000	800	5300	400	3000			12	12	100	800
P. W. Nash...........	1860	39	500	1227	14,000	300	4395	100	2500			42	10	150	900
Henry															
William A. Thorpe**..	1850	105	900	2600	15,000		2160		6000		50,000				
William A. Thorpe....	1860	94	1500	3438	74,000		7300		6000		80,000				
James Cowan..........	1860	74	600	1250	46,500		3380		4000		16,000				
P. G. Haynes.........	1860	53	250	400	10,600		2460		2000		20,000				
J. J. Cook...........	1860	77	1050	1540	63,000		5890		7000		102,000				

†In 1860, William Bonner owned 241 slaves and 7,000 improved acres in Mississippi; Moses had 150 slaves and 2,500 improved acres in the same state.

‡Cockrill was awarded the medal at the London Exposition in 1851 for the finest wool in the world. He imported Merino sheep in 1824 and Durham cattle somewhat later, and he had a cotton plantation with 135 Negroes in Mississippi. In 1860, he owned 3,500 sheep, sheared 10,000 pounds of wool, and produced 2,000 tons of hay.

§Many of Bell's slaves were employed in the manufacture of iron.

ǁBaxter was listed as an "iron master."

**Not all these details were taken from the records on the individual farmers of Henry, Gibson, and Dyer counties.

Some Large Slaveowners and Planters from Several of the Sample Counties (cont.)

County and Name	Year	Slaves	Im-proved Acres	Unim-proved Acres	Value of Farm	Value of Farm Imple-ments	Value of Live-stock	Bu. of Wheat	Bu. of Corn	Bu. of Oats	Pounds of To-bacco	Bales of Cotton	Bu. of Irish Pota-toes	Bu. of Sweet Pota-toes	Value of Slaugh-tered Animals
Gibson															
Solomon Shaw.........	1850	29	300	2200	$ 20,000		$ 4000		2500			75			
Solomon Shaw.........	1860	36	800	3907	94,140		7020		7500			65			
William Jordan.........	1850	53	500	690	11,900		2700		4000			45			
William Jordan.........	1860	73	700	659	33,310		4315		3000			70			
Lillian Mays..........	1850	65	400	500	8,500		2000		4000			115			
Asa Robinson.........	1860	30	3000	3700	70,000		4000		2000			90			
William D. Fly........	1860	74	600	400	25,000		600	600	3000			70	200	600	
J. B. Bowen	1860	72	700	700	40,000		9000		3500			90			
Dyer															
Henry Fowlkes.........	1850	35	310	720	6,000		2626		4000		26,600				
Henry Fowlkes.........	1860	39	400	800	30,000		6450		3750		35,000				
D. E. Parker..........	1850	29	500	6300	5,000				3500		14,000				
D. E. Parker..........	1860	41	600	2700	66,000		6420		3000		50,000	8			
W. P. Fowlkes.........	1860	55	300	800	33,120				3000		37,000				
E. Haskins...........	1860	49	400	400	25,000		3375		3250		40,000	1.5			
Haywood															
William Miller.........	1850	84	600	2000	13,000	$1000	2435	50	3750	1000		175		300	$ 550
William Miller.........	1860	116	900	8314	50,000	2500	4540	900	4500			190		100	1450
Hiram Bradford........	1850	63	750	1250	12,000	700	2700	200	6000	700		189	200	1400	350
William Johnson.......	1850	80	750	4711	10,000	360	1610		4000			324		150	550
Samuel Oldham........	1850	87	1200	2660	9,000	150	4600	450	4000	1800		125	50	300	720
Samuel Oldham........	1860	146	2100	2600	85,000	2280	11,980	3100	11,000			338	500	700	1735
William Huffman.......	1850		500	1700	25,000	300	5000	200	2500			139		50	1450
Thomas Shepard.......	1860	73	1400	3000	88,000	1650	6340	1000	6000			188	200	300	1840
Nathan Adams.........	1860	202	2000	5152	159,800	2500	9400	100	9500			487	50	1100	905

	Year													
William Anthony	1860	150	1200	1700	58,000	1225	2455	350	6000		247	550	50	2460
James Bond*	1860	221	4150	12,857	339,175	4000	15,675	170	21,700		1053	100	975	3700
W. P. Bond	1860	75	600	390	25,000	625	3500	100	3000		488		200	360
Fayette														
Martha Douglas	1850	91	430	1195	7,100	600	2575		1000		120		200	600
Joseph P. Littlejohn	1850	91	700	723	7,900	775	2000	54	3500	25	133	40	100	410
John Granberry	1850	68	750	493	8,700	570	2245		3500	200	168			570
John Granberry	1860	105	800	443	18,645	770	4090		2500	300	124			900
James A. Haslett	1850	86	1200	2000	20,200	2150	6185	60	7500		250	50	2000	300
James A. Haslett	1860	71	1500	6500	100,000	10,000	10,000	1000	10,000	1000	400	250	3000	1000
Charles Michie	1850	80	1200	1800	21,000	1000	2470		3500	1000	203	20	200	500
Charles Michie	1860	98	2500	1000	75,000	3000	6700	500	7250		300	200	500	1750
John Parkam	1850	77	550	550	7,000	800	3000		3000		140	100	1000	800
John Parkam	1860	114	900	600	15,000	1100	3000	700	5000	600	183	100	1000	1050
John W. Jones	1850	235	2200	1820	30,000	2000	6700	100	12,500	1000	875	50	1000	1800
John W. Jones	1860	182	2000	1500	52,000	1000	12,000	32	12,000		800	50	500	4000
J. G. Shaw	1860	70	750	350	24,000	2200	5050	500	3600		250			500
B. W. Williamson	1860	102	450	120	6,840	300	300	130	1500		65	100	100	100
O. Bland	1860	105	900	600	30,000	2000	5410	200	5000		140	50	50	420
F. Harvel	1860	85	1100	850	30,000	400	9282	350	3250		197	50	100	780
John H. Mabone	1860	104	1400	1960	60,000	1670	7550	250	4000		245		500	1500
W. B. Jones	1860	93	1100	900	20,000	1000	8240	250	5000		360	100	600	1820

*Hamer, *Tennessee*, IV, 380, says that Bond was "accounted the richest man" in Tennessee in 1860 and that he owned "over six hundred slaves." Bond was the father of nineteen children and built the first female college in Brownsville.

NOTES

INTRODUCTION

1. The best of these accounts are: Ralph B. Flanders, *Plantation Slavery in Georgia* (Chapel Hill, 1933); Charles S. Sydnor, *Slavery in Mississippi* (New York, 1933); Ulrich B. Phillips, *American Negro Slavery* (New York, 1918); and *Life and Labor in the Old South* (Boston, 1929).

2. Blanche Henry Clark, *Tennessee Yeomen, 1840–1860* (Nashville, 1942); Herbert Weaver, *Mississippi Farmers, 1850–1860* (Nashville, 1945); Frank L. Owsley, *Plain Folk of the Old South* (Baton Rouge, 1949); James B. Sellers, *Slavery in Alabama* (University, Alabama, 1950). An earlier work, Harrison A. Trexler, *Slavery in Missouri, 1804–1865* (Baltimore, 1914), shows some use of the unpublished census records, but this source was not exploited.

3. Much of the other information, as well as some of that enumerated, has been used by Clark in her significant study, *Tennessee Yeomen*.

4. Clark used a slightly different basis for her selections, and thus her figures do not always agree with those in this study.

5. The information concerning the geographical and topographical divisions of Tennessee is based on *History of Tennessee from the Earliest Time to the Present* (Nashville, 1887), chap. I. This work is hereinafter cited as Goodspeed (publisher).

CHAPTER 1: Legal Status of the Slave in Tennessee

1. *Annals of Congress*, 1st Cong., 1st sess. (1789–1791), 2226-27.

2. Walter Clark, ed., *The State Records of North Carolina*, XXIII (Laws 1715–1776) (Goldsboro, 1904), 62-66. The 1715 act was replaced by a more detailed statute of 1741. *Ibid.*, 191-204.

3. *Annals of Congress,* 1st Cong., 2nd sess. (1789–1791), Appendix, 2211.

4. John Haywood and Robert Cobb, *The Statute Laws of Tennessee of a General and Public Nature* (Knoxville, 1831), I, 321. (*Acts of the General Assembly of North Carolina,* 1753, c. 6, sec. 10). These works will hereinafter be cited as Haywood and Cobb and *Acts of G.A.N.C.* To avoid confusion it is to be noted here that all references to Haywood and Cobb are to North Carolina legislation applicable to Tennessee, and the succeeding parenthetical reference to North Carolina Acts is to show the growth of the slave code in that state even before Tennessee became legally competent to legislate for herself.

5. Helen T. (Mrs. R.C.H.) Catterall, ed., *Judicial Cases Concerning the American Negro and Slavery* (Washington, 1926–1937), II, 515, (Britain v. State, 3 Humphreys 203-04). The only instance discovered of an owner being ordered to take better care of slaves was in 1864. E. A. Paine, Brig. Gen. Comdg., wrote to "Tim" Walton of Sumner County, Tennessee, "Sir: You will at once without delay take measures to furnish good serviceable clothing to all the *black people* on your plantation or in charge." Walton Papers, Microfilm in Joint Universities Library, Nashville, Tennessee.

6. Catterall, *Judicial Cases,* II, 545. (Worley v. State, 11 Humphreys 174-75).

7. *Ibid.,* 549. (State v. McCarn, 11 Humphreys 497).

8. *Acts of Tennessee,* 1799, c. 10, sec. 1, 2. Italics added. For a discussion—rather unsatisfactory—of the Tennessee slave laws see H. M. Henry, "The Slave Laws of Tennessee," *Tennessee Historical Magazine,* II (1916), 175-203. An article of less value is William L. Imes, "The Legal Status of Free Negroes and Slaves in Tennessee," *Journal of Negro History,* IV (1919), 254-73.

9. *Acts of Tennessee,* 1813, c. 55, sec. 1.

10. It will be remembered that all North Carolina legislation herein mentioned was applicable to Tennessee.

11. Haywood and Cobb, I, 321. (*Acts of G.A.N.C.,* 1741, c. 24, sec. 45).

12. *Acts of Tennessee,* 1819, c. 35, sec. 1.

13. Haywood and Cobb, I, 322-23. (*Acts of G.A.N.C.,* 1741, c. 24, sec. 29, 31-33, 39). To release the county of further responsibility, an iron collar bearing the initials "PG" (abbreviation for "Public Gaol") was put on the Negro's neck. The sheriff was to forfeit $12.50 if he refused or failed to comply with the advertising regulation.

14. *Acts of Tennessee,* 1844, c. 129, sec. 1.

15. Haywood and Cobb, I, 323. (*Acts of G.A.N.C.,* 1741, c. 24, sec. 34-38). There was no established church in Tennessee, so the forfeits—it seems—went to the county coffers.

16. *Acts of Tennessee*, 1831, c. 103, sec. 9.

17. *Ibid.*, 1852, c. 97, sec. 4. A state desiring rendition for a fugitive had first to pay all expenses that had been incurred by Tennessee. *Ibid.*, 1850, c. 105, sec. 1.

18. Caleb P. Patterson, *The Negro in Tennessee, 1790–1865* (Austin, Texas, 1922), 42.

19. *Acts of Tennessee*, 1852, c. 97, sec. 13. The fee for apprehension within the corporate limits was $1 instead of the customary $5 for out-of-town "captures."

20. Catterall, *Judicial Cases*, II, 540. (Morehead v. State, 9 Humphreys 635-38).

21. Haywood and Cobb, I, 315. (*Acts of G.A.N.C.*, 1753, c. 6, sec. 2-4).

22. Haywood and Cobb, I, 315. (*Acts of G.A.N.C.*, 1799, c. 7, sec. 2, 4).

23. *Acts of Tennessee*, 1806, c. 32, sec. 5. Equal punishment was provided for free Negroes taken up at unlawful hours or in the company of slaves. A similar power of appointment was given to the commissioners of towns. *Ibid.*, sec. 6, 7.

24. *Ibid.*, sec. 8. The fines were to be used toward the lessening of taxes and the repairing of streets. The Minute Books of the various county courts give the names of the individuals appointed as patrols.

25. *Ibid.*, 1817, c. 183.

26. *Ibid.*, 1831, c. 103, sec. 11. Later it was made the duty of the justices to appoint patrols for their respective districts. *Ibid.*, 1838, c. 141, sec. 2.

27. *Ibid.*, 1831, c. 103, sec. 1.

28. *Ibid.*, sec. 10. This money was to be taken out of the Negro poll taxes.

29. *Ibid.*, sec. 13.

30. *Laws of the Corporations of Nashville to Which are Prefixed the Laws of North Carolina and Tennessee Relating to the Town of Nashville* (revised edition), 1837, c. 3.

31. *Ibid.*, c. 17. The fine for neglect of duty, intoxication, or refusal to serve was $5, and the patrol had to give bond for $500 for faithful execution of duty. Failure to so perform worked forfeiture of the appointment and the offender became liable on his bond.

32. *Ibid.* These provisions were re-enacted on February 26, 1850. *Revised Laws of the City of Nashville*, 1850, c. 34. The day police were not established until 1851 when they were given practically the same powers as the patrol. They served from sunrise to sunset. *Revised Laws of the City of Nashville*, 1854, c. 13.

33. *Laws of the Corporation of Nashville . . .* (revised edition), 1837,

c. 18, sec. 5-7. This act also contained some strict regulations concerning the free Negroes.

34. *Acts of Tennessee,* 1856, c. 80, sec. 1-4. All the provisions of this act, except the one relative to the plantation patrol, were repealed the following year. *Ibid.,* 1857, c. 3, sec. 1.

35. Haywood and Cobb, I, 314. (*Acts of G.A.N.C.,* 1741, c. 24, sec. 43). Negroes wearing liveries were always excepted. The pass "system" regulations were very loosely enforced. See pp. 92–93.

36. Haywood and Cobb, I, 314. (*Acts of G.A.N.C.,* 1741, c. 24, sec. 40). The reward for apprehending and returning such a slave was the same as if he were a runaway.

37. Haywood and Cobb, I, 314. (*Acts of G.A.N.C.,* 1741, c. 24, sec. 41, 42).

38. Haywood and Cobb, I, 314. (*Acts of G.A.N.C.,* 1753, c. 6, sec. 28).

39. *Acts of Tennessee,* 1799, c. 28, sec. 1.

40. *Ibid.,* 1836, c. 65, sec. 1.

41. J. E. Rains, comp., *A Compilation of the General Laws of the City of Nashville,* 1857, c. 26.

42. *Ibid.,* 1858, c. 27, sec. 1; c. 28.

43. John McLeod Keating, *History of the City of Memphis and Shelby County, Tennessee* (Syracuse, 1899), I, 381.

44. Haywood and Cobb, I, 309. (*Acts of G.A.N.C.,* 1741, c. 24, sec. 14).

45. Haywood and Cobb, I, 316. (*Acts of G.A.N.C.,* 1788, c. 2, sec. 7). Later the fine was reduced to $10. *Acts of Tennessee,* 1799, c. 28, sec. 1.

46. *Acts of Tennessee,* 1803, c. 13, sec. 4.

47. *Acts of Tennessee,* 1830, c. 34, sec. 1, 2, 4.

48. *Ibid.,* 1842, c. 141, sec. 1, 2.

49. *Ibid.,* 1836, c. 57, sec. 1, 2.

50. *Daily Appeal,* June 11, 1859.

51. Catterall, *Judicial Cases,* II, 522. (Sword v. State, 5 Humphreys 102-03).

52. *Republican Banner,* July 20, 1860. An 1846 statute forbade the granting of a liquor license to a free Negro. *Acts of Tennessee,* 1845–46, c. 90.

53. *Acts of Tennessee,* 1852, c. 174, sec. 6, 7, 10. These provisions were re-enacted eight years later. *Ibid.,* 1860, c. 26.

54. Haywood and Cobb, I, 315. (*Acts of G.A.N.C.,* 1741, c. 24, sec. 47).

55. *Acts of Tennessee,* 1819, c. 35, sec. 1.

56. *Ibid.,* 1803, c. 13.

57. *Ibid.,* 1831, c. 103, sec. 4, 8.

58. *Ibid.,* 1836, c. 44.

59. For accounts see: Amos Dresser, *The Narrative of Amos Dresser*

(New York, 1836); Benjamin Lundy, *The Life, Travels and Opinions of Benjamin Lundy.* . . . (Philadelphia, 1847), 277-79; Philip M. Hamer, ed., *Tennessee, A History,* 1673–1932 (New York, 1933), I, 466; W. T. Hale and D. L. Merritt, *A History of Tennessee and Tennesseans* (New York, 1913), II, 299.

Nine days later, August 30, 1835, the committee which tried Dresser held a meeting, and "resolved, that the merchants of Nashville and the State of Tennessee be requested to hold meetings and express their views upon the subject of trading and dealing with Arthur Tappan and Company or any other abolitionist." Hale and Merritt, *History of Tennessee,* II, 300.

60. *Acts of Tennessee,* 1858, c. 86.

61. Haywood and Cobb, I, 320. (*Acts of G.A.N.C.,* 1741, c. 24, sec. 27). In 1799 the former penalty was reduced to $50 plus damages; the latter remained unchanged. *Acts of Tennessee,* 1799, c. 28, sec. 2.

62. Haywood and Cobb, I, 329. (*Acts of G.A.N.C.,* 1786, c. 6, sec. 2); *Acts of Tennessee,* 1803, c. 13, sec. 3.

63. *Acts of Tennessee,* 1833, c. 3, sec. 1, 2. This did not apply to stow-aways who were to be deposited at the nearest jail and advertised. *Ibid.,* c. 62.

64. *Ibid.,* 1829, c. 23, sec. 22.

65. *Ibid.,* 1836, c. 5, sec. 2; c. 58, sec. 1.

66. Catterall, *Judicial Cases,* II, 490. (State v. Jones, 2 Yerger 22).

67. *Ibid.,* 531. (Duncan v. State, 7 Humphreys 151).

68. *Ibid.,* 540. (Morehead v. State, 9 Humphreys 635-38).

69. *Journal of the House of Representatives of the State of Tennessee,* 1838, p. 785.

70. *Laws of the Corporation of Nashville* . . . (revised edition), 1837, c. 18, sec. 7-8.

71. December 1, 1860.

72. Haywood and Cobb, I, 307, 326. (*Acts of G.A.N.C.,* 1741, c. 24, sec. 1, 23). The seller was to be committed to jail until he gave bond for $1,250.

73. *Acts of Tennessee,* 1806, c. 32, sec. 1. For a discussion of the free Negro in Tennessee, see J. Merton England, "The Free Negro in Ante-Bellum Tennessee," *Journal of Southern History,* IX (February, 1943), 37-58, and "The Free Negro in Ante-Bellum Tennessee," Ph. D. Thesis (Vanderbilt University, 1941).

74. *Laws of the Corporation of Nashville* . . . (revised edition), 1837, c. 18, sec. 17.

75. *Acts of Tennessee,* 1831, c. 102, sec. 1.

76. *Ibid.,* 1842, c. 191, sec. 1-6. Forfeiture of the bond invoked the penalties of 1831. This recognizance had to be renewed every three years, and if the court refused renewal twenty days were allowed for the colored

person to get out of the state. Also, such a freedman could not remove from his county without losing his favored status.

77. *Ibid.*, 1854, c. 50, sec. 1. Four years later Tennessee made it lawful for any resident free person of color, eighteen years of age or over, to choose a master and become a slave. After the circuit or chancery court had examined the petition and the prospective master, had satisfied itself there was no fraud, the master had paid to the clerk (for the school fund) one tenth the value set by three commissioners, and the master had given bond that the slave would not be exchanged, the master acquired the same property rights as if the Negro had been born a slave. The slave could not be attached by another in property settlements, and children born before commitment were not slave. *Ibid.*, 1858, c. 45, sec. 1-6. Several other states passed similar laws in the 1850's, but in contrast to some of the others no instance of a free Negro voluntarily becoming a slave in Tennessee was discovered.

78. *Ibid.*, 1826, c. 26, sec. 1-7. This act went into effect on March 1, 1827; the money from the sale of any slaves was to go into the state treasury; and anyone offering to sell a free person who had been bound for crime forfeited $500.

79. *Ibid.*, 1855, c. 22, sec. 1.

80. Haywood and Cobb, I, 328. (*Acts of G.A.N.C.*, 1777, c. 6, sec. 2). One fifth of the proceeds of these sales went to the apprehender of the Negro and the remainder went to the state. Perhaps, an "other than prescribed" method would be involved in the case of the man whose mind became diseased in 1825, and he "got a fancy that something was in his head . . . offered his slave his freedom if he would split his head open with an axe." Catterall, *Judicial Cases*, II, 529. (Alston v. Boyd, 6 Humphreys 505).

81. *Acts of Tennessee*, 1801, c. 27. The bond usually required was $1000 for each slave. See Will Books and Quarterly Minutes of the County Court of Davidson County for these early years, and Legislative Papers, *passim*. In Tennessee State Archives.

82. *Acts of Tennessee*, 1829, c. 29, sec. 1. For such cases see Catterall, *Judicial Cases*, II, *passim*.

83. *Acts of Tennessee*, 1831, c. 102, sec. 2. This provision was not to be applicable to a slave who had contracted for his freedom before the passage of the act, provided the court saw fit to grant freedom in those cases. *Ibid.*, 1833, c. 81, sec. 2. That the Legislature gave support to this exception before the passage of the 1833 act is attested by the action on petitions by individuals who had contracted for their freedom prior to 1831. See Box 93, Legislative Papers, 1825 to 1847. In Tennessee State Archives. The Constitution of 1834 forbade the General Assembly to make any laws for the emancipation of slaves without the owner's consent. Article II, sec. 31.

84. *National Banner and Nashville Daily Advertiser,* October 5, 1833.

85. Nashville *Republican and State Gazette,* October 29, 1833.

86. *Ibid.* Jacob B. Foote (Blount, Monroe, and M'Minn counties) was gratified to note that none of the opponents of changing the 1831 law argued the "abstract right of involuntary servitude." *National Banner and Nashville Daily Advertiser,* November 21, 1833.

87. *Acts of Tennessee,* 1852, c. 300, sec. 2, 3. An act of February 4, 1842 (c. 191) had given to the county courts the discretion of granting free persons of color the right to remain in the state. A group of Williamson countians said that "crowds of slaves" had been emancipated since this act which was "in principle the same with that policy which urges abolition of slavery." Their prayers of petition to revert to the law of 1831 were designated "unreasonable" by the legislative committees. Box 92, Legislative Petitions, 1843. In Tennessee State Archives.

88. *Acts of Tennessee,* 1854, c. 50. In 1860 Negroes who had been set free but not deported were given the "privilege" of voluntary slavery. *Ibid.,* 1860, c. 128, sec. 1. These emancipation restrictions were avoided in various ways. On this point see England, "The Free Negro." In 1860 the issue of expelling free persons of color from Tennessee arose in the legislature. Jordan Stokes (Davidson County) ridiculed the proposal as a safety device. He said such persons were too few, too dispersed over the state, and "too feeble in moral, mental, and physical powers to form even the nucleus of a conspiracy. . . . Senators would make Tennessee a laughing stock among her sister states, if they were to rest their support of the measure upon such grounds." He contended the legislature did not have the power to take such action, it would not be expedient, and concluded with "May a higher Sense of Truth, Justice and Mercy lead you all to such a conclusion as will plant no thorn on your pillow in the hour of death." *Speech of Jordan Stokes . . . on the Bill for the expulsion from the State of Free Persons of Color* (Nashville, 1860).

89. Catterall, *Judicial Cases,* II, 501. (Blackmore v. Negro Phill, 7 Yerger 452-65).

90. Haywood and Cobb, I, 315-16. (*Acts of G.A.N.C.,* 1741, c. 24, sec. 48, 50). Again note that only the North Carolina legislation that was applicable to Tennessee is mentioned.

91. Haywood and Cobb, I, 316. (*Acts of G.A.N.C.,* 1783, c. 14, sec. 2).

92. *Acts of the Territory Southwest of the River Ohio,* 1794, c. 1, sec. 32. A slave, however, was a competent witness against any freed Negro. *Acts of Tennessee,* 1813, c. 135, sec. 5.

93. J. D. Wheeler, *A Practical Treatise on the Law of Slavery* (New Orleans, 1837), 212-13. The other states were Kentucky, Maryland, Georgia, and Alabama.

94. *Acts of Tennessee,* 1819, c. 35, sec. 2, 3.

95. *Ibid.,* 1825, c. 24, sec. 1, 2, 4, 8. The bond was always to be double

the value of the slave. Murder, arson, burglary, rape, and robbery were designated as capital offenses punishable by death.

96. *Ibid.*, 1836, c. 19, sec. 9-11. Subsequently the master was made liable for the fee of the court-appointed counsel, if he did not furnish legal advice and consultation. *Ibid.*, 1838, c. 103, sec. 1. The only Nashville regulation relative to the trial of slaves provided that slaves convicted in a magistrate's court were to have the right of appeal to the Criminal Court of Davidson County. *Revised Laws of the City of Nashville*, 1850, c. 29, sec. 2.

97. Catterall, *Judicial Cases*, II, 509-10. (Elijah (a slave) v. State, 1 Humphreys 102-05).

98. *Acts of Tennessee*, 1820, c. 11, sec. 2.

99. *Ibid.*, 1821, c. 10, sec. 1-4; *ibid.*, 1823, c. 20, sec. 1.

100. *Ibid.*, 1825, c. 79, sec. 1, 2.

101. *Ibid.*, 1856, c. 83. This was not required if there was no paper in the county where the sale occurred. *Ibid.*, 1858, c. 94, sec. 1.

102. *Ibid.*, 1823, c. 17, sec. 1.

103. *Ibid.*, 1839, c. 47, sec. 1.

104. For an evaluation of the land speculators' role in taxation matters, see Gordon Chappell, "Land Speculation and Taxation in Tennessee, 1790–1834," M.A. thesis (Vanderbilt University, 1936).

105. *Acts of the Territory Southwest of the River Ohio*, 1794, c. 3, sec. 1, 2.

106. *Ibid.*, 1795, c. 2, sec. 1.

107. Article I, sec. 26.

108. *Acts of Tennessee*, 1797, c. 2, 3. The lower age limit for taxable slaves was raised from ten to twelve years.

109. Article II, sec. 28. Slaves between the ages of 12 and 50 were taxable. James W. Smith of Jackson County could see no justice in exempting slaves under 12 and over 50. He said that one of his most valuable slaves was over 60, and that slaves from 1 to 12 years old were worth from $100 to $300. "Now to vote for a system of taxation that will put a tax on everything the nonslaveholder owns, and exempt himself from paying a tax on his own negroes under 10 and over 50 years, he could not and would not do it; if for no other reason his conscience would forbid it." Nashville *Republican and State Gazette*, August 30, 1834. These remarks were made in the convention on August 29, but were not entered upon the journal.

110. *Acts of Tennessee*, 1860, c. 30, sec. 1. Nashville legislation provided that if the owner lived in the city, the slave was to be assessed to him; but if the owner were a nonresident, the slave was to be assessed with the person having him in his possession at the time of assessment. *Revised Laws of the City of Nashville*, 1850, c. 23, sec. 29.

111. *Acts of Tennessee*, 1819, c. 35, sec. 1. Attempt to rape a white

woman was later added to the list of capital offenses. *Ibid.*, 1833, c. 35.

112. Catterall, *Judicial Cases*, II, 534. (Tom (a slave) v. State, 8 Humphreys 86-87).

113. *Ibid.*, II, 516-17. (Jacob (a slave) v. State, 3 Humphreys 521).

114. *Ibid.*, II, 516. (Sydney (a slave) v. State, 3 Humphreys 478-80).

115. *Ibid.*, II, 551. (State v. Dan Cherry, 1 Swan 164).

116. *Ibid.*, II, 537. (State v. Brady, 9 Humphreys 47-54).

117. See the *Eagle and Enquirer*, May–June, 1852; *Republican Banner*, November–December, 1860.

CHAPTER 2: Hire, Sale, Flight, and Theft of Slaves

1. Catterall, *Judicial Cases*, II, 487. (Hicks v. Parham, 3 Haywood 224, 228). Slaves on hire were generally released to return to their owners just before Christmas. What decision a court might have made concerning liability for death between release and the end of the contract term must remain a matter of speculation.

2. *Ibid.*, II, 561. (Bell v. Cummings, 3 Sneed 285.)

3. *Ibid.*, II, 563. (James v. Carper, 4 Sneed 402). Catterall also contains some incidental information on the price of slave hire.

4. Accounts of Joseph Hooper and Wife, 1794–1804. John Claybrooke Papers. In Tennessee Historical Society. Many of these papers deal with the affairs of John Overton.

5. Memorandum. John Overton Papers. In Tennessee Historical Society.

6. Nashville *Whig and Tennessee Advertiser*, November 21, 1818.

7. Nashville *Whig*, December 15, 1819.

8. *Ibid.*, January 5, 1820.

9. *Ibid.*, February 2, 1820.

10. *Tennessee Gazette and Mero District Advertiser*, October 24, 1804; from Ulrich B. Phillips, ed., *Plantation and Frontier Documents* (Cleveland, 1910), II, 349.

11. Edward Ward to John Overton, February 22, 1816. John Overton Papers.

12. James Winchester to John Overton, December 11, 1816. John Overton Papers.

13. John S. Bassett, ed., *The Southern Plantation Overseer as Revealed in his Letters* (Northampton, 1925), 161-63. Frederic Bancroft says that Harry's master "received $487 annually for his hire," but this does not seem to be the case. *Slave Trading in the Old South* (Baltimore, 1931), 160.

14. *Impartial Review and Cumberland Repository*, May 24, 1806.

15. Samuel Stackens to John Overton, October 18, 1824. John Overton Papers.

16. George Skipwith to John Overton, January 23, 1833. John Overton Papers.

17. From Phillips, ed., *Plantation and Frontier Documents,* II, 45-46.

18. *Journal of the House of Representatives of the State of Tennessee,* 1833, pp. 114-18; *Journal of the Senate of the State of Tennessee,* 1835, pp. 70-83; Thomas P. Abernethy, *From Frontier to Plantation in Tennessee* (Chapel Hill, 1933), 286.

19. Randolph *Recorder,* July 1, 1836.

20. John Claybrooke Papers.

21. *Eagle and Enquirer,* January 5, 1858.

22. Schedule II, "An Enumeration of Slave Population," 1860 Census (unpublished), for Davidson, Fayette, Haywood, and Lincoln counties.

23. *Acts of Tennessee,* 1823, c. 17, sec. 1; *ibid.,* 1839, c. 47, sec. 1.

24. Receipt in the John Claybrooke Papers.

25. Thomas Overton to John Overton, November 22, 1795. John Overton Papers.

26. Receipts, 1802 to 1832. John Claybrooke Papers. Overton bought Wood on June 28, 1823, from William Day. On June 27, the latter had paid $700 for Wood—possibly in different type bank notes. At least six of these slaves were bought outside the state, and the majority were under fifteen years of age. Between 1794 and 1797 Joshua Coffee of Rockingham County, North Carolina, bought several dozen Negroes. In August, 1797, John Coffee recorded a memo indicating the purchase and sale of fourteen Negroes at £540 and £793, 16s., or a "clear profit" of $864. It seems that these fourteen may have been purchased by Joshua. John Coffee Papers. Tennessee Historical Society.

27. See John Claybrooke Papers, January 7, 1813. For additional data concerning the purchase of slaves and litigations over the sale of unsound slaves, see Catterall, *Judicial Cases,* II, 482-601, *passim.*

28. John Overton Papers.

29. Eliazar Hardeman to John Overton, October 27, 1830. John Overton Papers.

30. R. H. Barry to John Overton, August 13, 1831. John Overton Papers.

31. Phillips, *Life and Labor,* note, 275-76. Walker was one of the first United States senators from Alabama.

32. R. H. Barry to John Overton, January 25, 1831. John Overton Papers.

33. Same to same, February 6, 1831. John Overton Papers.

34. *Acts of Tennessee,* 1826, c. 26, sec. 1, 2. This act prohibiting the interstate slave trade went into effect on March 1, 1827. *Ibid.,* sec. 7.

35. R. H. Barry to John Claybrooke, June 2, 1834. John Overton Papers.

36. Same to same, October 17, 1834. John Overton Papers.

37. Same to same, August 24, 1836. John Overton Papers.

38. *The Anti-Slavery Record*, II (1836), 59. In 1831 the city of Nashville had purchased some slaves to work on the streets and at the waterworks. *National Banner and Nashville Whig*, July 27, 1831. In 1860–61 the slave department of the city government showed disbursements of $11,410.45, evidently for purchase and hire. J. P. Campbell, comp., *Nashville Business Directory, 1860–61*, p. 86.

39. *National Banner and Nashville Whig*, October 16, 1829.

40. *Ibid.*, November 7, 1831.

41. Keating, *Memphis*, I, 328.

42. *Hunt's Merchants' Magazine*, XLI (1859), 774. At Franklin, Kentucky, on August 12, 1859, ten slaves, ranging from three months to twenty-seven years of age, were sold at an average price of $1,243.50. *Ibid.*

43. *A Century of Population Growth* (Washington, 1909), 133.

44. Phillips, *American Negro Slavery*, 370.

45. *Ibid.*, 371.

46. *Ibid.;* Phillips, *Life and Labor*, 178.

47. *Report of the Tennessee Comptroller to the House of Representatives*, 1857, p. 37; *ibid.*, 1859, p. 17.

48. *National Banner and Nashville Whig*, September 26, 1831.

49. Nashville *Republican and State Gazette*, October 5, 1833.

50. Phillips, ed., *Plantation and Frontier Documents*, II, 55-56.

51. W. A. Provine, "Lardner Clark, Nashville's First Merchant and Foremost Citizen," *Tennessee Historical Magazine*, III (1917), 46.

52. See Davidson County Will Books for this early period.

53. John Bostick to John Claybrooke, May 16, 1835. John Claybrooke Papers.

54. Joseph Meek Letters. Fisk University Library.

55. Samuel Logan to Joseph Meek, February 9, 1835. Joseph Meek Letters.

56. Same to same, March 5, 1835. Joseph Meek Letters.

57. C. Haynes to Joseph Meek, May 30, 1835. Joseph Meek Letters. In the 47 there were one "yellow" and two "motatto."

58. Haynes meant that Julian was a handsome, smart mulatto, seventeen years of age, but that competition in bidding had run the price to $550.

59. C. Haynes to Joseph Meek, May 30, 1835. Joseph Meek Letters.

60. Same to same, August 7, 1835. Joseph Meek Letters.

61. *Ibid.*

62. C. Haynes to Joseph Meek, May 25, 1836. Joseph Meek Letters.

63. Samuel Logan and C. Haynes to Joseph Meek, August 19, 1836. Joseph Meek Letters.

64. *Ibid.* In this letter Logan expressed his dislike for Jackson: "I think it would be well that Providence would permit Genl Jackson to die, before his policy ruins the country."

65. C. Haynes to Joseph Meek, October 6, 1836. Joseph Meek Letters.

66. Samuel Logan to Joseph Meek, November 30, 1836. Joseph Meek Letters.

67. Same to same, January 4, 1837. Joseph Meek Letters.

68. Same to same, May 28, 1837. Joseph Meek Letters.

69. M. D. Cooper Papers. In private possession.

70. J. P. Campbell, comp., *The Nashville, State of Tennessee, and General Business Directory*, 1853, p. 94.

71. *Ibid.*, 100. It is not known whether the latter firm dealt in slaves.

72. Phillips, *American Negro Slavery*, 190. It is entirely possible, and even probable, that some of these individuals or firms were engaged in local sale and hire of slaves. In 1841 Samuel Johnstone of East Tennessee said there was near him a "slave dealer by the name of Upton who had collected about 30 which he had in a private prison awaiting their removal to Louisiana." W. Freeman Galpin, ed., "Letters of an East Tennessee Abolitionist," *East Tennessee Historical Society Publications*, III (1931), 147.

73. J. P. Campbell, comp., *Nashville Business Directory*, 1857, pp. 38, 103.

74. J. P. Campbell, comp., *Nashville City and Business Directory*, 1859, p. 251. One of Haynes' "scouts" was H. J. Lyles, who became connected with G. H. Hitchings the next year. The *Directory* for 1859 also designates Thomas G. James as a slave dealer, S. H. Bugg as a trader, four others as agents, and eight as auctioneers. The last included both general agents and other commission merchants. *Ibid., passim.* James later was a prominent figure in the Natchez, Mississippi, slave trade. Bancroft, *Slave Trading*, 305-06.

75. J. P. Campbell, comp., *Nashville Business Directory, 1860–61*, pp. 130, 188, 192, 216, 274. G. H. Hitchings was the same man who was in the firm of Lyles and Hitchings, and E. S. Hawkins was one of the 1859 "agents."

76. Nashville *Daily News*, February 1, 1859. Perhaps Hawkins' desire to sell in "this or adjoining counties" was a sop to local business. The same may be said of one of Haynes' advertisements. *Republican Banner*, December 31, 1858.

77. Nashville *Daily News*, June 19, 1859.

78. *Republican Banner*, January 6, 1860.

79. Bancroft, *Slave Trading*, 249.

80 *Ibid.*, 250.

81. Memphis *Enquirer*, November 4, 1836.

82. *Weekly American Eagle*, November 25, 1845.

83. *Eagle and Enquirer*, January 3, 1852; Bancroft, *Slave Trading*, 251.

84. *Daily Eagle*, March 14, 1846.

85. *Weekly American Eagle*, September 23, 1846.

86. *Ibid.*, December 24, 1846.

87. *Weekly Eagle*, May 18, 1848. The next year Saffarans and Son wanted to hire 50 men who would be paid "liberal wages, if engaged immediately." *Ibid.*, April 12, 1849.

88. *Memphis Directory and General Business Advertiser*, 1849, p. 15.

89. *Weekly Eagle*, August 30, 1849.

90. *Ibid.*, December 20, 1849.

91. John Hallum, *Diary of an Old Lawyer* (Nashville, 1895), 76. Bancroft correctly says that " 'Diary' is a misnomer for his inaccurate recollections." *Slave Trading*, 252.

92. Bancroft, *Slave Trading*, 252. Jefferson Bolton died in 1852. Hallum, *Diary*, 78.

93. *Daily Eagle and Enquirer*, February 23, 1852.

94. *Daily Appeal*, July 20, 1854.

95. *Ibid.*, June 21, 1856.

96. For accounts of this, see: Bancroft, *Slave Trading*, 253-56, 267; Hallum, *Diary*, 76-86; Keating, *Memphis*, I, 397-99. The Bancroft account seems the most reliable; Hallum has many inaccurate statements, among which is his recollection that the mob actually got the rope around Bolton's neck, and N. B. Forrest rushed in to save him. It was John Able, a gambler-murderer, that was almost hanged. Keating, Bancroft, and the Memphis papers attest this fact. None of the Boltons appear as slave dealers in the 1859 *Directory*, but in 1860 Washington Bolton is listed as such on p. 83.

97. Bancroft, *Slave Trading*, 258.

98. *Ibid.* Hallum says that Forrest was once connected with the Boltons, but no evidence has been found to corroborate this statement. It seems that Forrest's first partner was Byrd Hill, who had started out alone, and was later to take his son in with him. Bancroft, *Slave Trading*, 258.

99. *Daily Appeal*, July 20, 1854, and January 1, 1856.

100. *Ibid.*, June 13, 1856.

101. *Eagle and Enquirer*, January-June, 1857, from Bancroft, *Slave Trading*, 258.

102. Bancroft, *Slave Trading*, 262.

103. *Weekly Appeal*, January 6, 1860. Bancroft (p. 263) has substantially the same notice, from another paper.

104. Bancroft, *Slave Trading*, 263-64. Andrew Nelson Lytle, *Bedford Forrest and His Critter Company* (New York, 1931), 27-28, describes Forrest as a very humane trader.

105. *Daily Appeal*, August 12, 1854.

106. *Ibid.*, March 16, 1856.

107. *Ibid.*, April 14, 1859. Associated with Hill were his son and John D. Ware of Brownsville. This group was known as Hill, Ware and Co. *Williams' Memphis Directory, City Guide, and Business Mirror*, 1860, pp. 193, 335.

108. *Memphis City Directory and General Business Advertiser,* 1855, pp. 110, 112, 152, 185.

109. *Memphis City Directory for 1859,* p. 220.

110. *Williams' Memphis Directory, City Guide, and Business Mirror,* 1860, pp. 107, 144, 204, 312, 350.

111. *Daily Appeal,* February 24, 1856.

112. *Evening Ledger,* October 27, 1857.

113. Philo Tower, *Slavery Unmasked* (Rochester, 1856), 53. Alice D. Adams, *The Neglected Period of Anti-Slavery in America, 1808–1831* (Boston, 1908), 198, also places Tennessee in the breeding class.

114. Winfield H. Collins, *The Domestic Slave Trade of the Southern States* (New York, 1904), 75-77.

115. Bancroft, *Slave Trading,* 403.

116. The Nashville *Intelligencer,* August 28, 1799.

117. *Tennessee Gazette and Mero District Advertiser,* November 7, 1804; from Phillips, ed., *Plantation and Frontier Documents,* II, 87-88.

118. Nashville *Whig,* August 9, 1820. The Nashville *Gazette* also carried this advertisement on September 30, 1820.

119. Phillips, ed., *Plantation and Frontier Documents,* II, 80-81; from the New Orleans *Bee* of June 16, 1825, reprinted from the Memphis *Enquirer.*

120. Nashville *Republican and State Gazette,* July 5, 1833.

121. *Ibid.,* August 26, 1833.

122. William T. Hale, *History of DeKalb County, Tennessee* (Nashville, 1915), 103-04.

123. *Tri-Weekly Appeal,* September 4, 1845.

124. *Daily Appeal,* February 16, 1856.
Miss Mildred Ferguson of Trenton, Kentucky, stated to the writer that Jeff, slave of her great-grandfather, Charles N. Meriwether, was a frequent absconder because he liked to be "jailed" in the cellar where he could sleep on the cotton bales. She says the slaves were "notoriously no good" and badly spoiled. Meriwether lived on the Tennessee–Kentucky line in Montgomery County, Tennessee.

125. Why should he need to purchase his wife? She was already free according to his account; so were the children, as they took the status of the mother. Perhaps Burrell meant that he desired to raise money to pay transportation costs for his family.

126. Levi Coffin, *Reminiscences* (Cincinnati, 1876), 144-47.

127. Benjamin Drew, *The Refugee or a North-Side View of Slavery* (Cleveland, 1856), 77.

128. *Ibid.,* 183-85.

129. *Ibid.,* 123-29.

130. J. W. Loguen, *As a Slave and a Freeman* (Syracuse, 1859), 22.

131. Loguen later became a bishop of the African Methodist Episcopal

Zion Church. Carter G. Woodson, ed., *The Mind of the Negro as Reflected in Letters Written During the Crisis, 1800–1860* (Washington, 1926), 540.

132. *Ibid.,* 217-18.

133. *Ibid.,* 218-19.

134. *Ibid.,* 537-39. Jourdan and his family were living at Dayton, Ohio.

135. Louis Hughes, *Thirty Years a Slave* (Milwaukee, 1897), 12. This was possibly the same Edward McGehee who, later, was rather prominent in the colonization movement in Mississippi. See Sydnor, *Slavery in Mississippi,* 208-09.

136. Hughes, *Thirty Years,* 63.

137. *Ibid.,* 81-86. The reward for him was $500, or half that amount for "knowledge that he has been killed." *Ibid.,* 82.

138. *Ibid.,* 87-89.

139. *Ibid.,* 122, 127-37, 139-46, 164, 188, 191, 198, 209.

140. *Eighth Census of the United States: 1860,* I (Population), xv-xvi.

141. William H. Siebert, *The Underground Railroad from Slavery to Freedom* (New York, 1899), 342-43.

142. Nashville *Whig and Tennessee Advertiser,* May 1, 1819. This paper on March 6, 1819, carried a short item to the effect that Samuel Thurman, previously convicted of Negro stealing, had at the last term of the Rutherford Circuit Court been sentenced to execution on June 1. Thurman had been in the army during the War of 1812 and was a native of Blount County.

143. Nashville *Gazette,* September 23, 1820.

144. Nashville *Republican and State Gazette,* July 5 and August 26, 1833.

145. Phillips, *American Negro Slavery,* 381.

146. *Ibid.,* 382. Park Marshall thinks that Murrell's and Crenshaw's offenses were minor, and that they have been given too high a place in the crime world. "John A. Murrell and Daniel Crenshaw," *Tennessee Historical Magazine,* VI (1920–21), 3-9. Both Murrell and Crenshaw were born in Williamson County. Crenshaw was Murrell's chief lieutenant.

147. See H. R. Howard, comp., *The History of Virgil A. Stewart and his Adventure in Capturing and Exposing the Great "Western Land Pirate" and his Gang* (New York, 1836). Murrell had started out as a horse thief and had served a year in the penitentiary for such an offense. Robert M. Coates, *The Outlaw Years* (New York, 1930), really adds nothing to the Murrell story as related by Howard. Coates terms Murrell "that erratic Napoleon of the outlaws." Stewart, while capturing Murrell, was known as Hues, and is very probably the same Hues, or Hughes, who recovered some runaway slaves for the James K. Polk Fayette County plantation. Bassett, ed., *Plantation Overseer,* 55, 60.

148. Marshall, "Murrell and Crenshaw," 4.

149. June 21, 1834.

150. Randolph *Recorder,* September 25, 1835.

151. *Journal of the House of Representatives of the State of Tennessee,* 1838, p. 785.

152. Siebert, *Underground Railroad,* 174-75; Nashville *Daily Gazette,* April 13, 1849. The *Gazette* said that Dillingham was a Quaker school-teacher belonging to a respectable family, and was not without the sympathy of those who attended the trial. "It was a foolhardy enterprise in which he embarked, and dearly has he to pay for his rashness."

153. *Niles' Register,* XLI, 340-41; Patterson, *Negro in Tennessee,* 49.

154. Howard, comp., *Virgil A. Stewart,* 54-55.

155. *Ibid.,* 57-58. After his capture, Murrell gave the strength of his clan as follows: Tennessee 60, Mississippi 47, Arkansas 47, Kentucky 25, Missouri 27, Alabama 28, Georgia 33, South Carolina 35, North Carolina 32, Virginia 21, Maryland 27, Florida 16, Louisiana 32, and transient members 22. 452 in all! *Ibid.,* 116-18.

156. Memorials and Petitions to the Legislature of Tennessee, 1835; Phillips, *American Negro Slavery,* 485-86. "Insurrections" were often nothing more than rumors. As an example, *Niles' Register* of February 27, 1836, carried a note from the Philadelphia *Herald* reporting an insurrection of slaves in Nashville, causing the "utmost consternation." The "intelligence" purportedly came from J. & R. Yeatman & Co., via Mr. Harris. It held that the Planters' Bank had been "forced" into and all the communicants asked was to be able to "save our lives." A postscript noted that the Union Bank had been burned. *Niles* noted that it was needless to say that "the whole story is a *lie*—A WICKED LIE" and that a large reward was offered for the author. XLIX, 441.

157. John Claybrooke Papers. The dots, in this instance, indicate portions made illegible by mutilation.

158. M. D. Cooper Papers. In private possession.

159. Patterson, *Negro in Tennessee,* 49-50; Harvey Wish, "The Slave Insurrection Panic of 1856," *Journal of Southern History,* V (1939), 206-22, especially 209-13.

160. W. F. Cooper to M. D. Cooper, December 29, 1856. M. D. Cooper Papers.

CHAPTER 3: Antislavery Sentiment

1. John Allison, *Dropped Stitches in Tennessee History* (Nashville, 1899), 80. One should be careful about accepting Allison's statements. He states elsewhere that Lundy moved from East Tennessee to Ohio between 1815 and 1820, but Lundy nowhere says that he had been to Tennessee at that time. Lundy, *Life, Travels and Opinions.* James W. Patton in "Progress of Emancipation in Tennessee," *Journal of Negro History,* XVII (1932),

68, unreservedly accepts Allison's statement relative to the 1796 Constitutional Convention.

2. Asa E. Martin, "The Anti-Slavery Societies of Tennessee," *Tennessee Historical Magazine,* I (1915), 262. Thomas was the father of Elihu Embree. See pp. 67–69.

3. *Ibid.,* 261.

4. Stephen B. Weeks, *Southern Quakers and Slavery* (Baltimore, 1896), 236. The charter members were Charles Osborn, Elihu Swain, John Swain, John Underhill, Jesse Willis, John Canady, David Maulsby, and John Morgan. Martin, "Anti-Slavery Societies," 262, note 3.

5. Martin, "Anti-Slavery Societies," 263; Oliver P. Temple, *East Tennessee and the Civil War* (Cincinnati, 1899), 85.

6. Martin, "Anti-Slavery Societies," 264; Temple, *East Tennessee,* 86; William Birney, *James G. Birney and His Times* (New York, 1890), 76; Alice D. Adams, *Neglected Period,* 31.

7. Martin, "Anti-Slavery Societies," 266; Weeks, *Southern Quakers,* 236; Ruth A. Ketring, *Charles Osborn in the Anti-Slavery Movement* (Columbus, 1937), 16-17. Charles Osborn first began publication of *The Philanthropist,* a weekly, at Mt. Pleasant, Ohio, in August, 1817. "He was the first man in America to proclaim the doctrine of immediate and unconditional emancipation . . . and this was the first journal in America to advocate unconditional emancipation." Weeks, *Southern Quakers,* 235-36. Ketring, *Charles Osborn,* 86, disagrees with this statement. Coffin concurs with Weeks, but says that this credit has long been given to Lundy for the publication of his *Genius of Universal Emancipation* in East Tennessee. *Reminiscences,* 266. Lundy's paper was started in Ohio in January, 1821. Lundy, *Life, Travels and Opinions,* 20. Was either of these the first periodical devoted exclusively to antislavery?

In 1825 John Rankin published his *Letters on Slavery* which went through "many editions and exerted a very great influence." He has been called the "father of abolitionism," and again the "Martin Luther of the cause." Birney, *James G. Birney,* 168; Martin, "Anti-Slavery Societies," 264. Rankin said in 1820 that it was "safer to make anti-slavery speeches in Tennessee and Kentucky than in the North." Patton, "Progress of Emancipation," 67.

8. Memorials and Petitions to the Legislature of Tennessee, 1819. MS., State Archives. Some of these petitions came from the Manumission Society. Elihu Embree, *The Emancipator* (Nashville, 1932, reprint), 4th month, 1820, p. 10. In August, 1825, the eleventh convention of this society presented a memorial bearing the signature of the president, James Jones, again requesting the adoption of some methods of gradual abolition.

9. Report of Committee on Abolition Petitions, 1819. MS., State Archives.

10. Martin, "Anti-Slavery Societies," 267; Patton, "Progress of Emancipation," 92-93.

11. He was only thirty-eight.

12. Martin, "Anti-Slavery Societies," 267; Patton, "Progress of Emancipation," 93. This rapid rise in subscribers is in sharp contrast with the lack of popularity of Garrison's *Liberator*.

13. Embree, *Emancipator*, 7.

14. *Ibid.*, 69.

15. Lundy, *Life, Travels and Opinions*, 20. Temple says that Embree purchased Osborn's *Philanthropist*, and then Lundy bought the rights of the *Emancipator*. *East Tennessee*, 93. Also, he states that John Rankin deserves a higher place in the abolition movement than Lundy. *Ibid.*, 95. This statement smacks of uncritical loyalty to a fellow Tennessean.

Lundy states that Osborn sold to E. Bates, and as "E. Bates did not come up to my standard of anti-slavery, I determined immediately to establish a periodical of my own." *Life, Travels and Opinions*, 19. Lundy had contributed articles on slavery in Missouri to Osborn's paper.

16. Lundy, *Life, Travels and Opinions*, 23; Patton, "Progress of Emancipation," 94. William L. Garrison was Benjamin Lundy's assistant at Baltimore in 1828 and 1829. In the former year Lundy was assaulted by a slave trader, and in the latter, Garrison was imprisoned for libel. "Older editors said that . . . though more severe than Garrison, I so selected my words that they could not be construed into libels." Lundy, *Life, Travels and Opinions*, 29.

17. Lundy, *Life, Travels and Opinions*, 21, 30.

18. Martin, "Anti-Slavery Societies," 264-65, 271; Patton, "Progress of Emancipation," 89.

19. Martin, "Anti-Slavery Societies," 270.

20. *Annals of Congress*, 17th Cong., 1st sess. (1821-1822), 709; *ibid.*, 17th Cong., 2nd sess. (1822-1823), 642.

21. *Ibid.*, 18th Cong., 1st sess. (1823–1824), 931.

22. Martin, "Anti-Slavery Societies," 270-71.

23. *Ibid.*, 271.

24. *Ibid.*, quoting Benjamin Lundy, *Genius of Universal Emancipation*, VIII, 93-94.

25. *Third Annual Report of the American Anti-Slavery Society* (New York, 1836), 99. The other organizations were in Kentucky and Virginia.

26. Martin, "Anti-Slavery Societies," 272.

27. *Ibid.*, 273-74.

28. Hamer, ed., *Tennessee*, I, 464.

29. Martin, "Anti-Slavery Societies," 274.

30. *Ibid.*, 275.

31. W. Freeman Galpin, ed., "Letters of an East Tennessee Abolitionist," *East Tennessee Historical Society Publications*, III (1931), 134-49.

Birdseye died soon after the war started. *Ibid.,* 134. The originals of these letters are in the Gerrit Smith Miller Collection in the Syracuse University Library.

32. *Ibid.,* 135-36.

33. *Ibid.,* 137.

34. *Ibid.,* 138. Ezekiel's brother, Victory, of Pompey, New York, was Congressman from 1841 to 1843. The Tennessean wanted to see him before he took his seat and "convince him that cringing to the South is not the way to gain their respect or to discharge his duty to the North." *Ibid.,* 139.

35. *Ibid.,* 142.

36. *Ibid.,* 143-44.

37. *Ibid.,* 138, 144, 148-49.

38. Martin, "Anti-Slavery Societies." Actually the "Moral, Religious Manumission Society of West Tennessee," formed at Columbia in December, 1824, never brought about any startling results. It probably dissolved in 1826 or 1827. *Ibid.,* 275-77.

39. *The African Repository and Colonial Journal,* VI, 74; Patton, "Progress of Emancipation," 99.

40. *The African Repository and Colonial Journal,* VI, 77. Cahal played an important role in the Constitutional Convention of 1834.

41. *National Banner and Nashville Whig,* August 8 and 10, 1831.

42. Birney, *James G. Birney,* 112. His territory included Alabama, Louisiana, Mississippi, Arkansas, and Tennessee.

43. James G. Birney to Ralph R. Gurley, December 27, 1832, from Dwight L. Dumond, ed., *Letters of James Gillespie Birney, 1831–1857* (New York, 1938), I, 49.

44. Birney, *James G. Birney,* 115.

45. *Ibid.,* 126-27; from one of his editorials in the Huntsville *Democrat,* about August, 1833.

46. Birney, *James G. Birney,* 127.

47. James G. Birney to Ralph R. Gurley, December 3, 1833; from Dumond, ed., *Letters,* I, 96.

48. *Ibid.*

49. Birney, *James G. Birney,* 130. James G. Birney was soon to become an "immediatist," for he considered slavery a sin, and ". . . if gradual emancipation be insisted on, the conscience of the slaveholder is left undisturbed, and you gain nothing." *Ibid.,* 139.

50. *Ibid.,* 159.

51. *Acts of Tennessee,* 1833, c. 44, sec. 1.

52. Memorials and Petitions to the Legislature of Tennessee, 1833. State Archives. This petition was signed by Philip Lindsley, David Crockett, Robert Weakley, and about 160 others.

53. *The African Repository and Colonial Journal, passim.*

54. *Ibid.*, II, 324; XXVI, 255.

55. Journal of Samuel Henderson. MS. in private possession.

56. *Memorial of the Semi-Centennial Anniversary of the American Colonization Society* (Washington, 1867), 182-90; Patterson, *Negro in Tennessee,* 210-11. It is entirely possible that these figures are not accurate. The Maryville, Tennessee, *Intelligencer* indicated in early 1833 that something over 100 freedmen from Tennessee were to be among the expected 350 to sail for New Orleans in April of 1833. They were late in leaving and there were 150 instead of 350. See, *National Banner and Nashville Daily Advertiser,* February 14, March 22, and May 1, 1833.

All the states colonized only 11,909. Virginia led with 3,733; North Carolina followed with 1,371; Georgia came next with 1,341; Tennessee was fourth with 870; and Kentucky fifth with 675. Of these, 5,957 were emancipated to go to Liberia; 4,541 were born free; 344 purchased freedom; some were from the Barbadoes, and others "unknown." The total cost of colonization was $2,141,507.77. *Memorial of the Semi-Centennial Anniversary of the American Colonization Society,* 190-91.

57. *The African Repository and Colonial Journal,* IV, 239.

58. Lundy, *Life, Travels and Opinions,* 287.

59. "Letters of Negroes Addressed to the American Colonization Society," *Journal of Negro History,* X (1925), 261.

60. *Journal of the Constitutional Convention of 1834,* pp. 125-30. The above facts are hardly consistent with the assertion of the opponents of slavery that *many* of the slaveowners were against the institution. For a fuller account of the activities in the convention see Chase C. Mooney, "The Question of Slavery and the Free Negro in the Tennessee Constitutional Convention of 1834," *Journal of Southern History,* XII (November, 1946), 487-509.

61. *Journal of the Constitutional Convention of 1834,* p. 15.

62. *Ibid.,* 76. Allen asked to be relieved of duties on the committee; he was replaced by Samuel B. Fogg of Davidson County. *Ibid.,* 72. It should be noted that the committee members were from East, West, and Middle Tennessee, respectively.

63. *Ibid.,* 87-88.

64. *Ibid.,* 88.

65. *Ibid.*

66. *Ibid.,* 88-90.

67. *Ibid.,* 91.

68. *Ibid.,* 92.

69. *Ibid.*

70. *Ibid.,* 93.

71. These delegates were from Washington, Greene, Jefferson, Blount, and Bedford counties, respectively. M'Gaughey and M'Kinney still had different viewpoints in 1861; the former went with the Union, the latter

with the Confederacy. They were the only two still living who had taken an important part in the 1834 Convention. Temple, *East Tennessee*, 108.

72. *Journal of the Constitutional Convention of 1834*, pp. 98-99. With two exceptions the losers were from East Tennessee or Middle Tennessee areas where there were few slaves.

73. Nashville *Republican and State Gazette*, July 10, 1834. These remarks were made on June 24. Not all the speeches were entered into the *Journal*, and some must, therefore, be taken from other sources.

74. *Journal of the Constitutional Convention of 1834*, pp. 125-30.

75. *Ibid.*, 129. It seems that this was the first time the memorials had really been analyzed for source and signatures.

76. *Ibid.*, 147-51.

77. Constitution of 1834, Article II, sec. 31. This provision was first introduced by N. J. Hess, delegate from Dyer and Gibson counties, on June 6. *Journal of the Constitutional Convention of 1834*, p. 71. It was repealed in 1865. Amendments of 1865, sec. 1.

78. The Constitution of 1796, Article III, sec. 1, had extended this privilege to the free colored.

79. *Journal of the Constitutional Convention of 1834*, p. 37.

80. Nashville *Republican and State Gazette*, July 10, 1834.

81. *Ibid.*, July 5, 1834.

82. *Ibid.*

83. *Journal of the Constitutional Convention of 1834*, p. 171.

84. *Ibid.*, 208.

85. *Ibid.*, 210.

86. *Acts of the Territory Southwest of the River Ohio*, 1794, c. I, sec. 32.

87. From Hamer, *Tennessee*, I, 470. Nashvillians held meetings in May, 1844, and adopted resolutions to the effect that if Texas was not admitted to the Union they would attempt secession. John Wooldridge, ed., *History of Nashville, Tennessee* (Nashville, 1890), 170-71.

88. Frederick L. Olmsted, *A Journey in the Back Country* (New York, 1860), 239.

89. Part of the article was a reprint from the Nashville *Republican*.

90. Randolph *Recorder*, August 5, 1836.

91. Randolph *Whig*, April 7, 1838.

92. D. T. Herndon, "The Nashville Convention of 1850," *Transactions of the Alabama Historical Society*, V (1905), 230-32.

93. Charles Miller, comp., *Official and Political Manual of the State of Tennessee* (Nashville, 1890), 43.

94. Martin, "Anti-Slavery Societies," 279-80.

95. Carter G. Woodson, "Freedom and Slavery in Appalachian America," *Journal of Negro History*, I (1916), 145-46.

CHAPTER 4: Slave Life

1. James Stirling, *Letters from the Slave States* (London, 1857), 291.
2. See Diary of Harrod Clopton Anderson, I (1854–1860). In Louisiana State University Archives.
3. J. H. Ingraham, *Not "A Fool's Errand": Life and Experience of a Northern Governess in the Sunny South* (New York, 1890), 51. Miss Conyngham was the medium through which Ingraham related his own experiences and observations.
4. *Ibid.*, 59.
5. *Ibid.*, 143.
6. D. R. Hundley, *Social Relations in Our Southern States* (New York, 1860), 355.
7. Phillips, *Life and Labor*, 181.
8. Phillips, *American Negro Slavery*, 407-08.
9. *Ibid.*, 143.
10. Diary of Harrod Clopton Anderson, I, November 16, 1855.
11. Hundley, *Social Relations*, 356.
12. Phillips, *Life and Labor*, 248.
13. Ingraham, *Not "A Fool's Errand,"* 205.
14. Birney, *James G. Birney*, 159.
15. Hale, *DeKalb County*, 104-05.
16. Journal of Samuel Henderson, May 7, 1857. In private possession.
17. G. W. Featherstonhaugh, *Excursion Through the Slave States* (London, 1844), I, 189-90.
18. W. W. Clayton, *History of Davidson County, Tennessee* (Philadelphia, 1880), 412, 419.
19. John Overton Papers.
20. John Wooldridge, ed., *History of Nashville, Tennessee* (Nashville, 1890), 543.
21. From the *Daily Appeal*, January 29, 1861.
22. Ebenezer Jones to Atlas Jones, August 22, 1819. Calvin Jones Papers. In private possession. These papers were used several years ago by the writer; since that time some or all of them have been deposited in the University of North Carolina library. The letter quoted from here was written to Atlas and then forwarded to Calvin at Raleigh, North Carolina. From the contents of the letter, one would judge there was a sister living with Atlas. Calvin moved to West Tennessee soon after 1819.
23. Catterall, *Judicial Cases*, II, 569-70. (Jones v. Allen, I Head 626-38).
24. Mrs. Theresa Perkins, "Essay." This manuscript of some forty pages, bearing no date, is in private possession.

25. Mrs. Lucy Henderson Horton, "The Old South." Manuscript in private possession.

26. Hughes, *Thirty Years a Slave*, 94.

27. Phillips, *American Negro Slavery*, 313; Mrs. Lucy Henderson Horton, "The Old South."

28. Mrs. Theresa Perkins, "Essay."

29. Hughes, *Thirty Years a Slave*, 63.

30. *Ibid.*, 62.

31. *Ibid.*, 63, 67-68.

32. *Ibid.*, 188-89.

33. Carter G. Woodson, *The Education of the Negro Prior to 1861* (New York, 1915), 225.

34. William J. Simmons, *Men of Mark: Eminent, Progressive, and Rising* (Cleveland, 1887), 620-21.

35. *Ibid.*, 291-92.

36. *Ibid.*, 572.

37. *Ibid.*, 361-62.

38. Woodson, *The Education of the Negro*, 213; Drew, *The Refugee*, 123, 183. Pease later regretted that he would absent himself when his master wished to teach him.

39. Stirling, *Letters*, 56.

40. Mrs. Theresa Perkins, "Essay."

41. W. P. Harrison, ed., *The Gospel Among the Slaves, A Short Account of Missionary Operations Among the African Slaves of the Southern States* (Nashville, 1893), 91-92. The "softening" effect of religion upon the treatment of slaves is well depicted in Mary Church Wagner, "The Settlement of Zion Community in Maury County, Tennessee, 1806–1860" (M.A. thesis, Vanderbilt University, 1945), especially 73-78.

42. *Ibid.*, 167-70, 189. The two largest churches were at Charleston and Baltimore with 3,742 and 2,600 affiliates, respectively.

43. *Ibid.*, 194-96, 318-26. On these pages will also be found the number of missions established.

44. *Ibid.*, 341.

45. Wooldridge, ed., *Nashville*, 478. This was one of the three separate Negro churches in Nashville prior to 1860. The other two were Methodist.

46. Harrison, ed., *Gospel Among the Slaves*, 348-49.

47. Coffin, *Reminiscences*, 284.

48. Nehemiah Adams, *A South-Side View of Slavery; or Three Months at the South, in 1854* (Boston, 1854), 28.

49. Phillips, *Life and Labor*, 217.

50. Mrs. Theresa Perkins, "Essay." Mrs. Perkins lived in Franklin, Williamson County, Tennessee.

CHAPTER 5: Land Tenure and Slaveholding, 1850 and 1860

1. J. G. M. Ramsey, *Annals of Tennessee to the End of the Eighteenth Century* (Philadelphia, 1860), 648; John Haywood, *The Civil and Political History of Tennessee* (Nashville, 1891), 2nd edition, 484; A. W. Putnam, *History of Middle Tennessee, or Life and Times of General James Robertson* (Nashville, 1859), 531.

2. Avery O. Craven, *Soil Exhaustion as a Factor in the Agricultural History of Virginia and Maryland, 1606–1860* (Urbana, Illinois, 1925).

3. Abernethy, *Frontier to Plantation*, chap. 1.

4. These figures and ratios are based on statistics compiled from the following published reports of the United States Census Bureau: *Sixth Census or Enumeration of Inhabitants of the United States* (Washington, 1841); *The Seventh Census of the United States, 1850* (Washington, 1853); *Eighth Census of the United States, 1860* (Washington, 1860–1864); and *A Century of Population Growth, 1790–1900* (Washington, 1909).

5. *Sixth Census*, 272-73; *Report of the Comptroller of the Treasury of the State of Tennessee*, 1841, pp. 132-35; Nashville *Republican and State Gazette*, July 10, 1834; Carter G. Woodson, "Absentee Owners of Slaves in the United States in 1830," *Journal of Negro History*, IX (1924), 219-20; Carter G. Woodson, "Free Negro Owners of Slaves in the United States in 1830," *Journal of Negro History*, IX (1924), 75.

6. *Seventh Census*, ix; Owsley Chart. A chart showing the comparative number of improved and unimproved acres and value, livestock and value, and agricultural productions in all the Tennessee counties, as listed in the agricultural census for 1840, 1850, and 1860, has been compiled by Mrs. Frank Owsley. This chart has been found more usable for comparative purposes than the various census reports and is cited simply by the name of the compiler. It should be noted that a considerable amount of the land in Tennessee still belonged to the Federal Government.

7. All figures in the tables to follow are derived from the census schedules. Any differences between these and the comparable figures in Clark, *The Tennessee Yeomen*, and Owsley, "The Economic Structure of Rural Tennessee," are caused by the different criteria established for inclusion or exclusion.

8. A portion of the analysis which follows appeared in my article, "Some Institutional and Statistical Aspects of Slavery in Tennessee," *Tennessee Historical Quarterly*, I (1942), 195-228. The author does not claim absolute accuracy for the figures in this study: the methods of taking the census varied in spite of the fact that the same instructions were given to all enumerators; some enumerators were obviously careless; some of the sched-

ules are not in a perfect state of preservation; some "farmers" with less than $100 production were included on Schedule IV, instructions to the contrary notwithstanding. Others doubtless were not listed and constitute a sizable proportion of the "farmers" on Schedule I who are not on Schedule IV. While absolute accuracy is not claimed, the author is thoroughly convinced that the sample is sufficiently large to overcome most of the minor deficiencies of the census materials.

9. This trend is not to be discerned in all the counties with a relatively small number of slaveowners. The decrease in the number of heads of agricultural families in Davidson and Montgomery is accounted for by the fact that portions of those counties went to form Cheatham County in the 1850's.

10. For purposes of comparison, the percentages of landownership among the nonslaveholding group are included in Table II, and the percentages of slaveownership among the non-landowning group in Table III.

11. The long-standing opposition of the area to slavery probably helps to account for the decrease in slaveownership.

12. This is not to be explained by the large number of slaves that were held by the people of Nashville, for it is to be remembered that only agricultural *producers* are included in these figures.

13. For a detailed breakdown of the slaveholdings by counties, see Appendix A.

14. One other county in the state, Williamson, had a larger Negro than white population in 1860.

15. For the entire slaveholding area these percentages were 2.28 and 21.60. Appendix A will afford almost limitless opportunities for combinations and percentages.

16. The owners seem to have provided plentiful shelter for their slaves. In 1860, 6,532 of the 7,606 slaveowners had 15,725 slave houses, or an average of 2.41 houses per owner. All but two of the slaveowners of DeKalb County had slave houses; the ratio of houseowners to slaveowners in the other counties was almost identical with the ratio for all fifteen counties.The average number of houses ranged from 1.11 in Johnson to 3.72 in Fayette. Schedule II, "An Enumeration of Slave Population," 1860 (unpublished). The slave houses were not given in the 1850 Census, either published or unpublished.

17. *Eighth Census of the United States: 1860,* II (Agriculture), 238-39.

18. It should be noted that the amount of improved acreage reported in this table does not represent the total for the counties studied. The census enumerators failed to indicate the number of acres being cultivated in the case of 1,804 heads of agricultural families in 1850, and in 2,436 in 1860.

19. The amount of acreage in the above table does not agree with the acreage in the census reports; the above is only the taxable acreage. Nor is there an agreement on value: the comptroller's reports gave the value of

land as assessed for taxing purposes, while the census termed the worth of property as "cash value." There is no disagreement on the point that the land of the state nearly trebled in value in the last decade before the Civil War.

20. *Report of the Comptroller of the Treasury of the State of Tennessee,* 1859, pp. 65-67.

CHAPTER 6: Agricultural Production, 1850 and 1860

1. By far the best study on agriculture in this country is Lewis C. Gray, *History of Agriculture in the Southern United States to 1860* (2 vols., New York, 1941).

2. *Census of the United States: 1850,* lxxxiii. Tennessee ranked fifth in population in 1840 and 1850. *Ibid.,* ix, xxxiii. In 1850, 4,043 Tennessee farmers made five or more bales of cotton each, and in this respect Tennessee placed sixth. *Ibid.,* 178.

3. *Census of the United States: 1860,* II (Agriculture), xciv. The total production in the United States in 1860 was 5,387,052 bales as compared to 2,445,793 bales in 1850. Mississippi, Alabama, and Louisiana produced more than one half of the 1860 crop. *Ibid.,* xciii, xciv.

4. Owsley Chart.

5. *Ibid.*

6. Fayette led the state in 1840, 1850, and 1860; Haywood was second in 1860, taking over the place held by Shelby in 1850.

7. *Census of the United States: 1850,* lxxxv, lxxxii, 178.

8. *Census of the United States: 1860,* II (Agriculture), xcvi.

9. Of the 476 tobacco producers in Robertson County in 1850, only 16 did not own their land—2 slaveowners and 14 nonslaveowners. In 1860 only 40 of the 629 were not landowners; 8 of those owned slaves, 32 did not. By 1860 the landless slaveowners had a higher average production than either the landless or landed nonslaveowners.

10. Much of the 1840 tobacco land was probably put to corn in 1850, for the production of that crop jumped from 116,440 bushels to 893,328 bushels in the ten-year period.

11. See Appendix B.

12. For Dyer, see above under *COTTON.*

13. *Census of the United States: 1860,* II (Agriculture), xlvii.

14. It should be remembered that the decline in Davidson County resulted from the taking of part of that subdivision to help to create Cheatham County.

15. Owsley Chart.

16. Goodspeed (publisher), (Haywood County), 819.

17. *Census of the United States: 1850,* ix, xxxiii, lxxxii, lxxxiv-lxxxv;

Census of the United States: 1860, II (Agriculture), xxix-xxx, xlvii, xciv, xcvi-xcvii, cxxi, cxxiv. Perhaps more significant than rankings based on numbers is the per capita ranking of a state. For the position of Tennessee, especially in swine and cattle, see Owsley, *Plain Folk,* 50.

CHAPTER 7: Some Tennessee Planters

1. Diary of Harrod Clopton Anderson, vol. 3 (1886–1888); biographical sketch by his granddaughter, Cherry Bower (Mrs. Rundle) Smith, of Blanks, Louisiana. Harrod's father was professor of Greek at the University of Virginia.

2. Schedule IV, "Productions of Agriculture," (unpublished), Haywood County, 10th district. This schedule was combined with I, "An Enumeration of Free Inhabitants," and II, "An Enumeration of Slave Population," to determine the number of slaves Anderson held, and whether or not he was a landowner. It is entirely possible that the slaves—or most of them—should have been credited to Anderson's wife, for his granddaughter says that most of them were given to Mrs. Anderson by her father. Mrs. Rundle Smith to author, December 11, 1938.

3. Anderson thought "frequent doses of *Tar Sulphur* and *Copperas"* had cured his hogs. Volume 1 (1854–1862) is the only part of the manuscript dealing with the period of slavery, and will hereafter be cited merely as Diary.

4. Diary, February 21, 1854.

5. His cotton receipts for 1853 were: five bales @ 10¢, five @ 9¢, and six @ 7¢; total $789.10. The previous year he sold twenty-five bales at 6½ ¢ and 7½ ¢ and received $762.70 "or near it." *Ibid.,* April 21, 1854.

6. *Ibid.,* June 8, 1854.

7. *Ibid.,* July, 1854.

8. *Ibid.,* November 16 and 25, 1854. Anderson started building his own gin in August, and on July 18 had purchased "60 or 70 acres" of land from a Major Anderson.

9. *Ibid.,* April 2, 1856.

10. *Ibid.,* August 4, 1855.

11. *Ibid.,* December 1, 1855.

12. *Ibid.,* December 14, 1855.

13. *Ibid.,* April 12, 1856.

14. *Ibid.,* February 12, 1857.

15. *Ibid.,* July 26, 1856.

16. *Ibid.,* November 13, 1856.

17. This entry probably was made in the 1880's when he reread the first volume of his diary. Buchanan carried Haywood County by seventy-nine votes, "a great gain." *Ibid.,* November 7, 1856.

18. *Ibid.,* November 27, December 10 and 17, 1857. He kept seventy-three "stock" hogs for the next year. On January 4, 1858, Anderson said "cotton is flat 6 to 8½ ¢ pr lb," but on January 30 he sold four bales at 12½ ¢, four at 8¢, and four at 10¢: total $917.61.

19. *Ibid.,* July 28 and September 8, 1857.

20. On April 7 he said he had fifty-nine sheep.

21. Diary, March 16, 1858.

22. See entries of December 10, 19, and 20, 1858, and February 3 and 15, 1859.

23. Diary, November 26, 1859.

24. *Ibid.,* December 5, 1859.

25. *Ibid.* The thirty hogs weighed only 4,200 pounds. *Ibid.,* December 9, 1859.

26. Anderson was troubled by "distemper" among his horses in June and July, 1859.

27. Diary, September 22, 1859.

28. *Ibid.,* April 23, 1860.

29. *Ibid.,* November 1, December 12 and 24, 1860.

30. This does not include his recently purchased land in Lauderdale.

31. Schedule IV, "Production of Agriculture" (unpublished), Haywood County, 10th district. The number of slaves and slave houses was obtained from Schedule II, "An Enumeration of Slave Population," also unpublished.

32. This idea is no longer entertained by anyone who has studied the election returns.

33. Diary, July 22, October 12, December 5 and 6, 1861.

34. Biographical sketch, in Diary, vol. 3 (1887–1888), by his grand-daughter, Cherry Bower (Mrs. Rundle) Smith.

35. *Ibid.,* vol. 2 (1885–1886), May 3, 1886.

36. *Ibid.,* vol. 3, October 28, 1888. This was recorded, with a tribute, by his son, P. H. Anderson.

37. Polk-Brown-Ewell Collection (1803–1924), University of North Carolina Archives. Part of the Polk material used in this chapter is in the Polk-Yeatman Collection (1784——), also in the University of North Carolina Archives. These collections will be cited hereafter as P.-B.-E. and P.-Y., respectively.

38. Lucius Polk to William Polk, July 22, 1823. (P.-B.-E.)

39. Same to same, October 17, 1825. (P.-B.-E.)

40. William Polk to Lucius Polk, April 12, 1825. William Polk Letter Book, 1821–1832. In University of North Carolina Archives.

41. Same to same, August 19, 1826. William Polk Letter Book.

42. Same to same, October 4 and November 1, 1826. William Polk Letter Book.

43. Lucius Polk to William Polk, December 1, 1826. (P.-B.-E.)

44. William Polk to Lucius Polk, June 12, 1827. William Polk Letter Book.

45. Lucius Polk to William Polk, May 8, 1827. (P.-B.-E.)

46. William Polk to Lucius Polk, April 3, 1827. (P.-B.-E.)

47. Same to same, July 20, 1827. (P.-B.-E.)

48. Lucius Polk to William Polk, August 25, 1827. (P.-Y.)

49. Leonidas Polk to Lucius Polk, September 22, 1828. (P.-Y.) William wrote Lucius on January 8, 1828, that he had "just renewed the Nashville Republican containing nothing and worse than nothing." (P.-B.-E.)

50. Lucius Polk to William Polk, November 1, 1828. (P.-Y.)

51. Same to same, January 4, 1829. (P.-B.-E.)

52. Same to same, August 27, 1829. (P.-B.-E.)

53. Not to be confused with the wife, Sarah, of James K. Polk, Lucius' cousin. Lucius had eleven brothers and sisters and two half-brothers.

54. Lucius Polk to Sarah Polk, December 10, 1835. (P.-Y.)

55. The Booker mentioned here may have been the same one who bought James K. Polk's Fayette County plantation in 1834.

56. Lucius Polk to Sarah Polk, January 26, 1836. (P.-Y.)

57. Same to same, March 16, 1839. (P.-Y.)

58. Same to same, September 9, 1839. (P.-Y.)

59. M. D. Cooper and Company to Lucius Polk, December 24, 1839. (P.-Y.)

60. Same to same, February 20, 1840. (P.-Y.)

61. Same to same, December 24, 1840. (P.-Y.)

62. Same to same, January 10, 1842. (P.-Y.)

63. Schedules II and IV (unpublished), Fayette County, 9th district, 1850.

64. *Ibid.*, 1860.

65. *Ibid.*, Maury County, 19th district, 1850.

66. *Ibid.*

67. *Ibid.*, Maury County, 11th district, 1850.

68. *Ibid.*, Maury County, 10th district, 1860.

69. *Ibid.*

70. *Ibid.*, Maury County, 11th district, 1860.

71. *Ibid.*

72. Ashwood Farm Ledger, 1859–1872. (P.-Y.)

73. Niles Polk to Lucius Polk, July 29, 1855. (P.-Y.)

74. Bassett, ed., *Plantation Overseer*, 2. For terms of a sample overseer's contract, see *ibid.*, 23-24.

75. Phillips, *Life and Labor*, 316.

76. James K. Polk Papers. Library of Congress.

77. Bassett, ed., *Plantation Overseer*, 38-39. In 1834 only thirty-nine bales were made on eighty-five acres, "which was a small return from the time and labor involved." *Ibid.*, 39.

78. Polk was engrossed in his law practice and duties as national representative.

79. Bassett, ed., *Plantation Overseer*, 39.

80. *Ibid.*

81. This letter is found in *ibid.*, 53. All letters cited in connection with Beanland are contained in Bassett, ed., *Plantation Overseer*. The originals are in the James K. Polk Papers in the Library of Congress.

82. *Ibid.*, 55-56.

83. *Ibid.*, 57-58. This may have been the same Hughes (or Hues) who was instrumental in capturing John A. Murrell. His real name was Virgil Stewart.

84. Bassett, ed., *Plantation Overseer*, 59.

85. Ephraim Beanland to James K. Polk, February 1, 1834, from *ibid.*, 61-63.

86. *Ibid.*, 65.

87. Ephraim Beanland to James K. Polk, March 7, 1834.

88. Same to same, April 1, 1834. Jack's wounds were "not dangeres by any meanes."

89. Bassett, ed., *Plantation Overseer*, 71.

90. *Ibid.*, 73-74.

91. *Ibid.*, 81.

92. James K. Polk to Sarah Polk, September 26, 1834.

93. Bassett, ed., *Plantation Overseer*, 85-86.

94. *Ibid.*, 47-48. Half of the slaves were furnished by Polk and half by Caldwell. Bassett says, p. 49, that a second group of slaves probably soon followed.

95. *Ibid.*, 89-93. One of his five children, E. D. Beanland, became a physician, and others lived to be "persons of importance in their communities." La Grange is in Fayette County, but no Beanlands could be located in either the 1850 or 1860 census schedules.

96. *Ibid.*, 69.

97. *Ibid.*, 92.

98. *Ibid.*, 86.

99. Journal, December 10, 1847.

100. *Ibid.*, February 22, 1849.

101. *Ibid.*, March 7, 1850.

102. *Ibid.*, January 9, 1850.

103. *Ibid.*, January 21, 1851.

104. *Ibid.*, August 8, 1851, and September 1, 1852.

105. *Ibid.*, February 19, 1852.

106. See pp. 90-91.

107. Nancy had "Pulminary Consumption," and Jim died after a six-week siege of typhoid.

108. Journal, September 17, 1859.

109. The slave schedule is in Washington, and since Williamson was not used as one of the sample counties, the exact number of slaves Henderson held was not ascertained. The writer would judge that he did not have more than thirty.

110. Diary of Robert H. Cartmell, January 1, 1853, to September 30, 1858. Used through the courtesy of Cartmell Townes of Jackson, Tennessee. This is vol. 1 of the diary; vol. 2 deals with the Civil War period, and vol. 3 with the postwar period. Cited hereinafter as Cartmell Diary. The information on the operations from 1849 to 1853 was given in a memorandum at the beginning of the diary. Cartmell had attended law school at Lebanon.

111. *Ibid.*, summary for April, 1853.

112. In December of 1853 he sold 100 acres of this land to Robert I. Chester for $1,200. Cartmell remarked that he would not take $20 per acre for the remainder.

113. Cartmell Diary, January 7, 1854.

114. Deberry decided to go into business for himself and left the employ of Cartmell on December 18, 1854, two days before his time was up. Cartmell did not object to this, but decided after this experience: "I do not expect to have an overseer and do not want any."

115. Cartmell Diary, June 28, 1854. On July 4, Cartmell indicated his displeasure with "those who would sever this union, encourage civil war . . . lay violent hands upon the institutions of the South." To him the Federal Government had no authority in the internal affairs of a state, for both the states and the territories could regulate their own affairs provided always they were consistent with the Constitution of the United States.

116. It is not known whether Dave was still around in 1858, but on February 25 of that year Cartmell noted that "some scamp paid a visit last night & stole about all the *clothes* I had."

117. Cartmell Diary, late 1855 and February 5, 1856.

118. This entry is chronologically out of order, and is to be found in the middle of the diary.

119. Except two of the brothers of Lucius Polk, and there the only information obtainable was from the unpublished census schedules.

PRÉCIS

1. The reader is cautioned against applying these statements to any one section or region of the state; specific locales should be checked in the main body of the text or in the tables.

BIBLIOGRAPHY

Primary Materials

MANUSCRIPTS

Diary of Harrod Clopton Anderson, 3 vols., 1854–1888. Louisiana State University Archives, Baton Rouge, Louisiana.

Diary of Robert H. Cartmell, January 1, 1853, to September 30, 1858. In possession of Cartmell Townes, Jackson, Tennessee. This is Volume 1 of a three-volume diary.

John Claybrooke Papers, 1791–1881. Tennessee Historical Society Archives, Nashville, Tennessee.

M. D. Cooper Papers, 1830–1871. In possession of Miss Alice Stockwell, Nashville, Tennessee.

John Harding Plantation Records, 14 vols., 1820–1842. University of North Carolina Archives, Chapel Hill, North Carolina.

Journal of Samuel Henderson, 1834–1876. In possession of John Henderson, Franklin, Tennessee.

Calvin Jones Papers, 1813–1819. In possession of Ed Knox Boyd, Bolivar, Tennessee, when used. Now in Southern Historical Collection of University of North Carolina, Chapel Hill, North Carolina.

Legislative Papers, 1825–1847. Tennessee State Archives.

Joseph Meek Letters, 1835–1837. Fisk University Library, Nashville, Tennessee.

Memorials and Petitions to the Legislature of Tennessee, 1819, 1825, 1833, 1835. Tennessee State Archives, Nashville, Tennessee.

John Overton Papers, 1793–1834. Tennessee Historical Society Archives, Nashville, Tennessee.

Mrs. Theresa Perkins, "Essay." In possession of Mrs. W. R. Todd, Coshocton, Ohio.

Polk Plantation Account Books. University of North Carolina Archives, Chapel Hill, North Carolina. (There are eight of these books, but most of them are undated.)

William Polk Letter Book, 1821–1832. University of North Carolina Archives, Chapel Hill, North Carolina.

Polk-Brown-Ewell Collection, 1803–1924. University of North Carolina Archives, Chapel Hill, North Carolina.

Polk-Yeatman Collection, 1784———. University of North Carolina Archives, Chapel Hill, North Carolina.

Report of the Committee on Abolition Petitions, 1819. Tennessee State Archives, Nashville, Tennessee.

United States Census Bureau

  Seventh Census of the United States, 1850—Tennessee Original Returns of the Assistant Marshals (unpublished)
    Schedule I—"An Enumeration of Free Inhabitants"
    Schedule II—"An Enumeration of Slave Population"
    Schedule IV—"Productions of Agriculture"
  Eighth Census of the United States, 1860—Tennessee Original Returns of the Assistant Marshals (unpublished)
    Schedule I—"An Enumeration of Free Inhabitants"
    Schedule II—"An Enumeration of Slave Population"
    Schedule IV—"Productions of Agriculture"
Schedules I and II are deposited in the National Archives, Washington, D. C. Schedule IV is in the library of Duke University, Durham, North Carolina.

The three schedules listed above were used for the following Tennessee counties for 1850 and 1860: Davidson, DeKalb, Dyer, Fayette, Fentress, Gibson, Greene, Hardin, Haywood, Henry, Johnson, Lincoln, Maury, Montgomery, and Robertson.

OFFICIAL PRINTED MATERIALS

United States Census Bureau

  A Century of Population Growth. Government Printing Office, Washington, 1909.

  Statistical View of the Population of the United States from 1790 to 1830 Inclusive. Government Printing Office, Washington, 1841.

  Sixth Census or Enumeration of Inhabitants of the United States as Corrected at the Department of State in 1840. Government Printing Office, Washington, 1841.

  The Seventh Census of the United States: 1850. Government Printing Office, Washington, 1853.

  Eighth Census of the United States: 1860. 4 vols. Government Printing Office, Washington, 1860–1864.

United States Congress
   Annals of Congress, 1st Cong., 1st sess., 1789–1791.
                         1st Cong., 2nd sess., 1789–1791.
                         17th Cong., 1st sess., 1821–1822.
                         17th Cong., 2nd sess., 1822–1823.
                         18th Cong., 1st sess., 1823–1824.
States
   Walter Clark, ed., *The State Records of North Carolina,* XXIII (Laws
       1715–1776). Nash Bros., Goldsboro, North Carolina, 1904.
   Acts of Tennessee, 1799–1860.
   Acts of the Territory Southwest of the River Ohio, 1794, 1795.
   John Haywood and Robert Cobb, *The Statute Laws of Tennessee of a
       General and Public Nature.* 2 vols. F. S. Heiskell, Knoxville, 1831.
   *Journal of the Convention of the State of Tennessee Convened for the
       Purpose of Revising and Amending the Constitution thereof.* W. H.
       Hunt and Co., Nashville, 1834.
   Journal of the House of Representatives of the State of Tennessee, 1833,
       1838.
   Journal of the Senate of the State of Tennessee, 1835.
   Charles Miller, comp., *Official and Political Manual of the State of Ten-
       nessee.* Marshall and Bruce, Nashville, 1890.
   Report of the Comptroller of the Treasury of the State of Tennessee,
       1839, 1841, 1849, 1857, 1859.
City of Nashville
   *Laws of the Corporation of Nashville to Which are Prefixed the Laws
       of North Carolina and Tennessee Relating to the Town of Nashville*
       (revised edition), 1837.
   Revised Laws of the City of Nashville, 1850, 1854.
   J. E. Rains, comp., *A Compilation of the General Laws of the City of
       Nashville,* 1857.

NEWSPAPERS

The Appeal (Memphis), 1844, 1845.
Banner Advertiser (Nashville), 1833.
Daily Appeal (Memphis), 1854, 1856, 1859, 1861.
Daily Eagle (Memphis), 1846.
Daily Nashville True Whig, 1852.
Eagle and Enquirer (Memphis), 1852, 1857, 1858.
Evening Ledger (Memphis), 1857.
Gallatin *Journal,* 1828.
Impartial Review and Cumberland Repository (Nashville), 1806.
Memphis *Enquirer,* 1836.

Nashville *Daily Gazette*, 1849.
Nashville *Daily News*, 1859.
Nashville *Gazette*, 1820.
Nashville *Intelligencer*, 1799.
Nashville *Republican*, 1825, 1835.
Nashville *Republican and State Gazette*, 1831, 1833, 1834, 1835.
Nashville *Whig*, 1819, 1820.
Nashville *Whig and Tennessee Advertiser*, 1818.
National Banner and Nashville Daily Advertiser, 1833.
National Banner and Nashville Whig, 1829, 1831.
Randolph *Recorder*, 1834, 1835, 1836.
Randolph *Whig*, 1838.
Republican Banner (Nashville), 1858, 1860.
Tennessee Gazette and Mero District Advertiser (Nashville), 1804.
Tri-Weekly Appeal (Memphis), 1845.
Weekly American Eagle (Memphis), 1844, 1845, 1846.
Weekly Appeal (Memphis), 1860.
Weekly Eagle (Memphis), 1848, 1849.

CONTEMPORARY PERIODICALS

The African Repository and Colonial Journal, 67 vols. American Colonization Society, Washington, 1825–1892.
The Anti-Slavery Record. 3 vols. American Anti-Slavery Society, New York, 1835–1837.
DeBow's Review. 46 vols. J. B. D. DeBow, New Orleans, 1846–1864, 1866–1870, 1879–1880.
Hunt's Merchants' Magazine. 63 vols. F. Hunt, New York, 1839–1870.
Niles' Register. 75 vols. Hezekiah Niles, Baltimore, 1811–1849.

OTHER PRINTED MATERIALS

Nehemiah Adams, *A South-Side View of Slavery; or Three Months at the South, in 1854*. J. R. Marvin and B. B. Mussey and Co., Boston, 1854.
John S. Bassett, ed., *The Southern Plantation Overseer as Revealed in his Letters*. Northampton, Massachusetts, 1925.
J. P. Campbell, comp., *The Nashville, State of Tennessee, and General Business Directory*, 1853.
———, *Nashville Business Directory*, 1857.
———, *Nashville City and Business Directory*, 1859.
———, *Nashville Business Directory*, 1860–61.
Helen T. (Mrs. R. C. H.) Catterall, ed., *Judicial Cases Concerning the American Negro and Slavery*. 5 vols. Carnegie Institution, Washington, 1926–1937.

Levi Coffin, *Reminiscences.* Western Tract Society, Cincinnati, 1876.

Amos Dresser, *The Narrative of Amos Dresser.* American Anti-Slavery Society, New York, 1836.

Dwight L. Dumond, ed., *Letters of James Gillespie Birney, 1831–1857.* 2 vols. D. Appleton-Century Co., New York, 1938.

Elihu Embree, *The Emancipator* (Reprint). B. H. Murphy, Nashville, 1932.

G. W. Featherstonhaugh, *Excursion Through the Slave States.* 2 vols. John Murray, London, 1844.

W. Freeman Galpin, ed., "Letters of an East Tennessee Abolitionist," *East Tennessee Historical Society Publications,* III (1931), 134–49.

John Hallum, *Diary of an old Lawyer.* Southwestern Publishing Co., Nashville, 1895.

Louis Hughes, *Thirty Years a Slave.* South Side Printing Co., Milwaukee, 1897.

"Letters of Negroes Addressed to the American Colonization Society," *Journal of Negro History,* X (1925), 154-311.

J. W. Loguen, *As a Slave and a Freeman.* J. G. K. Truair and Co., Syracuse, 1859.

Benjamin Lundy, *The Life, Travels and Opinions of Benjamin Lundy.* . . . William D. Parrish, Philadelphia, 1847.

Memorial of the Semi-Centennial Anniversary of the American Colonization Society. Colonization Society Building, Washington, 1867.

Memphis Directory and General Business Advertiser, 1849.

Memphis City Directory and General Business Advertiser, 1855.

Memphis City Directory, 1859.

Ulrich B. Phillips, ed., *Plantation and Frontier Documents.* 2 vols. Arthur H. Clark Co., Cleveland, 1910.

James Stirling, *Letters from the Slave States.* John W. Parker and Son, London, 1857.

Third Annual Report of the American Anti-Slavery Society. William S. Dorr, New York, 1836.

J. A. Turner, *The Cotton Planters' Manual.* Orange Judd, New York, 1865.

J. D. Wheeler, *A Practical Treatise on the Law of Slavery.* Benjamin Levy, New Orleans, 1837.

Williams' Memphis Directory, City Guide, and Business Mirror, 1860.

Carter G. Woodson, ed., *The Mind of the Negro as Reflected in Letters Written During the Crisis, 1800–1860.* Association for the Study of Negro Life and History, Inc., Washington, 1926.

Secondary Materials

Thomas P. Abernethy, *From Frontier to Plantation in Tennessee.* University of North Carolina Press, Chapel Hill, 1932.

Alice D. Adams, *The Neglected Period of Anti-Slavery in America, 1808–1831.* Ginn and Co., Boston, 1908. (Radcliffe College *Monographs*, No. 14).

John Allison, *Dropped Stitches in Tennessee History.* Marshall and Bruce, Nashville, 1899.

Frederic Bancroft, *Slave Trading in the Old South.* J. H. Furst Co., Baltimore, 1931.

Charles A. and Mary R. Beard, *The Rise of American Civilization.* Macmillan Co., New York, 1930.

William Birney, *James G. Birney and his Times.* D. Appleton and Co., New York, 1890.

Gordon T. Chappell, "Land Speculation and Taxation in Tennessee, 1790–1834." Master's Thesis, Vanderbilt University, 1936.

Blanche Henry Clark, *Tennessee Yeomen, 1840–1860.* Vanderbilt University Press, Nashville, 1942.

W. W. Clayton, *History of Davidson County, Tennessee.* J. W. Lewis and Co., Philadelphia, 1880.

Robert M. Coates, *The Outlaw Years.* Macaulay Co., New York, 1930.

Winfield H. Collins, *The Domestic Slave Trade of the Southern States.* Broadway Publishing Co., New York, 1904.

Avery O. Craven, *Soil Exhaustion as a Factor in the Agricultural History of Virginia and Maryland, 1606–1860.* University of Illinois, Urbana, 1925. (University of Illinois *Studies in the Social Sciences*, XIII, No. 1).

Benjamin Drew, *The Refugee or a North-Side View of Slavery.* John P. Jewett and Co., Cleveland, 1856.

Ralph B. Flanders, *Plantation Slavery in Georgia.* University of North Carolina Press, Chapel Hill, 1933.

William T. Hale, *History of DeKalb County, Tennessee.* Paul Hunter, Nashville, 1915.

W. T. Hale and D. L. Merritt, *A History of Tennessee and Tennesseans.* 4 vols. Lewis Publishing Co., New York, 1913.

Philip M. Hamer, ed., *Tennessee, A History, 1673–1932.* 4 vols. The American Historical Society, Inc., New York, 1933.

W. P. Harrison, ed., *The Gospel among the Slaves, a Short Account of Missionary Activities among the African Slaves of the Southern States.* Southern Methodist Publishing House, Nashville, 1893.

John Haywood, *The Civil and Political History of Tennessee.* Methodist Publishing House, Nashville, 1891.

H. M. Henry, "The Slave Laws of Tennessee," *Tennessee Historical Magazine*, II (1916), 175-203.

D. T. Herndon, "The Nashville Convention of 1850," *Transactions of the Alabama Historical Society*, V (1905), 203-37.

History of Tennessee from the Earliest Times to the Present.... Goodspeed Publishing Co., Nashville, 1887.

Mrs. Lucy Henderson Horton, "The Old South." Manuscript in possession of Mrs. James Buford, Franklin, Tennessee.

E. E. Hoss, "Elihu Embree, Abolitionist," *American Historical Magazine,* II (1895), 113-38.

H. R. Howard, comp., *The History of Virgil A. Stewart and his Adventure in Capturing and Exposing the Great "Western Land Pirate" and his Gang.* Harper and Bros., New York, 1836.

D. R. Hundley, *Social Relations in our Southern States.* Henry B. Price, New York, 1860.

William L. Imes, "The Legal Status of Free Negroes and Slaves in Tennessee," *Journal of Negro History,* IV (1919), 254-73.

J. H. Ingraham, *Not "A Fool's Errand": Life and Experience of a Northern Governess in the Sunny South.* G. W. Carleton and Co., New York, 1880.

John McLeod Keating, *History of the City of Memphis and Shelby County, Tennessee.* 2 vols. D. Mason and Co., Syracuse, 1899.

Ruth A. Ketring, *Charles Osborn in the Anti-Slavery Movement.* Ohio State Archaeological and Historical Society, Columbus, 1937. (*Ohio Historical Collections,* VII).

Park Marshall, "John A. Murrell and Daniel Crenshaw," *Tennessee Historical Magazine,* VI (1920–21), 3-9.

Asa E. Martin, "The Anti-Slavery Societies of Tennessee," *Tennessee Historical Magazine,* I (1915), 261-80.

Frederick L. Olmsted, *A Journey in the Back Country.* Mason Bros., New York, 1860.

Frank L. Owsley, *Plain Folk of the Old South.* Louisiana State University Press, Baton Rouge, 1949.

Caleb B. Patterson, *The Negro in Tennessee, 1790–1865.* University of Texas, Austin, 1922. (University of Texas *Bulletin,* No. 2205).

James W. Patton, "Progress of Emancipation in Tennessee," *Journal of Negro History,* XVII (1932), 67-102.

Ulrich B. Phillips, *American Negro Slavery.* D. Appleton and Co., New York, 1918.

————, *Life and Labor in the Old South.* Little, Brown, and Co., Boston, 1929.

W. A. Provine, "Lardner Clark, Nashville's First Merchant and Foremost Citizen," *Tennessee Historical Magazine,* III (1917), 28-50.

A. W. Putnam, *History of Middle Tennessee, or Life and Times of General James Robertson.* Methodist Publishing House, Nashville, 1859.

J. G. M. Ramsey, *Annals of Tennessee to the End of the Eighteenth Century.* J. B. Lippincott and Co., Philadelphia, 1860.

James B. Sellers, *Slavery in Alabama*. University of Alabama Press, University, Alabama, 1950.

William H. Siebert, *The Underground Railroad from Slavery to Freedom*. Macmillan Co., New York, 1899.

William J. Simmons, *Men of Mark: Eminent, Progressive, and Rising*. George W. Rewell and Co., Cleveland, 1887.

Charles S. Sydnor, *Slavery in Mississippi*. D. Appleton-Century Co., New York, 1933.

Oliver P. Temple, *East Tennessee and the Civil War*. Robert Clarke Co., Cincinnati, 1899.

Harrison A. Trexler, *Slavery in Missouri, 1804–1865*. Johns Hopkins Press, Baltimore, 1914 (Johns Hopkins University *Studies in Historical and Political Science*, Series XXXII, No. 2).

Philo Tower, *Slavery Unmasked*. E. Darrow and Bro., Rochester, 1856.

Herbert Weaver, *Mississippi Farmers, 1850–1860*. Vanderbilt University Press, Nashville, 1945.

Stephen B. Weeks, *Southern Quakers and Slavery*. Johns Hopkins Press, Baltimore, 1896. (Johns Hopkins University *Studies in Historical and Political Science*, Extra Volume XV).

Carter G. Woodson, "Absentee Owners of Slaves in the United States in 1830," *Journal of Negro History*, IX (1924), 196-231.

————, *The Education of the Negro Prior to 1861*. G. P. Putnam's Sons, New York, 1915.

————, "Free Negro Owners of Slaves in the United States in 1830," *Journal of Negro History*, IX (1924), 41-85.

————, "Freedom and Slavery in Appalachian America," *Journal of Negro History*, I (1916), 132-50.

John Wooldridge, ed., *History of Nashville, Tennessee*. Methodist Publishing House, Nashville, 1890.

INDEX

Abolition crusade: effect on slavery legislation, 8, 15-17, 182; effect on antislavery sentiment, 64, 71; effect on South, 72, 79, 83, 96. *See also* Antislavery activities

Agricultural production: sectional variations in, 4-6, 145, 180; diversity of, 127, 133; summarized, 143-145. *See also* Corn; Cotton; Landowners; Livestock; Planters; Slaveowners; Tobacco; Wheat

Allen, Robert, 77

American Colonization Society, 73, 75, 76

Anderson, Almira A. C. (Mrs. Harrod C.), 147, 153, 156, 158

Anderson, Harrod C.: and slaves, 87, 89, 148-58 *passim;* planter, 89, 147-58, 181; land clearing, 148, 149, 151; economic status, 148, 149, 155-56; and wheat, 148, 151, 152, 155; farming problems, 148-55 *passim;* livestock, 148-57 *passim;* and corn, 148-58 *passim;* and cotton, 148-58 *passim;* builds gin, 150; political observations, 150-51, 156-57; builds ice house, 152; overseer for, 152, 153-54

Anderson, Isaac, 71

Anderson, Jourdan, 56-57

Anderson, P. H., 56, 57

Andrews, Jo, 175

Antislavery activities: in Constitutional Convention of 1796, 64; in East Tennessee, 64, 65, 66, 69, 72, 73, 77, 84; societies, 65-72 *passim;* in legislature, 66-67; attitude of slaveowners toward, 69, 77; in Constitutional Convention of 1834, 76, 77-80; effects of, 84, 183. *See also* Abolition crusade; Dresser, Amos

Barry, R. H., 35, 36-37

Bass, John M., 44

Baxter and Hicks, 37

Beanland, Ephraim: and punishment of slaves, 168-72 *passim;* plantation overseer, 168-74; and runaways, 170-73 *passim;* fight with slave, 172

Bell, Montgomery, 199

Bennett, John, 53

Birdseye, Ezekiel, 72-73

Birney, James G., 73-74

Black, John, 59

Blair, John, 69-70

Bolton, I. L., 46

Bolton, W. H., 46, 47

Bolton, Dickins and Company, 47-49

Bond, James, 201

Boswell, T. L., 97

Boyd, W. L., Jr., 44-45, 45-46

Bradshaw, Richard, 79

Briggs, Henry, 162

243